DACHAU
29 APRIL 1945

Prisoners at the barbed-wire fencing that delineated the western perimeter of the Inmates Compound, KZ Dachau, north of the guardhouse, 30 April 1945. Photograph courtesy National Archives of the United States, College Park, MD.

DACHAU

29 APRIL 1945

THE RAINBOW LIBERATION MEMOIRS

Edited by Sam Dann

Texas Tech University Press

This book was set in Serifa Light BT and Machine and printed on acid-free paper that meets the guidelines for permanence and durability of the committee on Production Guidelines for Book Longevity of the Council on Library Resources. ∞

All photographs and illustrations not otherwise identified are from the Rainbow Division Archives, which gratefully acknowledges those received from many of the contributors to this book and their families.

All photographs courtesy Col. John Henning Linden, U.S. Army (retired) are from the personal papers of Brig. Gen. Henning Linden, Assistant Division Commander, 42d Infantry (Rainbow) Division, U.S. Army.

Original negatives for all photographs by Raphaël Algoet, as news photographer for the Belgian government, are on file at the Center for Historical Research and Documentation on War and Contemporary Society (SOMA/CEGES), Brussels, Belgium. A number of these are reproduced from copies supplied courtesy Col. John Henning Linden, U.S. Army (retired).

Design by Rob Neatherlin

Printed in the United States of America

Library of Congress Cataloging-in-Publication Data
Dachau 29 April 1945 : the Rainbow liberation memoirs / edited by Sam Dann.
    p. cm.
    Includes bibliographical references and index.
    ISBN 0-89672-391-7 (alk. paper)
    1. Dachau (Concentration camp) 2. United States. Army. Infantry Division, 42nd—History. 3. World War, 1939-1945—Personal narratives, American. I. Dann, Sam, 1918-
    D805.5.D33D33 1988
    940.54'1273—DC21   98-13755
                                            CIP

98 99 00 01 02 03 04 05 04 / 9 8 7 6 5 4 3 2

Texas Tech University Press
Box 41037
Lubbock, Texas 79409-1037 USA
800-832-4042
ttup@ttu.edu

CONTENTS

FOREWORD

On April 29, 1945, when several hundred men of the U.S. Army's 42d "Rainbow" Division came upon Dachau, they did more than liberate a concentration camp and give new life to several thousand human beings who had been earmarked for death. They opened the eyes of the world to the horror of the Holocaust, and neither those brave men nor the world would ever again be the same.

We are now several years removed from the fiftieth anniversary observances of the liberation of Dachau and the other camps of Hitler's Final Solution. Each passing year means fewer survivors and liberators remain to provide first-person accounts of the genocide they witnessed. With a new millennium, and all its high-tech multimedia distractions, just around the corner, it becomes harder than ever to direct the attention of new generations to a brutal, primitive past when they would rather contemplate a bright, promising future.

But if the lesson of history is too well hidden, we are bound to confront once again the forces that set the Holocaust in motion. Indeed, even in the past twenty-five years, millions more innocent people have died in the fury of genocidal acts in Asia, Africa, and Europe. That is why *29 April 1945 Dachau: The Rainbow Liberation Memoirs* makes such an important contribution to humanity. In plain and powerful language, this book paints a moving portrait of historical reality that can help preserve our future. For it sets in immutable, irrefutable type the memories of those whose lives were forever changed on that day so long ago. And it serves as a permanent reminder of what can happen when we close our eyes to evil, and close our hearts to the fate of our fellow human beings on this planet.

I have had the honor of meeting some of the veterans of the Rainbow Division. As heroic as they were in fighting the Nazis and liberating the victims of the Holocaust, to a man they deny any special attention. Like so many of their generation, they simply say, "We had a job to do, and we did it." But in doing it so courageously and so well, they demonstrated that to be human was to be capable of great acts of courage and goodness, even in the face of unspeakable cowardice and evil.

There is another, more personal reason for my gratitude to the men of the Rainbow Division. A beautiful young woman named Ella Wieder was a prisoner of a subcamp of Dachau, in Allach. It, too, was liberated by the Rainbow Division on April 29. Ella Wieder found her way home to Czechoslovakia, where she met and married another survivor, Rabbi Samuel Freilich. Soon thereafter, they had a daughter, Hadassah, who is today my wife and the mother of our child, Hana.

Had the men of the Rainbow not arrived in Allach and Dachau that day in late April 1945, Ella Wieder might not have lived to marry her beloved Samuel, and neither Hadassah nor Hana would ever have been born. Such is the circle of fate that binds all our lives together on this earth.

I have no doubt that Hana will carry with her the memory of her grandparents, what they experienced in the Holocaust, and how they found freedom and made a new life for themselves in the United States. But what of the countless other young people who have no one to tell them in such immediate and compelling terms what happened at Dachau so many years ago? If they do not find instruction from a parent, or a teacher, or a visit to a museum, I hope they find their way to *29 April 1945 Dachau: The Rainbow Liberation Memoirs.*

If they read this book, I am sure their lives, like those of the men of the Rainbow Division, will never be quite the same.

Joseph I. Lieberman
U.S. Senator, Connecticut
April 1998

PREFACE

THE 42D RAINBOW INFANTRY DIVISION

The 42d Infantry Division of the United States Army was formed at the start of World War I in April 1917. It was made up of National Guard units from twenty-six states and the District of Columbia. The sight of all the colorful state flags inspired Major Douglas MacArthur to say it resembled a rainbow across the country. From then on, the 42d has been known as the Rainbow Division.

The Rainbow fought in most of the major battles after the U.S. entry into World War I and achieved a most impressive record. One of its regiments was the old New York "Fighting Sixty-ninth," known in Rainbow as the 165th Infantry Regiment. Its members included Wild Bill Donovan, Father Duffy, and Joyce Kilmer. General Douglas MacArthur was brigade commander and served as division commanding general before the armistice.

The original Rainbow patch was a half-circular arc, like the rainbow in the sky. However, after World War I, before the 42d Division went home its members cut their patches into two equal parts and left one in Europe to memorialize their fallen comrades. Our patch ever since has been the arc of a quarter circle.

In World War II, the Rainbow went into combat during the last days of December 1944. It turned back the final German offensive (code named Nordwind by the Germans) in the Alsace area. It breached the Siegfried line; crossed the Rhine; advanced through Würzburg, Schweinfurt, Fürth, Donauwörth; and liberated the concentration camp at Dachau on its way to the capture of Munich. During combat, the Rainbow served in the U.S.

Seventh Army. After V.E. Day, it was a major part of the U.S. occupation forces in Austria.

HOW THIS BOOK WAS WRITTEN

For more than half a century, some Rainbow soldiers have
been loath to talk or even think about Dachau. For them, that
day, those hours, or perhaps just the few minutes they spent
there were intensely personal and private. Dachau destroyed
their peace. To dwell on it could make one lose all faith in our fellow human beings and abandon all hope for a better world.

Rainbow soldiers sometimes would not discuss Dachau even
with their wives for a long time afterward. In telling contrast,
however, some members of the SS[1] not only informed their wives
of the atrocities they were committing but invited them along to
share in the experience. They were members of "police battalions," actually death squads. One of the most notorious was Police Battalion 101. One of its officers, Captain Julius Wohlauf,
brought his wife to a day-long massacre at the town of Miedzy-
rec in Poland. She happened to be pregnant at the time, and because of that, some of the men thought it was not quite proper
for her to attend. She was not the only lady present.[2]

But many other Rainbow soldiers have always believed that
the twenty-ninth day of April, 1945, was more than a day of
death and despair. It was also a great day of liberation and
therefore a day to celebrate, not with cheers, parades, and fire-
works but with thoughtful remembrance of a time when life pre-
vailed over death.

In 1993, the Rainbow Division Memorial Foundation decided
to compile a book that would tell the story of the capture and liberation of the concentration camp at Dachau by the officers and
enlisted men who were the first to enter and bear witness. The
effort was initiated by, among others, Sol Feingold, Art Lee, Dee
Eberhart, and Ted Johnson. Sam Dann was appointed editor.
Nearly four years were required to gather the necessary material
and prepare it for publication. Requests for eyewitness, personal stories were made at our annual and midyear reunions and
at gatherings of regional and state chapters of the Rainbow Division's Veterans Association. Our Division newspaper, the *Reveille*, and our regimental journals also publicized the project.
Most important, many who responded sent the names of buddies who were there that day.

All the stories in this volume appear essentially as they were written (by hand or typewriter); no attempt was made to modify, clean up, or interpret, except for minor changes in punctuation or spelling. In addition, some comments were edited for length. All changes were made with the consent of the men involved. Complete citations for the contributions appear in a note at the end of each. All testimonies are housed in the archives of the Rainbow Division.

What follows might be considered "Dachau in the raw," as witnessed by the men (although a considerable number weren't even old enough to vote) who saw it, felt it, smelled it, and have never been able to forget it.

WHY WE WROTE THIS BOOK

This book appears more than fifty years after Dachau. But why didn't we write it as soon as we came home? After all, none of the facts have changed. We could say that we were very much younger. We faced the prospect of getting our lives in order. We were starting families and jobs, finishing educations. We could say that we just didn't have the time. But perhaps the real reason is that we didn't think this book would be necessary. Dachau? The Holocaust? Everybody knew. It was in all the media: the pictures, the facts, the Nazi confessions, the Nuremberg trials. But as the years went by, there were stirrings of serious revisionism. And we became aware that the war might not be over.

People were arguing that there was no Dachau, or stating that it existed, but as a sort of rest and rehabilitation area. They were insisting that Hitler was not the monster wrongheaded people claimed but a misunderstood, high-minded idealist victimized by an insidious cabal of Zionists. Further, the war was actually forced upon Germany, and so on.[3]

If these revisionists gain credibility, then we know the war is not over. The battle we must fight now is to preserve the memory of Dachau so that evil will be recognized and remembered. If we allow this memory to be destroyed, then evil will have triumphed.

We recall Adolf Hitler's phrase *"Nacht und Nebel,"* Night and the Fog, which is where he would drive his enemies—into the everlasting darkness, with all memory of them blotted out. In effect, this is what the revisionists have in mind for the Holocaust. This must not happen. Our generation of Americans fought against Hitler. It is our hope that this generation will help us in the fight to remember why.

Although this is the history of a military operation, it is not a military history in the traditional sense. Military histories, as a rule, are concerned with the grand strategy and the big picture. We may say, therefore, that they are written from the top down. This book, however, is written from the bottom up, because it gives names and faces to the individual soldiers who put an end to the abomination that was Dachau.

The twenty-ninth day of April, 1945, became the Day of Dachau—a day so many Rainbow Soldiers will never forget; nor shall we allow it to be forgotten by the rest of the world. The memory of such depraved and maniacal cruelty and destruction must not be dimmed nor dissipated by the passage of time and allowed to fade away into the dark and impenetrable abyss of the past.

We write this book with a sense of urgency. All of us are now old soldiers. Some of us have grandchildren who are older than we were on April 29, 1945. Oh, how unbelievably young we were! So many of us still teenagers! Although it is more than fifty years ago, the horrors of Dachau stay with us still.

Our book is not intended as a scholarly analysis or an in-depth study of Dachau and the Holocaust. We were the spearhead of the Seventh U.S. Army racing toward Munich. We were just combat soldiers who happened to be passing through. We can only describe what we saw, what we heard, what we smelled, and how we felt. We offer eyewitness reaction from the heart and the gut. Therefore, this is more than just a description or an accounting. It is a testimony.

WHO WILL EVER BE FREE OF DACHAU?

Not the inmates who
Somehow survived.
Not the Americans of '45.
Not the visitors who come to see.
Not the old guards with
Their secret thoughts.
Not the townsfolk of ancient Dachau.
Not Germany.
Not the rest of the world.
And not the spirits
Who stand in rows
In the Appell Platz
Waiting for the last transport call,
Or who stir the leaves of the memorial birch
And breathe gentle sighs on the candles' flames.

Dee R. Eberhart

INTRODUCTION

Fifty-three years have gone by, more than half a century, since the gates of the Nazi concentration camps opened and the people of the world were confronted with images of unimaginable crimes. Those images since then have been associated throughout the world with the names Dachau, Auschwitz, and Buchenwald. Dachau was the first concentration camp in Nazi Germany, opening in March 1933 and becoming the model for the entire concentration camp system. Twelve years later, on April 29, 1945, American soldiers liberated more than thirty thousand survivors there. The Dachau camp was one of the last places of mass deaths under the National Socialist dictatorship.

In the Federal Republic of Germany, people long kept quiet about the Nazi government's crimes. The places where the crimes were committed were put to new uses or forgotten. The following generation first began to pose questions and to follow traces. In Dachau, thanks to the efforts of the International Committee of Surviving Prisoners, there came into being—twenty years after liberation—the first impressive memorial in West Germany. From the beginning, it was the place where surviving victims could tell their stories, where their voices would be heard.

During the eighties a very strong interest emerged worldwide in the history of National Socialism's practice of genocide, which then began to be called the Holocaust. At the same time, however, in many lands voices were raised that denied the murder of the Jews and sought to relativize the crime. Among the witnesses who in growing numbers countered these voices were soldiers of the Allied armies, particularly of the American forces, which had conquered Hitler's Germany and liberated the prisoners in the concentration camps. For many of them, this traumatic experience had a decisive influence in their future lives.

Introduction

The predominantly sick prisoners of the Dachau concentration camp, many of whom were at the point of death, had waited in despair during the spring of 1945 for the arrival of their liberators. For thousands, these came too late. Many survived after being liberated only for a few hours or a few days. According to accounts given by survivors, the ecstasy of joy in the roll call square at the sight of the first American uniforms was reserved for the healthy among the prisoners.

Fifty years later, in the spring of 1995, on the anniversary of the liberation, prisoners and liberators met once again at the former roll call square of the Dachau concentration camp to commemorate the victims and to remind coming generations to be vigilant. Both groups spoke about their shared feeling of responsibility to report on their experiences in order to spare coming generations such horrors. The present volume, edited by Sam Dann, telling the story of the day of liberation of the Dachau concentration camp as seen by members of the 42d Infantry Division (called the Rainbow Division), is also dedicated to the cause of further elucidating the past. One hopes that it will have many attentive readers.

Barbara Distel
Director, KZ-Gedenkstätte
Dachau Concentration Camp Memorial Site
Dachau, December 2, 1997

The silent, colossal National Lie . . . the clammy stillness created and maintained by the lie of silent assertion—the silent assertion that there wasn't anything going on in which humane and intelligent people were interested.

Mark Twain

ACKNOWLEDGMENTS

More than half a century has gone by since the twenty-ninth day of April, 1945. Many of our comrades have "passed over the Rainbow." It has required hundreds of letters, telephone calls, and visits to gather the information that fills these pages. As editor, I have been gratified by the enthusiastic and heartfelt responses from everyone we have been able to reach after all these years. It has also been a wonderful opportunity to renew old friendships and make new ones.

Most of us did not know one another back in 1945. After all, our division numbered some fourteen thousand, and infantry soldiers exist in rigid compartments. Your immediate family is usually your squad, perhaps your platoon. Your extended family is the company. Some members of the battalion may be acquaintances—but ascending from there, one really knows very few people. But the shared Rainbow patch, the missions, perils, experiences, and support, made us all buddies. It's a bond that endures for life. That same spirit of cooperation that made possible our Rainbow Division's magnificent success as a combat unit in World War II lives on to this day.

Special credit must be given to Charles G. Paine, G Company, 242d Infantry Regiment, who worked tirelessly with me to handle the mass of day-to-day details needed to organize the project. Without his wise and patient guidance, this work might never have risen above ground zero. Special mention must be made of Art Lee, Headquarters Company, 1st Battalion, 242d Infantry Regiment, who has spent years assembling all the historic data on our Rainbow Division's activities at Dachau. Sol Feingold, Anti-Tank Company, 242d Infantry Regiment, also has devoted many years to the study of the Holocaust and Dachau. Sol has compiled one of the most detailed collections of files on the subject. He has been most prompt and generous in sharing his knowledge with us, and his information has been of inestimable value. Dee Eberhart, I Company, 242d Infantry Regiment, and Ted Johnson, H Company, 232d Infantry Regiment, who serve as officers and trustees of the Rainbow Division Veterans Association Memorial Foundation Committee, have made significant contributions.

Once again, thanks to all my Rainbow buddies who dug deeply into memory to relive that twenty-ninth Day of April, 1945.

Sam Dann, H Company, 222d Infantry Regiment,
42d Infantry Division, the Rainbow

EDITOR'S INTRODUCTION

"UNDETERRED BY PALTRY SCRUPLES"

On March 21, 1933, this item appeared in a Bavarian newspaper, *Munchner Neusten Nachrichten:* "On Wednesday, March 22, 1933, the first Concentration Camp will be opened in the vicinity of Dachau. It can accommodate 5,000 people. We have adopted this measure, undeterred by paltry scruples, in the conviction that our action will help restore calm in our country, and is in the best interests of our people. Heinrich Himmler, Commissioner of Police for the City of Munich."[1] This was Himmler's original order establishing Konzentrazionslager (KZ) Dachau. His final order, which called for its destruction, would be issued twelve years and twenty-four days later.

Dachau is nine miles from Munich. In 1945, it was difficult to imagine that this quaint, quiet, picturesque Bavarian town would be the site of the Third Reich's first concentration camp, a prototype for the other charnel houses soon to come into existence.[2]

Dachau, technically speaking, was not a death or extermination camp like Auschwitz, where the basic purpose was to put its inmates to death in its gas chamber as soon as possible. Instead, at Dachau, many prisoners were worked to death—some swiftly, some slowly—in a complex of factories and repair shops that turned out a variety of products, ranging from shoe polish, delicate porcelain, and clothing to war materiel. In the process, thousands were also shot, beaten, tortured and starved to death. And so many perished of the diseases, especially typhus, that raged unchecked through the camp during its last days. Murders were also committed on an allegedly "higher and more enlightened level" by men and women of science who induced

Dachau 29 April 1945

Aerial view of the concentration camp at Dachau 27 May 1945. Photograph by 1st Lt. Harold L. Valentine, 163d Signal Photographic Company. Courtesy of the National Archives Still Picture Branch Photo ID
Number 111-SC-327754.

death by using human victims as guinea pigs in experiments
conducted "for the benefit of mankind."

How many perished here may never be known. The Nazis
succeeded in destroying many of the records. But the figures can
be doubled, if not tripled, if they include those who died en route,
and uncounted others who, half dead already, were shipped to
other camps for their "final solution." Although there was a gas
chamber at Dachau, it was never used.[3] Candidates for gassing
were sent to extermination camps elsewhere, including Austria,
Hitler's birthplace.

Dachau was also the control center for as many as three hundred subsidiary places of confinement, called Kommandos and
Auskommandos. Located in both Germany and Austria, they
were mostly hard-labor camps involved in construction, factory
work of all sorts, farming, metallurgy, and munitions. As of April
26, 1945, the total number of prisoners controlled by Dachau was
about sixty-seven thousand; of this number, more than half—

Organizational Chart—Dachau Concentration Camp

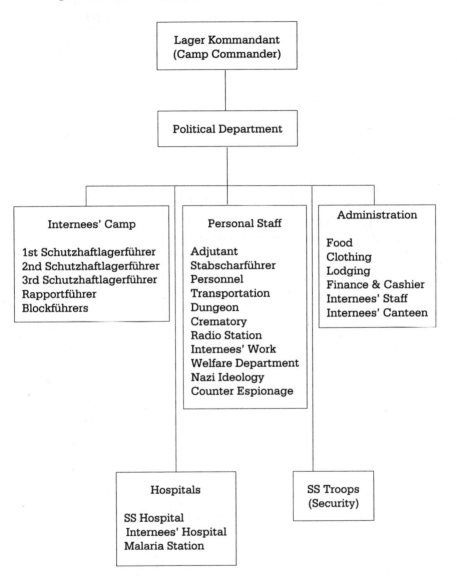

Reproduction of chart prepared by the Office of the Assistant Chief of Staff, G-2, Seventh U. S. Army, from the booklet *Dachau,* printed May 1945, by the 649th Engineer Topographic Battalion. Courtesy Dachau Collection, Hoover Institution Archives, Stanford, California.

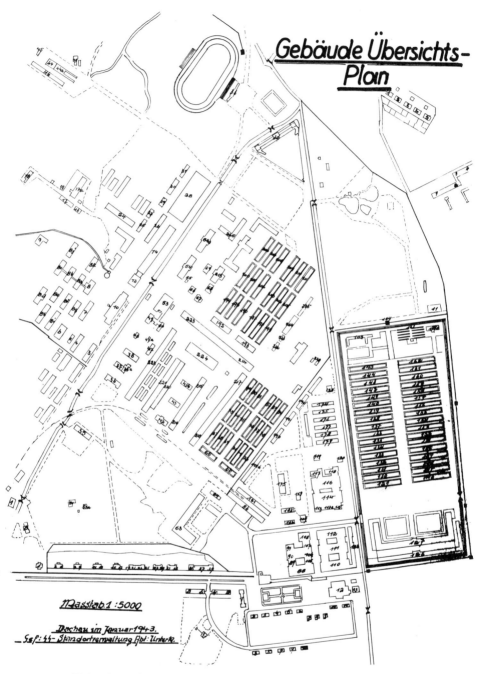

This plan of Dachau operations dated January 1943 shows not only the concentration camp but also the separately operated SS administrative and training camp. Courtesy Dachau Collection, Hoover Institution Archives, Stanford, California.

over thirty-seven thousand—were in the outside Kommandos. Included in the overall figures were twenty-two thousand Jews and more than twelve hundred clergy. The rest were Germans, Gypsies, Serbs, Croats, Slovenes, Poles, Czechs—indeed, citizens from practically every nation in Europe. There were even one Iraqi, one Irani, and three Turks.[4] At that particular moment in April 1945, in the main camp itself, Jews were in a minority, some 2,500 out of about 32,000. Although their numbers were constantly being augmented, they were used up faster and shipped out more frequently to the extermination centers.

THE SPEARHEAD

On April 29, 1945, the United States Seventh Army was in hot pursuit of what was left of the German Wehrmacht—the armed forces of Nazi Germany—in our sector. We were racing to Munich, where they either would or would not make a last, desperate stand. But when we were less than ten miles from our military objective, we ran into an installation many of us had never heard of, Dachau—swiftly to become known as one of the most infamous of the German concentration camps. Then, however, many of us had no idea what a concentration camp was; who could even dream that such a place might exist!

But no army that was fighting for freedom, justice, and human dignity could afford to disregard this devil's den of misery and murder. The 42d Infantry Division, "the Rainbow," moved in to clear and capture roughly the eastern section of the camp, which contained the inmates' enclosure. The 45th Infantry Division, "the Thunderbird," cleared and captured the western part, where the SS barracks were located.

Because of the action we performed on that day, we are called liberators of Dachau. The Rainbow; our comrades-in-arms, the Thunderbirds; and the attached units, the 692d Tank Destroyer Battalion (Rainbow) and the 191st Tank Battalion (Thunderbirds) constituted the spearhead that destroyed the diseased, evil heart of the beast that was Dachau on the twenty-ninth day of April, 1945.

Back home, the newspapers, newsreels, and radio broadcasts were filled with stories of Allied victories on every front: "Rebellion in the Wehrmacht!" "Nazi Soldiers Deserting in Droves!" "Seventh Army Sweeps into Austria!" "Berlin Tottering!" "Escape Routes in Italy Cut Off!" "Plans in Place for the

Occupation of Germany!" And just the day before, April 28, Benito Mussolini, the discredited dictator of Italy, was captured by partisans in Dongo Village on Lake Como and executed with his mistress, Clara Patacci.

If the war in Europe was considered "just about over," this was news to most front-line soldiers, certainly to those in the Rainbow Division, who had been in a fierce firefight less than twenty-four hours earlier. And so the twenty-ninth day of April, 1945, was just another day in the war, just another day to kill or be killed.

We were aware that the nature and the tempo of the struggle had changed. Obviously, we were winning. The enemy troops were falling back, and they were rapidly running out of room. At this rate, the war would have to be over in a matter of weeks, even days. But for now, our mission was to proceed with all possible speed to Munich. Our advance led us directly to the town of Dachau, and several units arrived at the camp somewhere around midmorning—perhaps, earlier or later, we cannot be sure: war is not a neat and orderly process, and most regimental orders were verbal, delivered to the battalions by liaison officers. Of course, as verbal orders proceed down a chain of command, there is ample opportunity for misunderstanding, or misinterpretation. Thus, in the real world of war, members of a given unit often have no accurate idea of time or place.

On April 14, Himmler had charged the commandant of Dachau to evacuate the camp: "There is absolutely no question of surrendering. The camp must be evacuated immediately. *No prisoner must fall into the hands of the enemy alive.* At Buchenwald, the prisoners have committed atrocities against the civilian population."[5] But Himmler's order was not obeyed. The Nazi garrison did surrender, and over thirty thousand prisoners did fall into our hands.

Himmler's order was not a sudden decision. It was actually a reminder to proceed with more speed and greater effort to execute an existing plan to "liquidate" the camp at Dachau and two Jewish labor camps, Muhldorf and Landsberg, because they were in the path of the advancing Allied armies. The area around Muhldorf and Landsberg had already been bombed by Allied air forces. Therefore, it was decided to have the Luftwaffe destroy them from the air, and nobody would know the difference. According to testimony given at the Nuremberg trials, the Landsberg prisoners would be marched to Dachau, to be exterminated with the inmates already there. All inmates, with the exception

Surrender of the SS *Übermensch* (Supermen) at Dachau. At far right is Maggie Higgins of the *New York Herald Tribune*. Photographed 29 April 1945 by Brig. Gen. Charles Y. Banfill, Deputy Commander for Operations, Headquarters, Commander Eighth Air Force. Courtesy Col. John Henning Linden, retired.

of "Aryan Nationals of the Western Powers," would be poisoned. The special code name for the Dachau murders was Action Wolkenbrand.[6]

Officials sabotaged the overall plan—but certainly not out of a sense of decency and a feeling of humanity. They were seasoned, veteran Nazi bureaucrats. They all had blood on their own hands, but they also had highly developed instincts for survival. It was painfully obvious that they were on the losing side, and soon there might very well be a day of reckoning.

In Dachau, many of the officers and men decided to slip away quietly and lose themselves in the civilian population. We were told by many of the inmates that those were the worst of the lot, although it is difficult to see how they could have been any worse than some of the specimens we captured. Some of the guards decided to stay and fight. Some decided to stay and surrender. Some decided to let events take their course.

In any case, when we arrived, Dachau was still standing intact. The more than thirty thousand prisoners—the alive, the half-alive, and the dead—were all in place. There would be some scattered skirmishing, a few brief firefights. We would enter the camp. And now, for us, the horrors would begin.

Most of what we saw was the main camp. At first, it was impossible to believe that this fiendish enterprise was located not in some nightmare, nether region of Hell itself but hardly a mile and a half away from the comfortable, genial town of Dachau. As the reader will learn later from firsthand accounts, most Dachauers steadfastly, even indignantly denied that they were aware of anything at all amiss on their doorstep. But, of course, the camp was the town's major industry, a boon to the economy, a plentiful supply of cheap labor—and this might have had something to do with it. How could they not know? The camp was in plain view of the town, practically in its backyard. Is it possible that no one saw those walking skeletons? No one heard the screams of the tortured? Burning human flesh has a particularly nauseating odor. Certainly, there must have been times when the wind carried the noxious smoke to every part of the town.

As our soldiers moved through this thriving, little town of Dachau, so many asked one another, "How could these people have lived with it?"[7] Obviously, they managed, especially if they were "undeterred by paltry scruples."

[Editor's note: In the testimonies that follow, each of our Rainbow witnesses is introduced by the rank he held as of April 29, 1945. Some, however, are referred to in other testimonies by ranks they assumed later.]

KZ Dachau

Nazi dawn—Dachau's gate opened wide,
Swallowing prisoners for a dozen years,
Incubator for the Holocaust.
Long, hard roads and a collision course:
For victims in their gray/blue stripes;
For black SS and their Kapos;
For Seventh Army,
XV Corps—
Rainbow 42nd;
Thunderbird 45th

All of their dead
Pointing the way.

Explosion for the world to see,
Skeletons alive and dead.
Liberators tears of rage.
SS sprawled in the coal yard, in the moat.
Death head guards had slunk away,
Replaced by Waffen SS-Viking,
Who believed the lies and chose Valhalla,
Unmourned by those behind the wire.

Grill iron work gate swung open.
Crematorium doors clanged shut.
Nazi twilight at the end of April.
One final plume of oily smoke,
In an outer yard of the Berlin Bunker,
Pilot beacon for the fires of hell.

Dee R. Eberhart

SIX OFFICIAL REPORTS

We captured Dachau on the twenty-ninth day of April 1945. Now, more than fifty years and some nineteen thousand days later, we must capture it again.

But where is Dachau? Not the present Dachau of the carefully preserved bricks and mortar—not the sterile, silent monument—but our Dachau of the living, the dying, the dead; the Dachau of the murdered and the martyred?

It still exists, as it always will, in the hearts and minds and memories of those of us who were there. And in the "official reports."

Although official reports are usually considered the most reliable of historical documents, many of them are signed by high-ranking officers who were not actually at the scene during the action. They are compiled by subordinates who may not have been there, either, and therefore the reports can be contradictory. After all, the same picture may be viewed from different perspectives. Reports from the field to a higher headquarters can also be influenced by various prejudices and personal positions which have to be protected. Thus, many reports are first interpreted and distilled. The basic facts are usually present, but at best they are secondhand recitals. They are devoid of subtext and emotion.

In the following pages, we offer six official reports. But these were written by officers who were both observers and participants. At Dachau, they were under enemy fire. They were there when the corpses were still fresh, the odors foul; and when wasted, diseased, and starved prisoners died before their eyes. Theirs, then, are more than routine military reports. They were written by men who were completely unprepared emotionally

Building Number 104—the main entrance (*Hauptwache*) to KZ Dachau-faces the Eickeplatz, named for Theodor Eicke, Dachau's first commandant. Photographed 29 April 1945 by Raphaël Algoet, news photographer for the Belgian government. Collection Algoet— SOMA/CEGES, Brussels.

for what they would encounter. As officers, their duty was to present factual information. But they also had to deal with the doings of the day as human beings. And one may sense their underlying feelings of grief, horror, and pity.

THE GENERAL

The entire Camp was a factory designed to wear out,
destroy, and consume the prisoners.

Brigadier General Henning Linden, Assistant Commander,
42d Infantry Division

Henning Linden was born in Mound, Minnesota, on September 3, 1892. His heritage was Swedish American, and he spoke Swedish until he was six years old. Because of his bright and optimistic disposition, he was nicknamed Sunny. He was a star hockey player at the University of Minnesota. He entered the army as a second lieutenant in 1918, rising to the rank of brigadier general. He was assigned to the Rainbow Division in November 1944. In the same month he led the division's three infantry regiments (the 222d, 232d, and 242d) to Europe, where they fought as Task Force Linden until the rest of the Rainbow arrived in February 1945.

Linden was a strict disciplinarian, but the men who came in daily contact with him admired and respected him because he was eminently fair. Scott Corbett, a correspondent for the *Rainbow Reveille*, the Rainbow Division newspaper (his own account of Dachau appears in Chapter 2), gives us an insight into Linden's character:

Two or three of us correspondents were surrounded by liberated inmates who were hugging and kissing and slobbering all over us, and we made no attempt to stop them. I suddenly noticed that Linden was nearby, and he saw what was happening. He walked straight over to us, and into the mob, and let them give him the same treatment. He never flinched. Later, the Medics rounded up the lot of us and shot DDT Powder down the back of our necks and all over us. None of us were exactly unemotional during that terrible day—and that includes General Linden in spades![1]

Pfc William "Pat" Donahue, one of Linden's guards, offers an enlisted man's impression:

He was strict; he was made to command. He scared the daylights out of an eighteen-year-old kid (like me). But as we got to know and understand him, he became a father image to us. He has been a great influence on my life. When we would mess up, he would call us in and ask, "Gentlemen, when are you going to stop embarrassing me?" And that would be the end of it. At the beginning of each day, one of us would say, "How are you this morning, Sir?" His standard answer was, "One step ahead of a cold."[2]

Dachau 29 April 1945

Headquarters
42d Infantry Division
Office of the Assistant Division Commander

2 May 1945

Memorandum to the Commanding General [Major General
Harry J. Collins]

Subject: Report on Surrender of Dachau Concentration Camp.

Herewith is submitted a brief report on the surrender of the
notorious Concentration Camp at Dachau, Germany, in compli-
ance with your instructions.

At about 1500 on 29 April, I arrived at the Command Post [CP]
222d Regiment, in Dachau, as instructed, to check on the status
of the Concentration Camp, and to be sure the prisoners therein
were frozen in place. I then proceeded to cross the Amper River
. . . and discovered the Camp a half-kilometer south of the bridge
. . . . Along the railroad running along the northern edge of the
Camp, I found a train of some 30-50 cars, some passenger, some
flatcars, some boxcars all littered with dead prisoners—20-30 to
a car. Some bodies were on the ground alongside the train, itself.
As far as I could see, most showed signs of beatings, starvation,
shooting, or all three. I moved forward toward the Camp where I
expected to find Colonel Downard[Commanding Officer, 2d Battalion, 222d Regiment]. As we approached the Southwest corner, three people came forward with a flag of truce. We met them
about 75 yards north of the Southwest corner. They were a Swiss
Red Cross Representative, Victor Maurer, and two SS troopers
who said they were the camp commander [SS Lieutenant Wick-
ert] and his assistant. They had come here on the night of the
28th to take over from the regular personnel, for the purpose of
surrendering the camp to the advancing Americans. The Swiss
Red Cross representative said there were about one hundred SS
guards in the camp who had their arms stacked, except for the
people in the tower . . . . He had given instructions that there
were no shots to be fired, and that it would take 50 men to relieve the guards, as there were 42,000 "half-crazed" inmates,
many of them typhus-infected[3] . . . . He asked if I were an officer. I
replied: "I am Assistant Division Commander of the 42d Infantry
Division, and will accept the surrender of the camp in the name
of the Rainbow Division for the United States Army . . . . " As we

were talking, there were several shots fired in the northeast corner of the camp. When I asked about it, he said he knew nothing. He had given strict orders that there be no shooting. I sent Lt. Cowling and two of my guards into the camp to reconnoiter, and they sent back word a few minutes later that we could enter. I moved into the enclosure area and found that the firing in the northeast area had been American troops coming through, and the appearance of a lieutenant and his three guards had loosed a wave of joyous enthusiasm to the extent that the whole fence was lined with a yelling, seething mass of prisoners who had broken through it in some places; and, in this process, several were electrocuted on the charged wires. Windows and doors in the big gatehouse were burst open by prisoners coming from the far side. Soldiers from the 45th Division arrived from the Northeast corner of the Stockade, and commenced firing over the prisoners' heads, as did soldiers from the 42d. This did not stop the rush. The inmates simply threw their arms around the soldiers, hugging and kissing them. In an hour, we had most of the prisoners back inside the enclosure . . . and under control. We discovered an American major, a lt. commander of the British navy, and a Belgian major . . . they appeared to be leaders of the POW organization. [IPC, discussed later]. We allowed them outside the enclosure, and into the CP which we established in the gatehouse, and put Lt. Colonel Walter Fellenz, CO, 1st Bn 222d Infantry in command of the Prisoner Stockade. By 1600, we had the camp well quieted down and organized. By 1750, a Lt. Colonel Squires [editor's note: Linden means Lt. Colonel Sparks, a battalion commander from the 45th division; see page 20] of the 157th Infantry, 45th Division, whose outfit had been fighting its way down through the Camp from the Northwest Corner, had arrived. He said his orders were to clean out the Camp by shooting it out with the [SS] guards and keepers. I told him my instructions were to keep the prisoners in place, and that Lt. Col. Fellenz, who was already in command of the POW cage, would continue as such, and they could coordinate by having their CPs close together. This was agreeable to the Colonel, and that order was immediately put into effect . . . .

I then took three reporters, Mr. Olson of *Time-Life*, Miss Higgins of the New York *Herald-Tribune*, and Mr. Cowan of the Associated Press, with myself, four of my guards, the aide, and representatives of the Prisoners Committee on a brief tour of the camp . . . . We went through a small crematory, outside of which were shoes and clothing . . . we saw several stacks of dead bodies

The surrender of Konzentrations-lager (KZ) Dachau. Top: Brig. Gen. Henning Linden (facing left) accepting the surrender, as an unidentified SS enlisted aid (front left) and Victor Maurer, International Red Cross delegate (center front) look on. *Stars and Stripes* staff writer Sgt. Peter Furst (back) faces General Linden. Photograph by Raphael Algoët. Collection Algoet—SOMA/CEGES, Brussels.

Bottom: SS 2nd Lt. Wickert, acting commander KZ Dachau (facing left) surrenders to Gen. Linden, (facing right). *New York Herald Tribune* correspondent Marguerite "Maggie" Higgins (front right) looks on. Courtesy of Col. John Henning Linden, retired.

... each looking like a human skeleton with the skin stretched over it. We visited rooms in barracks, where bunks were stacked five and six high in a room 20 by 30 where 50 men were quartered in so-called hospital wards which were nothing more than a concrete barracks floor with straw strewn on it ... living skeletons were lying in ragged, dirty clothing and bedding. The outstanding picture I got from my inspection of this camp was the barbaric, infamous systematic effort of the camp routine to degrade the human to a point where he bordered on the animal. I would strongly recommend that all German citizens within marching distance of this concentration camp be forced to walk through (it), to the end that the German people could know and realize what form of government and philosophy they have been supporting during the Nazi regime .... I did not go through all of the camp, as my mission was to ensure that the POWs were frozen in place. The report I got from the 222d Regiment, and the reporters with whom I talked later in the evening, was that the entire camp was a factory designed to wear out, destroy and consume the prisoners entrusted to its gates; and the sadistic philosophy and background of the whole camp is summarized by the words over the gate of the concentration camp: "Arbeit Macht Frei"—the translation of which is—"In Work You Will Be Free."[4]

THE AIDE

They tried to smile and wave—but most were too weak to do more than just look.

Lieutenant William J. Cowling III

William Cowling was born in Leavenworth, Kansas, on February 20, 1922. He was an only child. His father was a mail carrier, and his mother worked in a retail store. He met his wife while attending the University of Kansas. Married in 1947, they had three children—Sandra Cornell, John Cowling, and Barbara Cuite—and six grandchildren. He worked at a variety of professions but eventually engaged in real estate in the Kansas City area. He died in 1991.

A brave and most resourceful officer who performed his duty courageously at Dachau, Lieutenant Cowling was the perfect aide. He reported the facts exactly as he saw them. He never allowed his personality to intrude. He expressed neither an opinion nor a personal reaction, unlike the other three officers whose reports appear here. Note that he never used the word "I." He referred to himself throughout as "Lt. Cowling" or "the Aide."

Headquarters
2d Infantry Division
2 May 1945

Report of the Surrender of the Concentration Camp at Dachau

On 29 April, General Linden, Assistant Division Commander of the 42d Division, General Banfill of the Eighth Air Force, and General Linden's Aide, Lt. Cowling, and guards and drivers, were en-route to the left flank of the Division in the area of the 222d Infantry, with the mission of locating Colonel Downard's battalion, and pushing them on toward Munich. While passing through the city of Dachau, a jeep bearing two newspaper reporters, a *Stars and Stripes* [the official U.S. Army newspaper] reporter and a Miss Higgins from the New York *Herald Tribune*, questioned Lt. Cowling as to the location of the concentration camp. At this time, General Linden directed the Aide to continue toward the camp . . . to continue to look for Col. Downard, and take a reading on the situation.

Lt. Cowling continued toward the camp. Upon approaching a railroad track, a large number of boxcars were observed on a siding. The lieutenant discovered they were stacked with dead bodies. The Aide and the two generals made a quick inspection of the cars. The bodies were in an emaciated condition from starving. Many showed signs of beating and had been shot in the head. The Aide then proceeded toward the camp. As his jeep approached within a couple of hundred yards from the entrance, a German lieutenant, a soldier, and a civilian wearing a Red Cross armband and carrying a white flag, stepped from around the corner of a building. The American Lieutenant [Cowling], the guard and the jeep driver covered them as they came near. At this point, General Linden arrived, and the German officer said he wished to surrender the camp . . . and that approximately 100 SS Guards still remained in the camp and they were armed. These guards had been ordered not to shoot at the American soldiers, but to keep only the prisoners in check. The Red Cross man [Victor Maurer] said there were some 40,000 inmates, many of whom were half-crazed. At this point, small arms fire came from the left flank. The group took cover immediately, and the General had the German officer and the soldier stand in the open facing the fire, which soon let up. The General now sent the Aide into the camp to check on the situation. He also sent an officer, Major Avery, to get two Companies of the 222d Infantry up to the camp as soon as possible.

Lt. Cowling went through one gate of the camp, and just off to the right, about fifty yards, observed a tower with German soldiers inside. He ordered them down. Twelve came out. They were sent back under guard. The Lieutenant, one of General Linden's guards and the two newspaper reporters [Sergeant Peter Furst of *Stars and Stripes* and Marguerite "Maggie" Higgins of the New York *Herald Tribune*], moved inside. The large enclosure was at that time clear of any human beings. About a minute and a half later, people began pouring from the low, barracks-type black buildings. They were thin, dirty, half-starved. They rushed to the American Officer and the two newspaper reporters and attempted to shake their hands, kiss their hands or face, or just touch them. They even grabbed them and threw them up in the air, shouting in many different languages at the same time . . . .

Now the square was completely filled with thousands of yelling, screaming prisoners. They were all crowded up to the edge of a ditch just inside the barbed wire fence surrounding the encampment. General Linden arrived just as some of the people threw themselves across the ditch onto the wire. It was charged with electricity and they died instantly. The Lieutenant personally saw three of them die this way. General Linden directed his guards to get all the people back inside the enclosure. At about this time, Colonel Fellenz, of the 1st Battalion, 222d Regiment, arrived with some of his men. There were also some men of the 45th Division present. German guards still remained in all of the towers surrounding the prison with the exception of the one previously mentioned, and the two right at the gate. As Colonel Fellenz's men and some of the 45th Division approached, some of the [SS] guards fired at some of the prisoners who were trying to break through the fence. The doughboys of the two divisions shot the SS guards who had commenced the firing and quickly rounded up the others from the rest of the towers[5] . . . .

Dachau 29 April 1945

There was still considerable disorder. A few American soldiers had a good deal of difficulty attempting to make the prisoners, who were of all nationalities, understand that they must
remain inside until the Americans could arrange proper facilities
for release. It was necessary finally to fire some shots in the air to
get their attention. After a while, everyone was back inside the
enclosure, and a semblance of order was restored . . . .

The next hour was spent by General Linden and his group, including a Lt. Colonel Sparks of the 45th Division, attempting to
calm the crowd and make them realize that they would receive
proper food, medical attention, delousing, etc . . . .

An Associated Press reporter, another reporter, as well, requested the General's permission to inspect the camp. General
Linden consented and offered to accompany them along with the
Lieutenant and one of his guards. The first place visited was a
large yard, in which piles of assorted clothing were stacked. In
one pile were shoes, another, pants, and so on. As the group
moved through the camp, we saw four large ovens in which bodies were cremated. The group saw numerous piles of bodies, in
piles of anywhere between twenty and fifty, stacked between numerous buildings; all showed signs of starvation and were mere
skeletons; many showed signs of beating. The barracks were
dirty, low squat buildings, with bunks stacked to the ceiling, four
high, and so close together, a man could hardly squeeze between
them. In one building were all typhus cases; many had to lay on
the bare floor—a few had dirty straw pallets. They tried to smile
and wave, but most were too weak to do more than just look.

The party returned to the enclosure. By this time, the German
guards had either been killed or taken prisoner; and the Americans had taken over the camp. The General and his party then
left and returned to the 222d Regiment CP. The General returned
a short time later to be certain things were under control.

He remained until he was certain that Colonel Fellenz had
things well in hand. The time was approximately 2130. He went
back to the Division CP.

William J. Cowling, III
1st Lt. ADC
Aide to Asst Div Cmdr[6]

Lieutenant Cowling's report may be described as factual, impersonal, dispassionate—even cold. Reading it, one might con-
clude that he was unmoved by the experience. But Bill Cowling

considered it his duty to write in that manner. He believed that an official report must be confined strictly to the facts. However, the one he wrote must have been composed with considerable effort, because Cowling did have strong—even overpowering—feelings of grief and rage that day at Dachau. His official report is dated May 2, 1945. But three days earlier he had written what can be considered an "unofficial report," in the form of a letter to his parents. Here we can see an entirely different Lieutenant Bill Cowling:

28 April

Dear Folks:

Boy oh boy am I having a heck of a time trying to find time to write. We are really moving. My days have been consisting of getting up between 6:30 and 7:30 eating, throwing my stuff in a Jeep and taking off. When visiting the regiments and sometimes the battalions and then head for a new CP. By time we get into the new CP and set up it is 11 o'clock at night or later and I am so tired I just hit the sack, so I really haven't had much time to write. I received the fruit cake the other day and boy was it good. That package contained all the right things. I have lost my chap stick and my lips were so chapped so it really came in handy.

Well I was interrupted at this point and it is now the 30th of April and the very first minute I have had to write. Since I started this letter I have had the most, I suppose you would say, exciting, horrible and at the same time wonderful experience I have had ever or probably ever will have. When I tell it to you you probably won't believe all the details. I knew when I heard such stories back in the States I never believed them and now even after seeing with my own eyes, it is hard for me to believe it. Well, to go on with the story as you know we have been moving very rapidly and oftentimes the boss [Linden] and I get into the towns just about the same time the front line troops do. Yesterday we started out to locate a company and a unit advancing down a road. Enroute we learned from civilians and two newspaper people that just off the main road was the concentration camp of Dachau, oldest largest and most notorious camp in Germany. These newspaper people were going up to see the camp so we decided to go up too. We rode in a Jeep with a guard out ahead of the boys and we were several hundred yards ahead as we approached the camp. The first thing we came to was a railroad track leading out of the camp with a lot of open box cars on it. As we crossed the track and looked back into the cars the most horrible sight I have ever seen (up to that time) met my eyes. The cars were loaded with dead bodies. Most of them were naked and all of them skin and bones. Honest their legs and arms were only a couple of inches around and they had no buttocks at all. Many of the bodies had bullet holes in the back of their heads. It made us sick at our stomach and so mad we could do nothing but clinch our fists. I couldn't even talk. We then moved on towards the camp and my Jeep was still several hundred yards ahead. As we approached the main gate a German officer and a civilian wearing an International Red Cross band and carrying a white flag came out. We immediately filed out and I was just hoping he would make a funny move so I could hit the trigger of my tommy gun. He didn't however, and when he arrived abreast of us he asked for an American officer. I informed him he was talking to one and he said he wished to surrender the camp to me. About that time the General arrived and got the story from the German Lieutenant (that the camp was still manned by German guards who were armed but had orders not to shoot at us but only to keep the prisoners in check). Well about that time somebody started shooting from over on our left flank and we ducked but made the Germans stand in front of us. Finally the fire let up and we sent one of the guards back for a company of infantry. The newspaper people said they were going on into camp and I got permission to go on with them with my guard leaving the others with the General. We went through one gate and spotted some Germans in a tower. I hollered in German for them to come to me and they did. I sent them back to the guards and General and got on the front of the newspaper people's Jeep and headed for the gate.

A man lay dead just in front of the gate. A bullet through his head. One of the Germans we had taken lifted him out of the way and we dismounted and went throughout the gate into a large cement square about 800 squares surrounded by low black barracks and the whole works enclosed by barbed wire. When we entered the gate not a soul was in sight. Then suddenly people (few could call them that) came from all directions. They were dirty, starved skeletons with torn tattered clothes and they screamed and hollered and cried. They ran up and grabbed us.

Myself and the newspaper people and kissed our hands, our feet and all of them tried to touch us. They grabbed us and tossed us into the air screaming at the top of their lungs. I finally managed to pull myself free and get to the gate and shut it so they could not get out. Then I felt something brush my shoulder and I turned to the left of the two block houses guarding the gate to find a white flag fluttering square in my face and on the end of it inside the house eight Germans. I looked around the house and entered. I got the same question, are you an American Officer and said Yes. They turned over their arms, pistols and rifles to me and I told them to sit tight. I then went back outside and sent my driver to get the Jeep. Then I went back into the Germans and took their arms and sent the pistols to my Jeep (I gave all away but two). When I came back out the General was there and the people inside the enclosure were all in the large square shouting and crying. Then a terrible thing happened. Some of them in their frenzy charged the barbed wire fence to get out and embrace us and touch us. Immediately they were killed by an electric charge running through the fence. I personally saw three die that way. Our troops arrived about that time and took the rest of the guards, Germans (who during all this time had remained in the towers around the prison). A number of them and I sincerely regret that I took the eight prisoners that I did after a trip through the camp which I shall describe in a minute. Well the General attempted to get the thing organized and an American major who had been held in the camp since September came out and we set him up as head of the prisoners. He soon picked me to quiet the prisoners down and explain to them that they must stay in the camp until we could get them deloused, and proper food and medical care.

Several newspaper people arrived about that time and wanted to go throughout the camp so we took them through with a guide furnished by the prisoners. The first thing we came to were piles and piles of clothing, shoes, pants, shirts, coats, etc. Then we went into a room with a table with flowers on it and some soap and towels. Another door with the word showers lead off of this and upon going through this room it appeared to be a shower room but instead of water, gas came out. Next we went next door to four large ovens where they cremated the dead. Then we were taken to piles of dead. There were from two to fifty people in a pile all naked, starved and dead. There must have been about 1,000 dead in all. Then we went through a building where fifty men were guarded in a room the size of your kitchen. There were hundreds of typhus cases and all through the camp men cheered us and tried to touch us. Incidentally many of the dead and living showed signs of horrible beatings and torture. It is unbelievable how any human can treat others as they were treated. One wasted little man came up and touched my sleeve and kissed my hand. He spoke perfect English and I asked him if he were American. He said no, Jewish and that he was one of the very few left, that thousands had been killed. He had been there six years. He was twenty-eight years old and looked to be sixty years old. The Germans I took prisoner are very fortunate they were taken before I saw the camp. I will never take another German prisoner armed or unarmed. How can they expect to do what they have done and simply say I quit and go scot free. They are not fit to live.

Well, that's my story. A day I will never forget. It will get a lot of publicity and you may see General Linden's name connected with Dachau but you can know in your own minds that it was your son who was among the first American soldiers to enter the famous Camp of Dachau. I know that sounds like bragging but I only say it because it is true and I know that the story won't come out that way but several thousand prisoners will remember me. Incidentally there was 32,000 prisoners in the camp. They were Polish, Jewish, French, German and even American. Well I must stop now. The next time I write I hope I can say that I got my first German and I don't mean prisoner.

Incidentally, your griping about my going to the South Pacific. I have only been in the Army a couple of years. Some of these people were in the hell hole of Dachau for years. If I spend ten years in the Army during war I will never go through what those people go through. Even if I were killed, I would be lucky compared to those people. So if you still feel the jitters remember the people of Dachau and think how lucky I am no matter what happens.

We will write and I will give you the rest of the story when I get home.

Love, Bill[7]

Lt. William J. Cowling III, in 1945. Courtesy Col. John Henning Linden, retired.

Dachau 29 April 1945

THE "GUEST"

*The sight of the few American uniforms that had arrived,
resulted in an emotional outburst of relief and enthusiasm
which was indescribable.*

**Brigadier General Charles Y. Banfill
Eighth U.S. Air Force**

Brigadier Charles Y. Banfill of the U.S. Army Eighth Air Force
was assigned to observation duty in the European theater of operations. He told General Linden that he wanted to get a
"ground's eye view" of what he had seen from thousands of feet
up in the sky. Actually, he came along for the ride. Thus he found
himself with the "spearhead" on that day. He entered the camp
with General Linden, and there he saw far more than he, or anyone else, could have possibly imagined.

The air force, because of its devastating weaponry, can inflict
the greatest damage on the enemy. But the flying crews have only
a distant view of the heaps of rubble they create. They see the destruction of "targets," but not of human beings. They are spared
the sight of shattered bones, spurting blood, and dismembered
bodies.

Many infantry soldiers had what might be called today an "attitude" toward the air force. To begin, its members lived well.
They were stationed in towns and cities hundreds of miles from
the front. True, they were subject to enemy bombardment. So?
Who wasn't? They had warm, dry living quarters. They could
bathe every night. They had hot meals and clean clothes. And
they could enjoy personal relationships with townspeople who
lived near the base. When they went out on a mission—after they
dropped their bombs and shot it out with enemy fighters, they
could return, those who weren't killed—yes, we gave them that—
to the comforts of home. What did *they* really know about war?

In the infantry, you could spend the whole day and half the
night battling for a few acres of mud. And if you took it, what was
your reward? You could lie down and try to sleep in it. But these
were not lasting animosities. It didn't take us long to learn—the
hard way—that war, like life and death, is never fair.

One of the reasons we include General Banfill's report is because he adds the testimony of an "outsider" to our own. Another
is because it shows how the Rainbow acquitted itself at Dachau.

26

"To clear and capture the camp" could be considered, in itself, a routine military operation. But once inside, how were we to control thousands of dazed, desperate, frantic human beings who were determined to break out of their torture chamber without delay, and to hold them all in place until they were medically fit to be moved? It required all of our officers and men, from the general down, to display sympathy, understanding, and also gentle pressure. We can be proud that our fighting division possessed those qualities.

Brigadier General Charles Yawkee Banfill, USAF, was born September 5, 1897, in Bonifay, Florida. He served as an enlisted man in the First Field Artillery of the Louisiana National Guard. He was then assigned to the School of Military Aeronautics at the University of Texas. His army career was just beginning, and the air service was in its infancy. It can be said that they grew up together. Through the twenties and thirties, he served at a number of schools and bases throughout the United States and Hawaii. He was even in charge of filming the motion picture *Flying Cadet* at Duncan Field, Texas.

Appointed brigadier general in 1944, he went overseas in February 1945 as director of Intelligence, 325th Photo Wing, Eighth Air Force. He spent four days with General Linden, and the enlisted men in Linden's party remember General Banfill as very kind, considerate, and easy to talk to. General Banfill retired from active duty on July 31, 1953. He died in 1966.

Headquarters Eighth Air Force
Office of the Commanding General
APO 634

28 May 1945

Subject: Surrender of German Concentration Camp, Dachau, 29
    April 1945

To: Whom It May Concern.

This is to certify that I was present at Dachau on 29 April 1945 as a member of a party headed by Brigadier General Henning Linden, Asst. Division Commander of the 42d Infantry Division. During the approximate period, 1430 hours-2130 hours, I was in position to observe every action taken by Brig. Gen. Linden, except for two periods of time, approximately 30 and 15 minutes, respectively, when in the first instance, he entered the prison enclosure for the purpose of making an inspection, and I left the immediate vicinity of the gate to locate a portable Public Address System in controlling the liberated prisoners.

I have examined the statements by 1st Lt William J. Cowling, Jr., and Brig. Gen. Henning Linden, dated 2 May 1945, and while both cover matters beyond the scope of my personal observations, in every instance in which I have had personal knowledge, they are both accurate and factual.

The critical period of surrender and liberation extended from about 1530 to 1630 hours. During this period, the SS guards who had been withdrawn from the guard tower, laid down their arms, the electric current had been turned off the wire surrounding the enclosure, and this wire had been breached in numerous places. With the small number of American personnel available, BG Linden succeeded in keeping all but a few inmates inside the outer moat which surrounded the enclosure outside the wire. At one time, the gatehouse was completely in the hands of the prisoners, but with the assistance of calmer members of the prisoner personnel, and American soldiers, the gatehouse was cleared and policed.

. . . It is my considered opinion that BG Linden did everything in his power to carry out his Division Commander's instructions to keep the prisoners in place within the enclosure. As determined by discussion with English-speaking prisoners, the camp had been under extreme tension for many hours. The prisoners did not know (a) whether they would be massacred by the Germans, (b) whether they would be caught in a fire fight between the German and American troops, or (c) whether they would be liberated by the timely arrival of the Americans. The sight of the few American uniforms that arrived . . . resulted in an emotional outburst of relief and enthusiasm which was indescribable. The fact that several prisoners hurled themselves or were pushed against the charged wire and electrocuted themselves at the moment of liberation, gives some impression of the intensity of feeling.

I feel that under the circumstances prevailing at the time, BG Linden should be commended for the measures he took.

Charles Y. Banfill
Brigadier General, USA
Deputy Commander for Operations[8]

THE BATTALION COMMANDER

No wonder the flowers were so beautiful.

Lieutenant Colonel Walter J. (Mickey) Fellenz,
Commanding Officer, 1st Battalion, 222d Regiment

Walter J. Fellenz was a member of a military family. His father was in the service for forty years, and so were his two brothers. His son and son-in-law are West Point graduates.

"Mickey" Fellenz was born November 21, 1916, in Kansas. He entered the United States Military Academy in 1936 and later graduated from the U. S. Army's command and general staff college.

Following World War II, he served in Korea in 1953. From 1959 until his retirement in 1962, he was commanding officer of the 101st Airborne Support Group. He was awarded the Silver Star, the Purple Heart, and the Bronze Star Medal with Oak Leaf Cluster for heroic achievement.

Mickey Fellenz "passed over the rainbow" June 1, 1978, in San Antonio, Texas.

Headquarters
Fighting First Battalion
222d Infantry

6 May 1945

Subject: Impression of The Dachau Concentration Camp

To: The Commanding General, 42d Infantry Division (Thru
Channels)

The following impressions are based on personal observation and conversations with the Inmates at The Dachau Concentration Camp . . . .

1. *The Dead Bodies in the Box Cars . . .*

It was like approaching a rail siding in any small-size Western town where the appearance of thirty or forty box cars on a single track, lonely and desolate, is not a sight uncommon. As I neared

Dachau 29 April 1945

Brig. Gen. Linden (left, atop wall) restoring order at the Gate to the Inmates' Compound. Extreme left, SS 2nd Lt. Wickert, who surrendered the Camp; T-5 Harry Shaffer, and International Red Cross Delegate Victor Maurer. Photograph by Raphaël Algoet, 29 April 1945. Collection Algoet— SOMA/CEGES, Brussels.

the cars, however, I saw death and destruction of human lives at its height. Each of the thirty to forty cars contained the skin and bones of men and women, thousands of them, half-clothed in rags—dead.

Upon closer inspection of the bodies, I found many contained bullet holes. I was later informed by inmates that the SS required the prisoners to lie flat in the cars. From time to time, they would inspect the cars; any person not in the prone position, was shot without question, and left in the car.

Except for the small percentage who were shot, they died from starvation and exposure, and having been on the train twenty-seven days without food. Their clothes were rags; some had crude shoes with wooden soles, some had rags on their feet, most were bare-footed. All were mere skeletons, weighing on the average of fifty to sixty pounds.

Apparently, these people had been dead but a short time. There was no foul odor; just death—fresh death—everywhere.

2. The First Impression of the Camp

Nearly a thousand yards from the rail siding, was the Camp, itself. The approach was a wide, two-lane road with a lawn

The infamous Death Train, outside KZ Dachau. Photograph by T-4 Sidney Blau, 163d Signal Photographic Company, 30 April 1945. Courtesy of the National Archives Still Picture Branch Photo ID Number 111-SC-207475.

down the middle. One could imagine from the impressive massiveness of the grey Administration Buildings and Barracks, the fine lawns, great walls and black iron-grilled gates, that you were approaching a wealthy girls finishing school in the suburbs of one of our great cities. All was so neat, so orderly, so beautiful.

At the main gate, I met Brigadier General Linden, Lt. Colonel Bolduc, and several staff officers and bodyguards. General Linden was waiting for a report from his aide, who had been dispatched inside the camp to see if it had been deserted by its Guards. Shortly after my arrival, the aide [Lt. William Cowling] reported that the SS had apparently deserted the camp. In we went, fully prepared to fight, however.

Several hundred yards inside the main gate, we encountered the concentration enclosure, itself. There before us, behind an electrically charged, barbed wire fence, stood a mass of cheering, half-mad men, women and children, waving and shouting with happiness—their liberators had come! The noise was beyond comprehension! Every individual (over 32,000) who could utter a sound, was cheering. Our hearts wept as we saw the tears of happiness fall from their cheeks.

3. Death, Seventeen SS Men

Amid the deafening roar of cheers, several inmates warned us of danger by pointing to one of the eight [sic—there were only seven] towers which surrounded the electrically charged fence. The tower was still manned by SS guards . . . . The SS tried to train their machine guns on us; but we quickly killed them each time a new man attempted to fire the guns. We killed all seventeen SS.

In the excitement of the shooting, in the full view of the inmates, the surging throng pushed one man against the barbed wire fence. It was heart-breaking to see the poor fellow electrocuted when freedom was within his grasp.

4. Establishment of Order in the Camp

With the last of the SS guards killed, the inmates broke down the gate . . . . Fortunately, more of our troops arrived, and in a short time, the liberated inmates were made to understand that they must all return to the enclosure . . . . Shortly, order was restored.

In addition to the men from the 42d Division, elements from the 45th Division, under the command of Lt. Colonel Sparks, had arrived. I was placed in command of the enclosure, itself. Lt. Colonel Sparks was charged with the searching and guarding of the buildings within the Camp—but exclusive of the Prisoner Enclosure.

5. The Committee of Six

. . . I was introduced to a Major [actually he was a lieutenant] Guirard, and five other members of the Prisoners Committee, by General Linden. Lt. Rene Jean Anare Guiraud, a native of Chicago, and a member of the United States Office of Strategic Services [OSS], was the only American prisoner there. This body [the Prisoners Committee]—with the exception of the President, a British naval commander, who was a Belgian national, and the Vice-President, Major Guiraud, represented the majority of the nationalities of the inmates. They had been secretly elected several days before in anticipation of our coming.

The Committee and I went into conference and I was informed of the following facts of immediate concern.

a. Nearly all the inmates had typhus, and contact with them must be avoided.

b. The water was typhus-ridden because over 4,000 inmates had been buried near the water reservoir of the city of Dachau.

c. There were over 4,000 bodies in a warehouse in the crematorium.

d. There were over 1,000 dead bodies in the barracks within the enclosure. These people had died and had not been removed at the time of our arrival.

e. There were 491 women inmates in 3 separate barracks.

f. The prisoners had saved enough food from their already inadequate diet to feed themselves for 6 days before help from the United Nations was needed.

Armed with these facts, and in conjunction with Lt. Col. Sparks, I immediately made a report to higher headquarters. With the arrival of my troops, guards were posted where necessary; order by this time had been completely restored.

6. *Inspection of the Female Barracks*

Shortly after the arrival of my troops, I was taken by Major Guiraud to inspect the women's barracks. There, in each of the filthy barracks with a normal capacity of sixty, were jammed over three times that number of women, crazed, half-clothed. The stench in those barracks was vile. At the sight of American soldiers, they wept and cheered with happiness. Major Guiraud informed me that all the women were of Jewish extraction, or else were Aryans accused of having had sexual intercourse with a Jew. The SS used these women freely for their own enjoyment.

7. *Inspection of the Crematorium and the Gas Chamber*

Early the following morning, in company with several members of the Committee, I inspected the crematorium. It was located several hundred yards from the Enclosure Gate. It consisted of several large buildings, entirely hidden from outside view by a large well-trimmed hedge over twelve feet high.

Passing through the arched gate, I was confronted by a formal garden; green grass neatly cut, beds of flowers along the cinder paths, a water fountain, and several large birdhouses from which turtle doves came and went.

First, I was led to the execution grounds, a small plot of ground, entirely enclosed by a hedge. There, I saw a mound of earth about thirty feet long and four feet high. Here, prisoners, six at a time, were lined up; required to kneel down facing the mound, while the SS nonchalantly murdered them by shooting them in the back of the head from a range of two or three feet. The mound of earth was still wet with blood. Many thousands of men, women and children had been killed on this very plot of ground.

Next, I was led to the storage warehouse. This large building contained the naked dead bodies of over 4,000 men, women and children, thrown one on top of the other like sacks of potatoes. The odor was terrific. I vomited three times in less than five minutes. It was the most revolting smell I had ever experienced . . . .

Next to the Warehouse of dead bodies, was the crematory, itself; a large, double furnace, each capable of being stuffed with five or six corpses at once. The dead bodies were dragged from the Warehouse, jammed into the red-hot furnace. But even then, the Nazis were not through! The ashes of the victims were used as fertilizer for the flower gardens and the vegetable gardens— no wonder the flowers were so beautiful!

8. The Reason for it All

Leaving the crematorium, I went back to my command post where Major Guiraud informed me that I was to be the guest of the Camp for lunch. I declined, saying that food for them was scarce enough—but nothing doing! I was to be their guest!

During dinner, I inquired as to the reasoning behind it all. Why the terror, the killings, the cruelty?

I was adequately informed by men who had been at Dachau for terms as long as twelve years. The gist of the reasoning was as follows: In Hitler's conception of conquering the whole world, he desired to enslave all peoples, not as mere slave labor, but, in addition, he tried to completely break the human mind; to put it on a level with common animals. By doing this, he could not only make the German a superman, but, in addition, he could raise the ego of the German to unheard of heights.

Many factors were injected into the concentration camp to accomplish this total destruction of the mind; no recreation of any kind, no reading matter, all individual thinking was beaten out of the prisoners; starvation to a point where a crust of bread would cause a struggle to the death among the inmates; a system of selecting prisoners to do the torturing, the killing and beating. In addition, Dachau even had prostitutes to further

destroy self-respect. The cunning German left not a stone un-
turned to accomplish his subtle plan.

Had the plan worked, all humanity would soon have been en-
slaved, body and soul—soon to be reduced to nothing but animals under the mind-destroying, mad scheme of Adolf Hitler
and his SS. Thank God, this plan shall never be fulfilled.

Walter J. Fellenz
Lt. Col., Infantry,
Commanding the 1st Bn, 222d Infantry,
42d Rainbow Division[9]

    In 1975, Colonel Fellenz sent a copy of his Official Report to his
children, along with this note: "I suggest that you preserve this
material so that your children will be able to see what it was like
in 1945, thirty years ago. This set of documents is part of your heritage, my children, and you must use it. You may duplicate it and
send it to your friends if you like.

    "If you don't believe how it was, I don't blame you. Yet, you
should believe your father's words. Trust me, for I saw it all with
my own eyes."[10]

THE INTERNATIONAL PRISONERS COMMITTEE

    The information that describes the International Prisoners
Committee (IPC) is an excerpt from an official document on Dachau prepared by the CIC Detachment, Seventh Army, May 1945:

When American troops entered Dachau, they found an International Prisoners Committee (IPC) functioning in the Camp.
The IPC was in complete control. Most of the SS Guards had fled
together with most of those prisoner elements who had co-
operated with the SS, and had, themselves, been guilty of mal-
treatment and murder of fellow inmates.

The origins of the IPC go back to sometime in September of
last year [1944] when Allied military successes in the West
promised the possibility of an early liberation. A small group of
inmates, employed in the Camp Hospital, served as a nucleus:
an Albanian (Kuci), a Pole (Nazewsi), a Belgian (Haulot) and a
British-Canadian (O'Leary). They established contact with representatives of other nationalities—Russian, French, etc.— and
also co-operated with one German, Oskar Mueller, a recent

Original caption for this photograph reads: *Here are a few of Dachau's 30,000 still living prisoners, clad in their blue and white striped prison garb. And one for whom deliverance came too late, but Dachau's people have become so used to the sight and stench of death his body is placidly ignored.* Photograph taken 29 April 1945 by Pfc William R. "Hap" Hazard, photographer for the 42d Infantry Division newspaper, the *Rainbow Reveille.*

arrival in the Camp. Aside from Mueller, the "hospital nucleus" of the future IPC did not work with any German prisoners. They were too much afraid of spies working among the Germans.

The aims of this group were simple. They wished to prepare for the advance of the Americans, save as many lives as possible in the last critical phase before liberation, and keep a record of original criminal SS activities and personalities. In this program, they seem to have been quite successful. Since last December, they tried to keep certain key inmates as "patients" in the Camp hospital where they enjoyed a certain protection. They likewise enlisted the help of a great number of block and cell seniors to control the activities of criminal elements among the prisoners, and nip in the bud any provocative action which the SS might use to unloose mass massacres. They prepared lists of crimes and criminals among the SS and their prisoner stooges. Finally, they tried to keep informed about the advance of the Allies, listening to foreign broadcasts, and spread the news by their men throughout the Camp. When American troops were near Augsburg, they even established contact through prisoners working on farms in that area.

The building up of this rather closely knit network of activities was facilitated by the gradual disintegration of SS controls during the last months, the replacement of old SS Guards, the comparatively small number of guards toward the end (about 251), and confusion created by orders and counter-orders from higher headquarters. In the last days, the IPC came practically out into the open. On April 27, a large transport of 6,700 Russians, Poles, Germans and Jews was scheduled to leave the Camp [they were to be sent to extermination centers]. By changing national identity patches, and padding Camp records, 1,000 Russians were hidden in the camp and escaped the transport and destruction. Of this transport, only 60 survived the massacre staged by the SS Guards on the road south of Munich.

On the following day, the IPC actually issued circulars, informing their fellow prisoners that the Committee had taken over, that they should stay in their barracks and maintain law and order to prevent provocations. An attempt by the SS to evacuate another transport on the evening of April 28 failed when the inmates simply did not leave their barracks. Besides this simple aim for the purpose of saving as many lives as possible, the IPC did not have any program. There was no political activity of any kind, and no social differentiations within the group. Thus, the activities of the one well-organized group emerging in the Camp proved that the only rationale for organizing any group activity under the conditions of Dachau was derived entirely from the primitive motive of personal survival, and not from any social, political or religious associations.

The IPC is now the highest prisoner authority in the Camp. It is headed, at present, by a former Soviet General Michailow. The Belgian Haulot is Vice-President. It holds daily meetings with the Army authorities and is charged with carrying out the orders of the American camp commandant. Sub-committees for all basic necessities—police, food, sanitation, work, discipline have been established. In this way, the Committee assists in maintaining order, and preparing conditions for the release and repatriation of the prisoners at Dachau.[11]

Dachau 29 April 1945

AN AMERICAN INMATE

Lieutenant Rene Jean-Anare Guiraud was integrated into the regular U.S. Army and attained the rank of major prior to being retired on May 31, 1952, for disability reasons. Mentioned in both Lieutenant Colonel Fellenz's report and the IPC document, Lieutenant Guiraud was reportedly a member of the OSS. He was captured behind the enemy lines and sent to Dachau, where he became the only known American POW in the camp. For some reason, the Nazis believed he was a major.

Information about Guiraud during the war was declassified several years ago. At our request, the Central Intelligence Agency (CIA) sent it to us. Guiraud died January 24, 1970.

Block 12 Supplemental Sheet

a. After undergoing extensive specialized training and operational testing, I was parachuted into Occupied France, accompanied by a radio operator. Upon arrival in France, we assumed identities and posed as French citizens who had been in Occupied France throughout the war. My mission was to organize a secret organization capable of collecting intelligence, harassing German Military units and occupation forces, sabotaging critical war materiel facilities, and protecting key military features for use by Allied Forces when they reached the area.

b. Though arrested on a charge unrelated to my activities, the mission was successful. Prior to my arrest, 1,500 guerrillas had been organized, equipped from "Local" stocks, trained and led in operations; intelligence and counter-intelligence works had been developed; numerous resistance cells for passive sabotage had been brought under our control and direction, and had been trained, and "security weeded" of penetrations; and my radio operator had been established with a secure system of transmission sites, couriers, etc. Upon my arrest, he carried on.

c. After undergoing two months of "forceful" interrogation by the Gestapo, and having successfully avoided compromising the mission, I became the permanent "guest" of the Nazis in the Concentration Camp of Dachau in Germany, where I remained until liberated by U.S. Forces in April, 1945. While in Dachau, I fostered and participated in a prisoner resistance movement which went undetected until liberation. At the moment of liberation, I was placed in command of the Dachau Camp and post area pending the arrival of U.S. Civil Affairs, etc., authorities. After orienting three different G-5s in two weeks, I "escaped" the assignment; and accompanied by five fellow "ex-prisoners" (all British agents), commandeering a disabled U.S. C-47 and crew, we arrived in Paris in time for the "V-E" celebrations that evening.[12]

THE RAINBOW DIVISION'S OFFICIAL CORRESPONDENTS

Dachau was a magnet for the media, which consisted mostly of the written word, pictures in the press, radio broadcasts, and films shown in the newsreels. The war made the reputations of many of the correspondents, among them Ernie Pyle, E. R. Murrow, Louis Lochner, Sid Olson, Howard Cowan, Walter Ridder, and Marguerite Higgins, who proved she could keep up with any of the male reporters in the field. Word that the capture of Dachau was imminent spread through the journalistic fraternity—and sorority; many of them arrived there practically on our heels.

Present on the scene also were Rainbow correspondents Sergeant Scott Corbett and Technician 3rd Grade (T-3) James Creasman.[1] Corbett, a member of the 242d Infantry Regiment, was also a reporter for the *Rainbow Reveille*, our official division newspaper, which is still being published today.

> *It doesn't make me sick to my stomach, or anything like that—it just makes me goddam mad!*
>
> **Sidney Olson, TIME-LIFE correspondent,**
> **as reported by Sergeant Scott Corbett, RAINBOW REVEILLE**

Scott Corbett was born in Kansas City, Missouri, in 1913. He attended Kansas City Junior College and then the University of Missouri, where he graduated with a degree in journalism. He married Elizabeth Pierce, and they moved to New York. There, he began his lifelong career as a writer.

After the war, he wrote for the *Saturday Evening Post* and comedy sketch material for radio and TV. He is the author of seventy novels; sixty are for children. In this field, his most successful work is a ten-volume series entitled *The Lemonade Trick*. Based on his experience in renovating a four-story brownstone building, he wrote a book called *The Reluctant Landlord*. This was purchased by Hollywood and made into a movie, *The Love Nest*, with Marilyn Monroe, June Haver, William Lundigan, and Jack Paar. Scott is the father of a daughter, Florence Lee Corbett Flusser, and has two grandchildren.

The first human beings ever to enter the infamous Concentration Camp at Dachau without despair and terror, entered it today. Infantrymen of the XVth Corps, 42d Division, are now in command of Dachau and they brought a new life to over 30,000 survivors among the prisoners of the horror camp.

What they found there bears out every atrocity told about the first great concentration camp in the twelve years of its existence. In the Crematorium, the skeleton-like bodies of the dead still lay in a room next to the furnace, stacked like cordwood. The cement floor slanted to a drain which carried off the blood, but not the unforgettable stench of death. Unlike Auschwitz, where the Gas Chamber and the Crematorium were demolished by the retreating SS, the destruction of this horrifying evidence at Dachau by a time bomb was prevented when doughboys discovered and severed the wire which would have set off the charge. In addition, the entire building was a maze of booby-traps.

There was a neat building which is the porcelain factory of Dachau, where political prisoners turned out dainty porcelain figurines, and busts of Hitler for German homes. Among these, were a German soldier holding a flagstaff with a Nazi flag, soldiers of all kinds and ages; medieval figures, drummer boys, peasants in costumes of various regions of Germany; horses, bears, and exquisite 18th Century courtiers—silk-stockinged and be-ruffed—playing flutes. Some of the figurines were beautifully colored. On one shelf, as if to symbolize Germany, stood two colored figurines: one, a Hessian Mercenary, the other, an SS Storm Trooper on horseback. Another popular figure was Frederick, the Great, also on horseback.

In each of the neat, orderly, well-appointed offices, throughout the Camp, large, framed photographs of Heinrich Himmler dominated the room. His photo also dominated a kitchen in an SS messhall where a Storm Trooper sat alone at a table. Nearby, water from a tap, over a basin, was running full blast and spilling onto the floor. In the kitchen was the sour smell of spoiled food still in pots on the stove. On the table before the Storm Trooper, was a half-eaten meal.

"What are you?" he was asked.

"SS," he replied bluntly and arrogantly.

"What are these others?"

He shrugged, contemptuously. "Luftwaffe" [German air force].

Someone whispered the question, "How could you do these things . . ?"

This time he just shrugged. "These human swine,"[2] he said.

Scott Corbett's piece on Dachau in the *Rainbow Reveille* is an official part of our division's military history. When Art Lee told him about our plans to write this book and asked him if he could add anything to his eyewitness account, Scott sent him a letter which touches the true heart of the story.

December 19, 1994

Dear Arthur:

Here is a copy of a letter I wrote to my wife, Elizabeth, two days after I visited Dachau on April 29, 1945. My wife was born in Dachau in 1911, when her father had come to Munich to study medicine. It was a terrible way to visit her birthplace, and now, more than ever, I wish she were still with me to help with all this. In 1990, just a few months after our 50th Wedding Anniversary, she died suddenly, the day before Thanksgiving. A lot of vignettes are as fresh today as the moment I experienced them. What the letter does is establish who was there, where we were, and when. I might add that there was no correspondent from any other Division with us. For that reason, if for no other, I am glad this has come up.

Dachau 29 April 1945

A Merry Christmas and Happy New Year to you—merrier and happier than we had in those years!
Yours

Scott

FROM: Sgt Scott Corbett
Div HQ Co 42d Div
APO 411 c/o PM
TO: Elizabeth G. Corbett
East Millstone, N.J.
c/o J. W. Pierce
New York, N.Y.

1 May 1945
Bavaria

Darling:
May 1st and it's snowing, some May Day.

At the moment, I'm wondering if you already know that I visited your birthplace, because the AP Correspondent, Louis Lochner, mentions me in his piece about Dachau. I was with him when he visited the camp the day after our troops took the place. That day, Sid Olson of Time-Life, a lad named Ridder of the St. Paul Dispatch, and I were the first newsmen in the Camp. Howard Cowan of the AP, and Jan Yitrick of the London News Chronicle turned up shortly. On our own, we poked around the kitchens, the porcelain factory, the Crematorium, and the Main Enclosure. Nothing can adequately describe the horrors we saw there.

On a railway siding just outside the camp, we saw those boxcars filled with the dead who had been penned up to starve to death.

Inside the grounds, a few dead SS men whom the prisoners had caught, dotted the landscape and floated in the canal beside the road that led inside from the Main Gate. They were beaten to a pulp, needless to say. I won't go over it all because I'm sure you'll read about all the incredible horrors in the papers.

When we left, we went back to Corps. The Corps Public Relations Office put us up, furnished us with typewriters and liquor, and we wrote our stories. We had to relax to get some of it off our chests for a while. A major and a lieutenant of a Signal Photo

Company [official army photographic unit] was assigned to take pictures for the War Crimes Commission, so we all talked till one. Finally, we all went to work. We would write, and then someone would exclaim about something, and we would all stop and talk about it. We drank steadily, I don't mind saying. All of us just wrote pages and pages and we didn't finish till five-thirty. We managed to squeeze out three hours sleep. We all agreed that once was enough. We never wanted to see Dachau again. But the next day, when they heard that I had already been to Dachau, Louis Lochner, Jack Bell of the Chicago Daily News, and Herb Plambeck of the Des Moines Register, and INS [International News Service] wanted me to go with them, so I found myself making a second tour.

The second day was much different from the first. Everybody was there by then; correspondents, photographers, officers of this and that . . . whereas the first day there was no one but us soldiers, freed prisoners and the dead.

After a time, General Linden and various staff people returned, and the General made a tour of the Main Enclosure to see the bodies of those inmates who had been shot and stacked up by the SS the night before they beat it. That part of the experience is unforgettable, for everywhere we went, the poor, miserable prisoners cheered us, kissed our hands, our cheeks, clung to us, or just maybe touched us, to see if we were real.

All the time, I felt how the final incredibility was that I was visiting a place just outside the town you were born in; the pleasant, little suburb I had just passed through. Thank God you were born an American there and not a German.

Today, I visited Munich with Louis Lochner, Bell, and Plambeck. Lochner is the top AP man in Germany. He won the Pulitzer Prize for his reporting there some years back. He knows all the background on Hitler and The Nazi Party history. He had been to all the landmarks before the war, so he gave us a tour of Munich such as few people will ever be able to make under such distinguished auspices. We started at the Burgerbrau Keller, where Hitler had made his first attempt to grab power, for which he spent two years in prison . . . writing *Mein Kampf*. Next, the Hofbrau where his henchmen frequently met after they had begun to gain prominence. We visited the great ruined shell of the Cathedral, The Frauenkirch. We visited the monument to the great German Field Marshall Tilly, in front of which 27 thugs fell in the 1923 Putsch, while Hitler fled in a waiting taxi. We went to The Koenigs Platz, where the fallen thugs are buried in ornate tombs in beautiful classic pavilions. On each side of the Square are Art Galleries, among Europe's finest.[3]

We talked our way into the Fuhrer House, although, the guards had orders to admit nobody. We went up the magnificent marble staircase to the sumptuous rooms where Hitler and his gang pulled off their great coups. We walked into the room where Chamberlain and Daladier sold out Czechoslovakia to Hitler for "Peace in Our Time." Louis Lochner was one of the correspondents waiting outside the room when Chamberlain came out with the announcement. He had also been to all the other places we had visited, drinking beer and watching the ceremonies.

We also saw what must have been Hitler's private rooms, with AH in the bronze back of the fireplace, and a magnificent bathroom still spotless and gleaming.

I can't write all I've seen these past three days, because I've seen a lifetime of incredible sights and places where terrible and monumental history was made. I'm sure you'll read a great deal about all this in the papers, but I wanted to write about it to you, myself, anyway. Read some of this to Louis and to anyone who is interested. The more people who finally get it through their heads that everything terrible told about these people is true, the better. I know that Louis, in particular, will be interested in knowing that I, of all people, happened to be one of the first to see these incredible horrible, and hideously immoral things.

Don't worry about its effect on me, because surprisingly enough, the effect on a person of any stability is not to give him the shakes or unbalance his mind or anything like that. Instead, it's as Sid Olson said, when we first looked at the dead in the boxcars:

"It doesn't make me sick to my stomach or anything like that—it just makes me goddam mad!"

All my love,

Scott

*Seasoned to stark reality . . . , trained observers saw
the freight cars full of piled cadavers no more than bone
and skin and could not believe what they saw.*

T-3 James Creasman, HQ Company, 42d Infantry Division

James Creasman was born in Tennessee in 1914. He graduated from Arizona State University. He has had a long and distinguished career in education. After the war, he worked with the
Voice of America. In 1947, he became alumni director at Arizona
State. He remained there until 1964, at which time he joined the
Peace Corps. He led a group of sixty-three volunteers in Brazil. He
spoke Portuguese and was able to teach and demonstrate the ba-
sics of health and sanitation. In 1966, he returned to Arizona State
University as an assistant to the president, a position he held until 1984.

Creasman was a member of 42d Division Headquarters Company, assigned to the staff of *World News*. This paper was very
important to our division commander, Major General Harry J. Collins. The general insisted on rigorous training in weapons and
tactics; he also felt that an informed soldier was a more effective
soldier. In his view, it was essential that we should learn not only
how to fight—we should also understand why.[4]

Thus, a news and information bulletin was published at regular intervals. It was distributed to each officer and enlisted man.
Creasman's eyewitness account of the action at Dachau is now
among our historical documents. Here are some excerpts:

42d Rainbow Infantry Division
World News
Vol. 1   Tuesday   1 May 1945   No. 43

Dachau is no longer a name of terror for hunted men. Some
32,000 of them have been freed by The Rainbow Division. The
crimes done behind the walls of the worst of all Nazi Concentration Camps, now live only to haunt the memories of the Rainbow
men who tore open its gates and first saw its misery, and to ac-
cuse its SS Keepers of one of the worst crimes in all history.
When Infantrymen of the Rainbow fought their way into Dachau,
against fanatical SS Troops who met deserved violent deaths
along the moats, behind the high fences, and the railyards littered with the bodies of fifty carloads of their starved victims,
these hardened soldiers expected to see horrible sights. But no

human imagination fed with the most fantastic tales that have leaked out from this earliest and most notorious of all Nazi Concentration Camps, could have been preparation for what they did see there . . . The keen descriptive powers of a score of ace correspondents who entered while the battle was still in progress, and through whose eyes the whole world looked upon that scene, could not do it justice. Seasoned as they were to stark reality, these trained observers gazed at the freight cars full of piled cadavers, no more than bones and skin, and they could not believe what they saw . . . Riflemen, accustomed to witnessing death, had no stomach for rooms stacked almost ceiling-high with tangled human bodies adjoining the cremation furnaces, looking like some maniac's woodpile . . . An officer pressed through mobs of forgotten men of all nations, wept unashamedly as limp ghosts under filthy blankets, lying in human excreta, tried to salute him with broomstick arms, falling back in deathly stupor from which most would never rouse . . . It was incredible that such things could happen today, but there were the men who did it—the SS. At least 25, and perhaps 50, were beaten to death by inmates who struck with all the fury of men who suddenly release years of pent-up hate . . . These once-swaggering Hitler worshipers would pocket no more of the profits from the hair-oil, shoe-polish, thermos bottles, notebooks, stationery, brushes, porcelain works of art, and cigarette paper manufactured there by men and women from all of Europe until starvation and disease made them worthless and then they were burned . . . Now, the SS Guards were dead. But their deaths could not avenge the thousands of dead and dying in Dachau . . . Those tortured dead can only be avenged when our world is aroused so much by what the 42d uncovered at Dachau, and by what others have found at all the other Dachaus scattered throughout Germany, that never again will any party, any government, any people be allowed to mar the face of the earth with such inhumanity.

GENERAL LINDEN'S GROUP

When General Henning Linden left for Dachau, he traveled in a small convoy of three jeeps. In addition to himself and Lieutenant Cowling, there were six enlisted men, three drivers, and three guards—all members of the 42d Division Headquarters Company. This group stayed together for the entire time the general was in Dachau, except for a few brief intervals when two or three of them might have gone a short distance away on a sudden mission. All of them shared the experience with Linden. They saw what he saw, they heard what he heard, and they took cover from enemy fire when he did. It isn't often that the enlisted personnel who were with a high-ranking officer can also present their memories of the same event. Evidently, they all saw the event in much the same way. However, they tell us things that Linden naturally wouldn't put in his report—for example, the fact that he was compelled to strike a recalcitrant Nazi officer with his stick. Likewise, they contribute something of the flavor of his language, as when he told John Veitch, "Veechems, go get that Kraut!"

In his report, the general says, "I sent Lt. Cowling and two of my guards into the Camp to reconnoiter . . . ." These guards, nameless in the report, were Carl Tinkham and Guido Oddi. Here, Oddi is able to tell us how they felt and what they did while they were inside. Oddi and his fellows Harry W. Shaffer, Carl Tinkham, and William Donahue were part of a roundtable discussion at a division reunion held fifty years later in Louisville. It was an informal give-and-take session that was videotaped.[1] What follows is exactly what they said to one another.

Dachau 29 April 1945

*We saw women who told us they were continually being raped
by the SS guards.*

T-5 Guido Oddi

Guido Oddi was twenty-six years old on the twenty-ninth day
of April, 1945. In civilian life, Guido had been in the construction
business, and he returned to that activity after his discharge. He
was seventy-six, and retired, when he set down his impressions.

Guido, an enlisted man, was one of General Linden's personal
guards. Thus, he was in the company of high-ranking officers and
had an insight into their characters and personalities. Of General
Linden, Guido says, "He was very interested in the people under
him; available for their comments; and listened to their views and
thoughts. He admired the young Lieutenant Cowling, who
"'watched over' the general and saw that he could get some rest
and quiet time."

As for himself, Guido says, "What I saw at Dachau made me
think more about people in all classes."

We left that day from division headquarters in a convoy of
three jeeps. Myself, Lt. Cowling, and Bauerlein as the driver, in
the first one. The general, with Harry[Shaffer] driving, and Carl
Tinkham, as guard. And the third, with John Veitch driving and
William Donahue as guard.

The day, as I remember, was on the cool side, and very quiet.
The road ahead was quiet and open. We came to a bridge where
a group of women were standing along the side. After examin-
ing the bridge for mines and explosives, we talked with the
women. They told us that a group of German soldiers had just
left. The women seemed to be of all different nationalities.

We crossed over the bridge, and I remember a wall on our left
side, and three persons came out of a gate, carrying a white flag.
They were the Red Cross man, the Nazi lieutenant, and some
German soldier. The Red Cross man said the Germans wanted
to surrender the camp to an American officer. There were also
German soldiers still in the camp.

The General told Tinkham and me to go inside for an inspection. On the way, we passed that railroad siding with the cars
that were stuffed with those dead bodies; some of them falling
out the doors. They were all piled one on top of the other. I don't
remember just how many cars I saw. I do remember that I tried
to listen for any sounds of life, but not hearing any. When we got

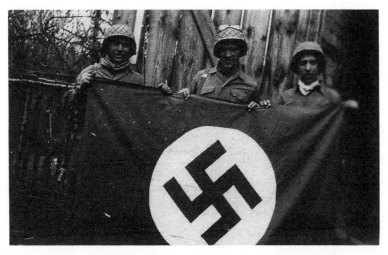

Left to right: T-5 Carl Tinkham, T-5 Guido Oddi, T-5 John Veitch, among the first G.I.s to enter Dachau.

inside the camp—and the inmates saw who we were and that we were American soldiers—great shouts of "Bravo!" went up from all of them.

Well, there were only two of us, and there must have been thirty or forty German soldiers up there in those guard towers. However, they began to come down from there, without their arms, and we turned them over to other Rainbow soldiers that were coming in.

At about this time, the General and Lt. Cowling joined us. We walked into the prison compound itself, which was a large, fenced-in area. The inmates told us that the fence was electrified. But they were so overjoyed to see us, and to try to come near us, and there was so much pushing and shoving, that one poor inmate wound up against the fence and was electrocuted. Someone then went into the gate house and turned off the current. Now, lots of people were arriving—and not just soldiers. One was a very famous reporter named Marguerite Higgins.

The inmates, as I now understand it, had formed a committee to take over the camp. They asked us if we wanted to see the place. We saw those ovens and more bodies just stacked up outside. We saw the gas chamber. We saw barracks where inmates who just couldn't get out of their beds were just left there. We saw women who told us that they were continually being raped by the SS guards. During all that time we were in the camp, I did hear small arms firing in other parts of it.

I remember when some of the women prisoners saw us coming in, they took out knitting and embroidering things.[2] They took down our names and the 42d Division and said they would embroider them. And so, if anybody comes across some of those knitted things in Germany or Austria, or any parts of Europe, they'll know that the Rainbow Division was certainly there in Dachau.

We left the camp and went on to Munich. I guess this ends that day, and as much of it as I can remember. It was fifty years ago, and parts of it will remain with me forever.

I shall never forget it as long as I live!

T-5 Harry W. Shaffer

Harry Shaffer was twenty-seven years old on April 29, 1945, which was the day he entered the camp. He was discharged from the army on June 1, 1946. He helped his wife organize and start a boutique, which she operated for the next forty years. In September 1947 he enrolled at Pennsylvania State University as a pre-med student. He was graduated from Temple University with the degree of Doctor of Podiatry. He practiced in Bedford, Pennsylvania. He later moved from a rented office to his own medical building. Here, he practiced until he retired in 1993. He reports, "My wife, Ruth, and I celebrated our fiftieth wedding anniversary in 1992—and we are both going strong!"

On the tape, Shaffer told us about a letter he wrote to his wife that day. It was dated April 29, somewhere in Germany (because we could not give an exact location):

Just a few lines because I am very tired and still have a long way to spend a Sunday, which is also my birthday! I shall never forget it as long as I live! Well, it started off early in the morning. We got on the Autobahn, a pretty nice road, macadam instead of concrete. After a short while, we left it and headed for a concentration camp, which we knew was nearby. A civilian led us to it. We came to a railroad siding that seemed to run alongside the camp itself. It contained many boxcars filled with dead people— most were emaciated; looked as if they had starved to death.

Then, we headed toward the camp itself. As we entered the main gate, we met a Red Cross rep and two German soldiers, and they surrendered the camp to General Linden. Inside, we saw the prisoners. We estimated there were about 30,000. We didn't meet with any resistance. After we were there a half hour, we heard shots from the other side of the camp. From then on, it was a scene of confusion. We stayed there the whole day. We left very late.[3]

I can't remember a lot after we passed through the gate.

T-5 Carl Tinkham

We got there real early—can't say for sure when—but it was real early. My story will have to go along pretty much the same as Shaffer's. I can't remember a lot after we passed through the gate.

It seemed to me that the firing we heard started not a half hour after we got there—but more like ten or fifteen minutes.

I went through the camp later with a man from the Red Cross [Victor Maurer]. He said he was from Switzerland. I was his guard. He wanted to tell the inmates they would be liberated in a day or two. That's all I can remember.

It went just about the way Oddi and Shaffer said . . . .

Pfc William "Pat" Donahue

William Donahue was born July 15, 1925, in Racine, Wisconsin. He entered the service in 1943. He was nineteen the day he saw Dachau.

When he came home, he worked for Massey Harris, a farm implement company, for fifteen years. He sold clothing for several years; then he was employed by American Motors.

He and his wife, Merle, have twin daughters and a son. When he took his family to visit Dachau at one of the memorial services his son, a U.S. Marine, said to him, "Dad, I never knew you had to go through all this!" "All this" had made a profound and lasting impression on Pat Donahue. He was one of the group that videotaped their story at the Rainbow Division's Louisville reunion.

Being a guard with General Linden, I can agree with Shaffer, Tinkham, and Oddi concerning what transpired until the shots were fired. At that time, the general asked Bauerlein [Lieutenant

Cowling's driver] and me to get Colonel Fellenz to report to him, which we did. As we were coming back to the camp, Tink and Oddi were coming up that road toward the main gate.

When we got to the main tower, some infantry from the 45th Division came into the prison area from the left side of the camp where the SS barracks were. From then on, things were in some confusion. There was a conversation between the general and a technical [tech] sergeant from the 45th, who'd been drinking. That was settled and the sergeant apologized, and from then on it was just a matter of moving people ᵣ ᵢ ᵢund. There was an American officer there, a POW. He had a French name. What was it, Guido? Oh, now I remember—Guiraud. I believe he later made major. There were also three Canadians and two British officers. Well, as for the rest of the things that happened, it went just the way Guido and Shaffer and Tinkham said. I do know we stayed till dark, and then we pulled out.

These are memories that are not pleasant to live through again.

T-5 William Veitch, brother of T-5 John Veitch

On April 29, 1945, John Veitch was twenty years old. He was discharged from the army on June 6, 1946. That year he enrolled in Westminster College in Fulton, Missouri. He graduated in 1950 and took a position with Mobil Oil in their marketing department. He married Marilyn J. Miller in 1948. In 1958, he and his wife and son moved to Denver. He became a manufacturer's representative in the Rocky Mountain area.

We received the story of John Veitch's Dachau experience early in 1996. It was written not by John but by his twin brother, William (Bill), who was also overseas with the Rainbow, but his unit did not happen to enter the camp. For over fifty years, John and Bill talked about it, and thus the event was always fresh in their minds.

When we asked John to write his account for this book, personal problems prevented him from doing so. William has set it down for us just as John has been telling it over the years:

To begin—twin brother John and I were drafted in September, 1943, when we were 18 years old. We were sent to Camp Gruber, Oklahoma. We were assigned to Headquarters Battery, 542d Field Artillery Battalion, Rainbow Division. We served together until March 19, 1945. I was assigned to Division Artillery.

John was transferred to Division Headquarters, and became a jeep driver for General Linden.[4]

On that fateful morning of the 29th, General Linden's party set out for Dachau in three jeeps [as described earlier by Guido Oddi]. John and Guard Carl Tinkham were in his jeep. At the 222d Regiment CP near Dachau, they picked up an Air Corps general, Charles Y. Banfill, Deputy Commander for Operations, U.S. Eighth Air Force. As Brigadier General Banfill put it himself, he wanted to see some action on the ground after having flown above it all those months. General Linden gave him permission to come along in John's jeep, as Linden's guest. As they approached the camp, they heard small arms fire. In the ensuing excitement, the Air Force General grabbed John's carbine. Everyone took cover. Then, as suddenly as it had begun, the firing stopped. No one knew from where it came.

Then, they moved on to the camp itself. The camp commandant came out carrying a white flag, evidently in an attempt to surrender. The general said to my brother, "Veechems, go get that Kraut!"

John did so and took the flag away from the officer.

Then General Linden said, "Tell that Kraut to put his hands on his head."

Either the "Kraut" didn't understand my brother's command, or he refused to obey. John then called back to the General, "I did, General, but he won't do it!"

The general strode over to the German and, with his stick, gave him a whack on the head. The German caught on.

Then they went inside the camp. There was a table where the German officers placed their sidearms. My brother "liberated" a German Luger (semiautomatic pistol). Later, he gave it to me. I still have it.

The camp was ringed with a moat and guard towers. Oddi and Tinkham, two of Linden's guards, then walked up into each tower and brought down the Germans who were in them. They collected all the guards till they came to the last tower. That German wouldn't come down. Oddi placed his foot in the German's back and gave him a shove. He went tumbling down the stairs, and stretching out his arms, grabbed two other Germans, and all three fell into the moat.

As for the rest of my brother John's story, it coincides pretty much with the other accounts that I have heard about the camp. My brother cried when he was at Dachau, and these are memories that are not pleasant to live through again.[5]

Dachau 29 April 1945

"Arbeit Macht Frei!" Work makes you free? Yes, Messieurs!
Free! Free of the SS!

Paul M. G. Levy, Interpreter

Paul Michel Gabriel Levy was born in Belgium in 1910. He has
had a distinguished career as an educator. He was a professor at
the University of Strasbourg and at the Catholic University of Leu-
ven. When the Nazis invaded Belgium, he was arrested and imprisoned in a concentration camp located in the old Belgian
fortress of Breendonck. Freed after a year, he made his way to
London, where he worked in broadcasting. He was chief of information services and war correspondent for the British Broadcasting Company. With the invasion, he returned to Europe as an
accredited correspondent. He was on his way to Dachau when
General Linden saw him and asked him to join his group as interpreter.[6]

When I was arrested by the Nazis and sent to Breendonck, I
was insulted by the Sturmbannfuhrer [a major in the SS] on the
day I arrived.

I was trying to fill a wheelbarrow with earth. He kicked me
three times while I was trying to work. At each kick, I made a
vow. One, to get free and tell the world how people were treated
in Nazi Concentration Camps. Two, to be among the first to enter a liberated Camp. Three, to take the Commandant of this
camp a prisoner, bring him to his former jail, and not treat him as
he had treated us.

My vows were favorably heard.[7]

Enroute to Dachau! I am living the most amazing hours of my
life! I am determined to arrive at a German Concentration Camp
with the first Liberators! I missed Breendonck. I have Buchenwald. I wanted to have Dachau. I knew about Dachau. I drive
quickly toward Camp. On the way, I pass Aichach Prison for
Women—a part of the Dachau System. Fifty from Belgium are
there. I recognize Louise de Lantsheere, and Ginette Pevtchin.
Both were members of the Underground Organization ZERO. I
had known Ginette many years. She was a barrister. After the
war she became a judge in the High Court of Justice in Brussels.
Louise was the daughter of the well-known Belgian journalist,
Paul de Lantsheere. I met her while in hiding. She helped me get
to London. I had promised her father I would try to track her

down in Germany. She was also a journalist. She became god-mother to one of my sons born after the war.

I stop for a while, and then proceed toward Dachau. But the road is narrow and cluttered. From time to time, a shell digs a hole in the ground, or hits a team. I am in the midst of a long line of vehicles. The M.P.'s will not allow me to pull ahead. Then, a miracle! Three jeeps are overtaking us! A large man standing in the first one, notices my Press Sign, and motions me to follow. He is General Linden, Second in Command of the Rainbow Division. At 4:30, we are in Dachau. [He could be a few hours off either way, because it was a most hectic day.]

The village is charming, peaceful and does not reflect the horror sparked by saying the name of that Mecca of the Concentration Camps. From some two kilometres away, we could hear machine gun fire.

We leave for the Camp. We stop at the railway station. Two trains are parked; full of cadavers. The last transport from Buchenwald and Kaufering—dead and anonymous, they will never be identified—jammed into cattle cars on the eve of freedom. We looked over the victims. They are horribly skinny; some are mutilated. An American lady correspondent, Marguerite Higgins, arrives. A white flag floats from a Guard Tower. A civilian with a Red Cross Flag comes to us. He is followed by two SS—one a lieutenant, the other, a plain trooper. They have come to surrender the Camp. I am the Interpreter. They are typically arrogant and impertinent. They still insult their victims: "These are dangerous prisoners. Watch out for your soldiers!" The Red Cross Man feels it necessary to add that they are also "crazy."

The Officer says he will only surrender to armed, uniformed Americans because he still insists that ". . . the prisoners are too dangerous!" Linden asks him to explain the train with the cadavers. He says he knows nothing about it. Just then, despite the White and Red Cross Flags, we are fired on. Linden, with blows from his cane, forces the officer to the ground.

Soon, the shooting stops. My duties over for the moment, I decide to go inside. There are still SS in the Towers. Just in case, I make sure of my side arm. Now, an immense clamor arises. Prisoners burst from their barracks. They yell, they cry, they sing! French, Dutch and Belgian priests were saying masses. I was hugged, kissed and tossed in the air because the inmates thought I was an American G.I. And in the crowd, I see my friend, Arthur Haulot! Dear Arthur in his zebra-striped uniform! The pestilence of the Camp has been swept away by the fresh

Reunion at Aichach, Bavaria, 30 April 1945. In the courtyard of the Nazi
prison liberated two days prior, Belgian war correspondent Paul Levy is
flanked by two of his newly liberated countrywomen: Belgian secret
agents Louise de Landsheere (left) and Ginette Pevtchin (right), who
later became a barrister and member of the Belgian high court. At right
is Minette Detige, also of the Belgian Resistance. Photograph by
Raphaël Algoet. Collection Algoet— SOMA/CEGES, Brussels.

air of freedom! Luminous smiles light emaciated faces! Allied flags—American, French, British, Belgian, Dutch, Russian, Luxembourg—made God knows how, come out from who knows where! Joy, enormous joy comes over that terrible place, even while people continue to die, full of typhus because the malediction of that evil Crooked Cross continues its foul work even after the Rainbow has blown away all the gates. The Gates where the SS had the effrontery to inscribe: "Arbeit Macht Frei!" Work makes you free! Yes, Messieurs—Free! Free of the SS!

I remembered my promise to Louise de Lantsheeres' father—to find Louise and bring her back. I returned to Aichach. An American Major was now in charge of the prison. I asked him to release Louise and Ginette Pevtchin. He agreed on one condition. I must sign a paper on which he typed: "Received, Two Belgian Girls." I signed it.[8]

THROUGH THE LENS OF THE PHOTOGRAPHERS AND THE ARTIST

A photograph is also an official record and is, perhaps, the most accurate of all. Robert Steubenrauch and Fred Bornet were members of the 163rd Signal Photo Company, Seventh Army, attached to the Rainbow Division. Since they were free to go after "targets of opportunity" (that is, find the action), they stayed with the Spearhead. They were with us at Dachau. Like everyone else, they reacted strongly to what they witnessed.

The best picture was the one I didn't take.

T-5 Robert Steubenrauch, 163rd Signal Photo Company

Bob Steubenrauch was born in New York City in 1924. Drawn to photography at an early age, he took his first job after graduation with *Collier's* magazine for twenty dollars a week. His unusual talent was recognized, and he was made a member of the 163rd Signal Photo Company. When Bob left the service, he took a job in Okinawa supervising the U. S. military photo lab. Although he was a civilian, he held a rank equivalent to major.

Bob's life has been devoted to photography. His greatest learning experience was working for the noted photographer Andre Cartier-Bresson. He has freelanced for *McCall's*, worked for Marathon Oil as photo editor of their publication, and served as corporate manager of photography for Goodyear. He is also a writer who has published four books of photo essays.

Bob retired in 1989. He and his wife Leah had two sons, now deceased. He spends a great deal of time lecturing on the

Holocaust for schools and community and religious groups. He attended our Rainbow Division Reunion in Louisville in 1994, taking part in the videotape of remembrances. He was twenty-one at Dachau and seventy when he recorded his reactions:

I think I got there early—but it was after General Linden arrived. I didn't enter through the main gate but through the one that had the lettering on the top—Arbeit Macht Frei—"Work Will Liberate You." I simply had no idea how monstrous it would be. I think I was there for about an hour. By this time, photographers from all over began to arrive. Among them was George Stevens, the noted Hollywood director. He had an incredible group with him. They had four trucks, twenty-eight men, and the latest and best Hollywood equipment. I'd had thirty months overseas by this time. I had experienced many grim sights in combat. I took more pictures than I can remember. But the best picture was the one I didn't take. I was about to photograph a group of inmates who obviously didn't have more than thirty minutes to live. I just couldn't bear to see the look in their eyes. So, I lowered my camera and simply walked away. My sergeant, Fred Bornet, said that we had to stay with the Spearhead. I knew that Dachau would get plenty of coverage and didn't need us, and so we left.

We were moving ahead, down the road, when we encountered a group of about fifteen Polish inmates who had just walked out of the Camp. Our jeep driver, a Polish-American, asked them where they were going.

"We are walking home," one replied.

"Where's home?"

"Warsaw," the man answered.

They were hardly more than skeletons. It was almost all they could do to put one foot ahead of the other. But they seemed gripped by a feeling of euphoria.

"Stay here," our driver said. "You'll be taken care of."

"No, no!" they insisted. "We are walking home to Warsaw." Of course, they all dropped shortly afterward.

Then, orders came directing us to spend the night in the town of Dachau. We liberated a villa, which evidently must have belonged to a high-powered Nazi—a *burgomeister* [mayor] or *gauleiter* [ruler of a state or province]. His wife was there, and she had placed signs in English: "Wipe your feet!" "Clean the tub!" What an arrogant Nazi bitch!

She insisted that she was innocent of all knowledge about the camp. But we found photos of her husband and her son in full Nazi regalia. We also discovered a cache of loot they had sent her from all over Europe. It consisted of marvelous delicacies— tins of fruits and meats and so on. We couldn't eat any of it. We loaded it all into duffel bags, and during the next days we passed them out to the liberated prisoners. We felt just like Santa Claus.[1]

There are those who don't believe there was a Holocaust.
Well let me startle you!

Second Lieutenant Ted MacKechnie

Ted MacKechnie is an accomplished artist. He is also a teacher and judge of watercolor painting. For our book, he contributed sketches that were made at the scene on the morning of April 30, 1945. These drawings are how Ted MacKechnie "saw" Dachau, following the time-honored calling of the combat artist. In just a few well-chosen lines, he succeeds in illuminating the crowded horrors of that ghastly concentration camp. At the time, he was twenty-two years old.

Ted was an enlisted man on the staff of the 42d Infantry Division's weekly newspaper, the *Rainbow Reveille*, prior to his graduation from Officers Candidate School at Fort Benning, Georgia. General Collins brought him back into the Rainbow Division as Collins's junior aide de camp. Ted had been an art student at the University of Illinois. He always carried a sketchbook, and most of his drawings were made at the scene of the action. After the war, he was commissioned into the regular army and retired a full colonel in 1969. Following an active army and business career, he says, "I happily paint and play golf."[2]

There was no snow in Dachau on the twenty-ninth of April 1945, but it did snow on the thirtieth when MacKechnie made the following sketches that appeared in the *Rainbow Reveille*.

The stark outline of one of the four crematory ovens at KZ Dachau. Many of our soldiers had expected huge furnaces,; these did seemed rather small for the daily volume of "business." These ovens were operated around the clock.

Articles of clothing piled up just outside the crematory. Camp personnel issued used shirts, shoes, trousers, and jackets to new arrivals.

Flatcars along the siding. Although it was almost May, snow had fallen in the Dachau area. While the bodies in the boxcars were plainly visible, those in the flatcars, in many cases, were snow-covered mounds.

Guard Tower B. The artist made this sketch after all the guards had been removed and the buildings on the left had been cleared out. It is a rare view of Dachau as lonely and deserted at that moment. Only a few hours before, SS guards were in that tower, firing machine guns in a final act of defiance.

Sketched on the spot, the artist's rendering serves as chilling witness to the Dachau "Waiting Room." Rarely empty, the "waiting room," which adjoined the crematory served as a holding area for the dead before they were sent to the ovens. MacKechnie quoted one American soldier as whispering "Like a maniac's woodpile."

Dachau 29 April 1945

[I saw] walking corpses in striped suits.

Sergeant Fred Bornet, 163 Signal Photo Company, Seventh Army

Fred Bornet was born in Belgium. He emigrated to the United States in 1939 and became an American citizen. During the war, he served as a sergeant with the 163rd Signal Photo Company, Seventh Army. Members of his outfit had considerable freedom to seek "targets of opportunity" in order to film the war up close. From Wurzburg through Munich, Bornet unofficially attached himself to our 222d Regiment. Even though he is not listed on our rolls, he shared the Dachau experience and can, therefore, be considered one of our own.

Sunday, April 29, 1945—Yesterday crossed the Danube. Heavy traffic. Evening with "charming" Kraut family. Daughters Ildegarde, Judith, sensuous brown eyes; charming mother, paralyzed. Piano. Today, chase of Rainbow Division to Aichach. Everything on wheels. Breathless rush to Munich. Troops reach Dachau. Visit to the Aichach Prison for Women. Iron galleries, like Sing-Sing. Emaciated women. Eyes wide, fevered hugs, trembling hands applauding. Had this ball in my throat. Stroke the cheek of little, old woman in her cell. Another kisses my shoulder. Then, meet woman lawyer from Brussels; friend of the Katlins, Blankensteins, all part of my Antwerp youth. Coincidence? Musso [Mussolini] hung yesterday in Italy.

Dachau, April 30, 1945. 1 P.M. . . . Ack-ack Sergeant tells us Munich has fallen. Everybody's in. Corps' signs are up all the way. Exhilarating ride along soft road. Walking corpses in striped suits, along road, waving, saluting, dazed. In town, large streets, mass of liberated British and Italian POWs and people greeting all incoming troops. Advance elements only. Some shells crash. Smoke in the streets. Liberated Yanks delirious . . . . Troops on tanks. Jeeps wait to move further through town. No resistance. . . .

Dachau, May 1, 1945. A house. Clean, cheerful. You can imagine this cozy German family sitting around a warm table. Smiling, pig-tailed, little girl; peaceful, familiar clink of silverware. And the town is Dachau. And I know that one Kilometre away, people are rotting; stacked up in ovens—dragging tortured bodies through a Camp dreaded by millions. And today, again, Munich. Free. Shell-pocked city. Snow flurries. Champagne in crowded cellar. Food riots. 1,500 Kraut P.W.'s filing through town. Seventh Army 20 miles from Innsbruck.[3]

COMPLETING THE PICTURE

Dachau did not fall after a bitterly fought pitched battle. Dachau fell like a poisoned fruit from a diseased and dying tree.

This is not to say that there wasn't any resistance. There was some fierce, if sporadic, fighting in various sections of the camp as groups or even individual "true believers" nursed a forlorn hope that *Alles* was not yet *Kaputt*. Even while General Linden was accepting the official surrender, there was a burst of gunfire. But this amounted to nothing more than some Nazi diehards making a final statement.

And so, on that Sunday, we entered the camp. Angered by the sight of it, we hauled down that Nazi flag and burned it! Angered, yes, and even more: furious, enraged—even dismayed, disoriented, and made violently ill. For we had just learned a most traumatic lesson. We found out why we were fighting this war. True, we were aware of the fact that we were fighting for our country, our freedom, our way of life—for justice and even to save the world. We believed it as an accepted truth. But we believed it in our heads. Now, suddenly, as if we had been struck by a bolt of lightning, it became a revealed truth. It had burned its way into our being. Yes, Dachau was a lesson, a most expensive lesson. We had to pay for it with our innocence. We were, by now, accustomed to violence and death. But when we killed, it was in armed combat—man to man. However, most of us were raised to believe in fair play, justice, mercy, the sanctity of life. Admittedly, there were violations of all these principles in our own country—but nothing that could even remotely approach this unspeakable place. How could we accept the fact there were people—human beings—who could be responsible for this insane slaughterhouse, this Dachau! Many Rainbow soldiers were still under twenty. They aged quickly, as did everyone else.

Many of us have tried so hard to forget Dachau. Reading through quite a few accounts, we come upon phrases such as "I have tried to believe it never happened"; "How could those bastards do it!"; "Over the years I kept hoping it was a bad dream." But Dachau cannot be denied. It remains deep in the psyche.

Our average age now is over seventy. We have lived long lives, crowded with incident and experience. With the passage of time, much has been forgotten. But not Dachau—never Dachau. The very mention of the name blows away so many of the mists that shroud the past. Suddenly, we see ourselves a half century younger—armed, steel-helmeted—standing by that death train or entering through the gate with that filigreed "*Arbeit Macht Frei.*" Once again, we gasp in horror at the ovens. We try not to weep at the sight of the living and dead masses of huddled skeletons. We try to say something comforting to a despairing inmate—but we don't know what. We offer someone a K-ration, a misguided act of kindness, because so much "food" at one time might just possibly kill him. And then there was that overpowering stench. Even now, it can sometimes induce a feeling of nausea.

These then, are the memories—the everlasting memories—that will enable us to capture that day at Dachau.

SUNDAY, APRIL 29

When our division went into combat in December 1944, we could see no end to the war. Although victory may have seemed inevitable to the experts, all we knew was that we were taking a beating in the foxholes. We were bending under the murderous fury of a Nazi counterattack. Yes, The Rainbow bent—but it didn't break. After a bloody January, we commenced the sweep that would carry us all the way to Munich and victory.

By April, we could see the bright light glowing at the end of the tunnel. As a matter of fact, we even believed we were finally out of that tunnel. We were optimistic—yes, and high spirited—because we knew that, despite some flareups of resistance here and there, it was all over.

And then came Dachau—and the worst day of the war.

Almost everyone who entered Dachau had an automatic response at first, and that was the refusal to believe it. And this quickly—or slowly—gave way to a sense of bewilderment: "This isn't happening," "I thought I had entered the Twilight Zone."

68

And then there was the difficulty, or the reluctance, to look at the enormous mass of emaciated dead and really believe they were once people just like us. (And the living didn't look very much better, either.)

Oh, we had seen dead bodies, but not like these, and never so many. Wherever one looked, heaps, piles, stacks! Some were just dumped helter skelter. There must have been thousands and thousands. Who could hope to count them? And these were just the ones who were here now, today. How many had been cremated and, thus, disappeared, yesterday, and the day before—and all the days before? As far as we were concerned, the evidence of our own eyes told us that the number must have been overwhelming. Later we would hear that inmates tried their best to confound the death machine, substituting, as often as they dared, the bodies of those who had already died of disease or starvation for prisoners scheduled for execution. We have since seen official death-toll figures, and though we are convinced that they are low, at least they capture the magnitude of the horror. But eventually, each Rainbow soldier accepted reality, although it was difficult—no, impossible—to make peace with it.

As we read about the Rainbow men's experiences at the camp, we realize that they tell as much about themselves as they do about Dachau. Some try hard to keep their feelings in check and simply relate the facts. Others give full vent to strong emotions: "This is when I started to hate the Germans!"

So many say they were "hardened" or "battle-hardened" to sights of gore. But that isn't the truth. To be hardened means that one has undergone a personality change and accepts cruelty as a matter of course. The Nazis were hardened. We were not. We were shocked and benumbed by what we saw. We were trying to block it all out, the idea being, "If I don't think about it, it didn't happen."

When we arrived at the Dachau gate, the war was still on. And we saw that right here and now there might very well be a battle. When Lieutenant Colonel Donald Downard told his machine gunner, Robert Flora, to "lead us in," Flora replied, "Colonel, I've come this far—do I have to get killed now?" We comment on this because it is a prevailing attitude among combat troops when a war is won but not yet quite over. A common prayer is, "Please, God, don't let me die now for nothing!" We call it the "last man to be killed in the war syndrome."

In the following accounts, that there will be some discrepancies as to exact times and places—who was where and when.

Dachau 29 April 1945

We had seen dead bodies . . . but never so many. Wherever one looked, heaps, piles, stacks! Some were just dumped helter skelter. Bodies in Building No. 172 (Krematorium), KZ Dachau, awaiting cremation, 30 April 1945. Photograph by T-4 Sidney Blau, 163rd Signal Photographic Company. The scene was first photographed the previous day by Pfc. William R. "Hap" Hazard, staff photographer of the *Rainbow Reveille,* after a bomb set to booby trap the building had been neutralized. Courtesy of the National Archives Still Picture Branch Photo ID Number 111-SC-206190.

Troops on the move who may have to pause now and then to fight have a tendency to lose track of time and place. Minutes, hours, and sometimes even days blur into one another. Troops in combat, as a rule, do not live lives on an orderly schedule. For them, at times there is neither day nor night; there is no clock, no scheduled routine. There is only dangerous improvisation. But we are fortunate in having multiple witnesses to the same events. Many were members of the same units and were present at the same time. Many had not seen each other since that day. And yet, when they were asked to describe the action at Dachau years later, they seemed to be remarkably in agreement.

The first Rainbow soldiers who entered the camp received the full shock of Dachau. They were completely unprepared for

Just inside the eastern perimeter barrier of the Inmates Compound, KZ Dachau. Visiting American newspaper and magazine correspondents view rows of corpses of prisoners in front of the camp's "hospital area," as were so designated the first ten of the thirty-four prisoner barracks. Photograph by T-4 (first name not known) Cunningham, still photographer, 3908th Signal Service Battalion, United Kingdom Base, Communications Zone, European Theater of Operations, APO 413, 4 May 1945. Courtesy of the National Archives Still Picture Branch Photo ID Number 111-SC-205450.

what awaited them. There may have been some rumor, some hearsay of a "concentration camp": "What's a concentration camp? A prison camp? A prisoner of war camp? A detention camp? A stockade?" If any of us thought about it at all, it would be in terms of the type of places that we had seen, read, or heard about at home. But a camp where thousands of people were systematically slaughtered by government fiat? No. Not even in the movies! But there it was. Dachau—without prologue or introduction. Not a warning or even a hint of what was in store.

Lt. Col. Donald E. Downard.

I believe there is no limit to what a man can do if he doesn't care who gets the credit for it.

**Lieutenant Colonel Donald E. Downard, CO,
2d Battalion, 222d Regiment**

Don Downard was born February 11, 1914, in Harland, Kansas. He attended schools in Oklahoma and Arkansas and college in Mountain Home, Arkansas. He was in the Civilian Conservation Corps before he joined the army. He spent more than eighteen years in the service, which he left because of a disability. After brief stints in the motion picture industry and in sales, he found the love of his life in veterans service work. He worked for the Texas Veterans Affairs Commission and later for the Disabled American Veterans (DAV) as supervisor of the San Diego office. After he retired, he moved back to Texas and did veterans service work from his home until his death in 1994. He was active in his community—volunteering in church, school, youth groups, and in the executive branch of the volunteer firemen.

Don married Eleanor Eichholz Miller in 1967. They have four children and nine grandchildren. He also had five children and seven grandchildren from a previous marriage. He was thirty-one at Dachau and eighty when he contributed to this volume.

Downard was a veteran combat officer long before he was assigned to the Rainbow, having been under fire in North Africa and Italy. He had an enviable reputation as an attack-oriented leader, constantly on the go and always in the forefront. He was usually "too busy" for the routine paper work and left most of it to his subordinates. His is the most frequently mentioned name in our Dachau history because of the train loaded with the dead on the siding outside the camp. Of all the thousands in the boxcars, there was just one person left alive. Downard carried him to safety and life (see Rahr, "Stories from Behind the Wire").

Downard, like Colonel Fellenz and so many Rainbow soldiers, was profoundly affected by his Dachau experience and spent the rest of his life helping to make sure that the world was fully aware of the evil that flourished there. He was a man of definite opinions and didn't hesitate to state them, as we can see by some of his memories of that day.

Yes, indeed, I was at Dachau. My soldiers were there before any of the other Rainbow units, or personnel, including General

[Linden] and his party, and the Red Cross, news reporters, and the rest of them. Mickey Fellenz was there pretty early, but not before my 2d Bn soldiers.

Earlier that day, we were about six kilometers from Dachau, when one of my sergeants brought a civilian to me who said there was a large Concentration Camp. It was the first I'd ever heard of Dachau. I passed the word along to my Companies that a) I'd received the report; b) it might not be true; c) it could be a trap; and d) if true, care must be taken because of possible disease, etc. At any rate, I moved quickly toward Dachau along a country road with my lead rifle company F, 222d, and my attached Tank Destroyer Platoon [2d Platoon, A Company, 692d Tank Destroyer Battalion]. We were well within my assigned zone of attack. We came under small arms fire at the foot of a long, not too steep hill. We halted, dispersed and dispatched the offending Krauts; about a platoon, maybe two. We remounted the Tank Destroyers and moved on. Then, to our left front, at the top of the hill, a tank, in full defilade, opened up on us.[1] It fired two rounds. Both missed by a mile. I had assumed it was a German tank. We could see no markings. The foot soldiers sought cover along the road. I ordered our Tank Destroyer to open up on the tank—which they did. Either the third or fourth round hit the tank and set it afire.[2] Its personnel bailed out quickly. It was a 45th Division Tank well out of its zone. Fortunately, there were no casualties—except for the tank, itself.

This matter was investigated, I suppose, at the request of the 45th Division, after the war. I told the Investigating Officer just how it happened—and that was the last I ever heard of it.

When we arrived at the Camp, the first thing I saw was that terrible train. I walked past car after car. It was all I could do to believe it. Suddenly, a soldier, about ten or fifteen yards behind me, yelled, "Hey, Colonel! Here's a live one!" Immediately, I ran back to the car. There, almost buried under a mass of dead bodies, was a hand that was waving so feebly you could hardly notice it. But it was moving! I climbed up into that car, and assisted by the TD Officer [Captain Roy Welbourn], managed to get him out of there. To make sure he got to the Aid Station, I decided to take him there, myself. We started for the Aid Station, but we came under some small arms fire. My driver cracked up the jeep, and I was thrown some distance. When I regained consciousness, I was lying on a litter in the Aid Station. On another litter, on my left, was the survivor. He wasn't hurt in the accident. I had a concussion and some contusions. I went back to my CP. I received verbal orders from my Exec, Major James A. Deane, to turn the Camp over to Col. Fellenz, and get moving toward Munich. I ascertained that Fellenz's First Battalion was there, so we moved out. There was no formal transfer since Mickey was already there. I was told about the 45th. I guess they arrived from another direction at about the same time my soldiers did. I'm not denying that they were there. I'm only saying that I, personally, never saw a Thunderbird patch.

It's interesting to note that a Negro Tank Battalion Company, or Battery, claims to have been at Dachau long before any other units. Further, a Field Artillery Battalion of Japanese-American soldiers also claims, "First there." Plus others, too numerous to mention. If all who claim they were there were actually at the scene, then the rest of the war had surely ceased, and no other outfit had anything else to do.

I never saw any other units at the Camp other than my 2d Bn soldiers, and the 1st Bn of the 222d Regiment of The Rainbow.

The sights at the Camp were so terrible that I have tried to block the whole thing out, and I have succeeded to some extent.

And I do know that we were first—but who cares! I believe there is no limit to what a man can do if he doesn't care who gets the credit for it.[3]

Some have wondered why Downard, who was the ranking officer at the time, should have personally taken the survivor to the aid station. Surely there were any number of enlisted men who could have been told to do it. But for those who knew him, his action was typical. To Downard, the war was personal—and he saw it in terms of people to whom he could relate. Note how he uses the phrase "my soldiers"—emphasis on the word *my*. All the soldiers in the 2d Battalion of the 222d Regiment remained "his" soldiers for fifty years after the war, until he died in 1994. Perhaps Downard saw the plucky survivor as one of "his" soldiers

What a horrible sight to see!

Corporal Robert W. Flora, H Company, 222d Regiment

Robert Flora was discharged from the army on June 12, 1946. He was twenty-two years old. That year he married Eloise Holmes. In 1948, he went to work as a machinist at the naval air station in Norfolk. He retired in 1979 at the age of fifty-five. He also

Dachau 29 April 1945

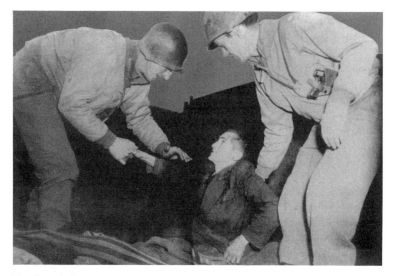

The Death Train's lone survivor. Only one in nearly two-thousand survived to be saved by Capt. Roy Welbourn, Company A, 692d Tank Destroyer Bn., left; and the Rainbow Division's Lt. Col. Donald E. Downard, right.

did radio and television repair. He has five grandchildren. The Floras celebrated their fiftieth wedding anniversary in 1996.

I was in on that battle for Dachau—and this is what I remember:

There wasn't very much resistance in the town, itself. But then, we moved along those railroad tracks. We saw the boxcars loaded with all those dead people inside. That is when we really started to hate the Germans. My machine gun was front-mounted on my jeep. Col. Downard said to me, "You're the man. Go out in front and lead us in."

I said to him, "Colonel, I came this far. Do I have to get killed now?" You could say things like that to Downard.

Well, we had put up a loudspeaker calling on the SS to surrender, but they wouldn't. And so, Downard said to me, "If we try to blast 'em out with artillery, we'll kill too many innocent people. It's Infantry time!"

So, we moved forward. A German machine-gunner, from a tower, pinned us down for a bit. We got rid of him and moved on through the Main Gate—I think it was. As we started in, we were held up again by a machine gun that was firing at us from a window in one of the buildings. He would give us a burst, duck away, and then give us another short one. I just set the sights of my Heavy-Thirty [thirty-caliber, water-cooled machine gun] on that window, and waited for him to rise up again. When he did, I got him. There was some—but not too much—fighting after that. Then, I remember that huge mass of prisoners just milling around. We saw terrible things—people lying in heaps—all dead. And, of course, all those corpses in the furnace room. What a horrible sight to see!

We captured some of the guards. They were lucky that we took them alive. The ones that we didn't kill or capture were hunted down by the freed inmates and beaten to death. I saw one inmate just stomping on an SS Trooper's face. There wasn't much left of it.

I couldn't tell his nationality, but he must have understood English because I said to him, "You've got a lot of hate in your heart."

He looked at me and nodded his head.

"I don't blame you," I said.

We only stayed there a short while, and then we moved out toward Munich.[4]

I just don't feel I can talk about it.

Sergeant Forrest C. Eckhoff, 2d Battalion, HQ Company, 222d Regiment

Forrest Eckhoff was born in Cole Camp, Missouri, in 1922. He attended Central Technical Institute in Kansas City and was married after leaving the army in 1946. He and his wife Margaret have already celebrated their golden anniversary. They have two sons and two daughters and six grandchildren. Forrest owned an electronics store in Kansas City for thirty years and then returned to operate another in Cole Camp. Right now, he is enjoying his retirement, and has an interest in veterans' affairs. He was twenty-three years old at Dachau and seventy-three when he recorded his experience.

I remember that morning. We were sitting on the back of Sherman tanks moving along in a column, when Col. Downard came along side in a jeep. He spotted me and yelled for me to get in the jeep with him. I hopped in and the jeep moved out quickly. I sat in the rear, and Col. Downard—as usual—stood up in the front seat, and held on to the windshield. Soon, we came to some open ground, and just before reaching the Camp, we passed General Linden and men in the group with him. They had taken cover because they were under small arms fire—possibly coming from the Camp Guard Towers. At least, it seemed to be from that direction. We swept around General Linden's party, and we went right into the Camp. I don't know which of us was the first inside the Camp. I only know for sure that I was third. First and second would have to be determined by whether Downard's pointing hand was ahead of the driver's foot. Since I didn't have the proper angle on it, I couldn't say. I don't know how, or if, they ever settled it between them.

As for what I witnessed inside that place—I just don't feel that I can talk about it. I will testify that all the terrible things everyone says about it are true.[5]

We saw all those piles of dead bodies all over. After seeing them, we didn't feel too good toward the SS.

Sergeant Olin L. Hawkins, F Company, 222d Regiment

Hawkins was twenty-four years old on April 29. He was discharged in November 1945. He worked at various jobs but found no satisfaction in any of them. He reenlisted in 1947 and received an appointment as second lieutenant. He served in Korea with K Company, 38th Infantry. In 1952, he was sent to Salzburg and later to Vicenza, Italy. He retired as a major after twenty years service. He worked for State Farm Insurance Agency as an insurance adjuster, and then for Farmers Insurance in Tulsa. He retired at age sixty-five and is now living in Sand Springs, Oklahoma. He says, "I've had no trouble keeping active, and right now I feel five years older than young and twenty years younger than old." Olin was seventy-three when he videotaped his Dachau experiences at the Louisville reunion.

It was early in the morning. We started walking down the road toward Munich. All of a sudden we got orders to "Load up!"

We loaded up on every available vehicle, and we charged ahead, hell-bent for election! The I & R platoon [intelligence and reconnaissance] was in front. I was platoon leader, 3rd Platoon, Company F 2d Battalion, and our battalion commander, [Lieutenant Colonel] Downard, was leading the way. We ran into little pockets of resistance, and the I & R gave them machine-gun bursts and we drove right through them. The German soldiers just looked at us. They couldn't understand it. Why didn't we want to stop and fight?

Then, without warning, we ran into some real resistance. We stopped. We unloaded. It was, as near as I can recall, some fifty SS troops; that's what they said they were later. We chased them into a dead-end draw just outside the Dachau camp. I sent a squad to the left and a squad to the right, and we fired machine guns into them, and mortars into them, and killed about two-thirds of them and took the rest prisoner. And that's when I saw General Linden and his aide [Lieutenant Cowling]. I can remember the aide saying to him, "General, we d better get! It's dangerous up here—there's shooting!"

And the general said to him, "The company commanders are up here—so why shouldn't we be?"

Then Colonel Downard told us to mount on the tank destroyers [TDs]. I had twenty-five men, and we got aboard. Downard pointed the way to go, and we went! We came to a canal with a little wooden bridge across it. It certainly wasn't strong enough to hold the TDs. So we just dismounted and walked across. Now on my left was the gate to Dachau. We headed for it. I remember the street was bricked. And I said, "If they start shooting at us, we have no place to hide." Then we saw those boxcars along the railroad siding. But I didn't think anything of it then, because I was just too busy watching that gate. I don't know which gate it was, but it had that big eagle on it.

Now, suddenly, one of my men said to me—I hate to take Christ's name in vain, but he said to me, "Jesus Christ, Sarge! Look at *this*!" Well, I turned around and I looked. And I saw those dead bodies in the boxcars. In one car, Colonel Downard had already taken that survivor out.

Well, we milled around there for a while. And then we moved inside. We saw all those piles of dead bodies all over. After seeing them, we didn't feel too good toward the SS.

In our march toward Dachau, F Company was the lead unit of the 2d Battalion. The only troops we passed were elements of

Rainbow soldiers open a Death Train car 30 April 1945. Photograph by Lee Miller. Copyright © Lee Miller Archives. Reprinted with permission.

the 20th Armored alongside the road, waiting for us to go by. And I remember we stayed in that camp until dark, and then we moved out. The next morning, Lieutenant Don Hathaway and 1st Sergeant Howard Benton went to a bake shop in the town of Dachau and loaded up with bread, and then we drove toward Munich.[6]

A medical corpsman looks into a Death Train car, one of fifty believed at first to be filled with dirty clothing that turned out to be piles of corpses. Courtesy of the National Archives Still Picture Branch Photo ID Number 208-129-J-26.

American soldiers make several boys whom they believed to belong to the Hitler Youth Movement examine a Death Train car filled with dead prisoners. Photograph by T-4 Sidney Blau, 163d Signal Photographic Company. Courtesy of the National Archives Still Picture Branch Photo ID Number 111-SC-264813.

Rainbow medics examine a corpse on the Death Train 30 April 1945.
Photograph by Lee Miller. Copyright © Lee Miller Archives. Reprinted
with permission.

*Startled, I remember dropping the [camera] case
and tugging at my carbine.*

**Sergeant William "Hap" Hazard, Staff Photographer,
RAINBOW REVEILLE**

William "Hap" Hazard was born in Berwin, Illinois, on February
11, 1923. The family moved to Madison where Hap earned his
bachelor's and master's degrees. He earned a doctorate at the
University of Iowa. After the war, he worked on the picture desk
of the Milwaukee *Journal*. He also taught journalism at the Uni-

versity of Wisconsin and later at the University of Texas. He is still active in satellite and imaging photography. He and his wife, Patricia, have two sons and two daughters. He was twenty-two years old at Dachau and seventy-two when he wrote of the experience.

I first heard of the coming strike against Dachau from one of the writers in our G-2 Group—probably Scott Corbett. Usually, a writer, a photographer and a G-2 jeep driver would be assigned to a team to accompany a Battalion on a particular mission, or occasionally, we would go out on our own without orders, if requested by a well-known Correspondent. To the very best of my recollection, this was the case on April 29. I believe Sid Olson of Time-Life asked for an Army photographer soon after he had heard that the 222d Regiment was to "take" Dachau. After receiving the call in our impromptu darkroom, I asked Fred Ziesk, the regular jeep driver for our unit to drive our writer, I think it was Scott Corbett [it was] and me to connect up with the 222d's 2d Battalion or wherever we could find Olson outside of Dachau. As I recall, the drive from Division Headquarters was about thirty or forty miles through an area of unknown risk.

After crossing a small river [the Amper] near Dachau, we spotted a long line of boxcars near the prison compound. Rifle and machine-gun fire could be heard from the general direction of the stalled train. As we approached, we could see a patrol working its way along the side of the tracks with a half-track and light tank moving nearby. After approaching cautiously next to the tracks leading toward the compound, we drove to a parked jeep about two hundred yards from the compound. From that point, we were on our own. I joined Colonel Downard as he made his way toward his patrol, which by this time had radio'd their findings in the boxcars. These were next to a side entrance to the Camp, itself. This is when Downard, joined by a T.D. Commander [Captain Roy Welbourn], was told that a survivor was in one of the cars filled with bodies.

I asked the Colonel to wait briefly until I could get into position, before rescuing the survivor. It took me less than fifteen seconds to get focused and insert the flash bulb in my 4 x 5 Speed Graphic. Sid Olson joined me just after the picture was shot.

After making pictures of the rescue operation, I worked my way along the tracks leading to the Compound Entrance, when the figure of a German soldier, on the run, appeared suddenly between two empty boxcars. He leaped over the coupling, about ten yards from where I was standing, and veered off to the left, slightly away from me. Startled, I remember dropping the case, and tugging at my carbine, which was slung across my left shoulder. Combat photographers usually carried carbines when in fighting zones.

Before I could bring my carbine to bear, he veered to the right, jumped the coupling of an adjacent rail car, which put him back to the side from where he had come. Almost immediately, a G.I. appeared on the scene from between two boxcars, and asked me, "Where in hell did he go?"

I pointed to the spot where the German had disappeared. The G.I. quickly followed. Within seconds, there were two or three quick shots, and the race was over, although I never did see the final outcome.

Other activity along the tracks convinced me to wait for one of the correspondents or army writers before entering that side entrance to the Dachau Prison—which momentarily had open gates; and nobody was around. Soon, I was joined by Howard Cowan [from the Associated Press] and Scott Corbett to photograph the Crematory and "Showerbath" Gas Chambers.

I'm not sure I returned to Dachau the next day, because I was under the gun to get my film processed and printed from the previous day, and I may have spent it in the Dark Room.

I suppose I haven't said much here that isn't already known. But even if I wanted to remember all the details of Dachau, it's hard to be nostalgic when your memory is short.[7]

Hey, Colonel! Here's a live one!

T-4 Anthony Cardinale, HQ Company, 222d Regiment

Tony Cardinale was exactly one month away from his twenty-fifth birthday (May 29) when he found himself at Dachau. He was seventy-four when he wrote down his experience at the camp.

In January 1946 he was discharged and went home to Oakland for a joyous family reunion. He returned to his previous job as a meat cutter. In 1950 he was married. He can't get over the fact that a year later he was able to buy a three-bedroom home in Danville, California, for $9,950! He says, "If I hadn't sold it, I'd be sitting on about $250,000 today! I cry a lot!"

He has four grown children, three boys and a girl. Jim, the oldest, was killed in Vietnam in 1968. He was a navy corpsman assigned to a marine battalion. He was a conscientious objector and refused to carry a weapon on patrol. Tony writes, "Although it's been 28 years since his passing, I still miss him. I know now the fear, anxiety, worry and stress that our folks felt when we marched off to war 50 years ago."

Tony retired at sixty-one but still keeps busy part-time. He sings with a small musical group of "senior musicians." He says they keep young by playing at old folks homes.

What follows is a true and factual account of my own personal experiences at The Dachau Concentration Camp. I was a member of the Headquarters Company of the 222d Regiment, Rainbow Division.

To the best of my memory, it occurred at the very end of April, 1945. What I remember is entering the Camp at the left end of the Main Entrance. We came upon a siding with rail cars, boxcars, on it, with open sides. I was with Sergeant Joe Balaban. As we walked along, we peered into each one of those cars. They were loaded with dead bodies. Then, in one car, I detected a movement. It was amidst all those bodies. It was a hand. It was poked up between some of the bodies on top of it. It was weakly waving back and forth. It was quite evident that its owner was alive, and had heard our voices, and was desperately trying to attract our attention. Well, I suppose I could have climbed up into that boxcar and picked him up. I don't know why I didn't. Instead, I called out to Colonel Downard, CO, of the 2d Bn, who had already passed that boxcar and was about fifteen or twenty feet ahead of me: "Hey, Colonel! Here's a live one!"

Colonel Downard and another officer—I think he was from the Tank Destroyer outfit attached to us, came running back to the car. They both climbed in the car, lifted that poor man up out of the pile of bodies to the opening in the car, and handed him down to me and Joe. There's a picture of them holding the prisoner—but it was snapped from behind me and above my head, so I'm not in it. In wide-eyed bewilderment, the man asked me, "Frei . . ? Frei . . . ?"

In my inadequate German, I tried to tell him that yes, he was now "frei" and in good hands. In another picture, there's a smaller photo of Joe Hazel, who took the man from me—once again snapped from above—so I missed my chance of being pictured once again. The only reason I would have liked to have my photograph taken, is because it would authenticate the

Dachau 29 April 1945

S. Sgt. Joe Balaban c. 1945.

experience of all this, which has been indelibly imprinted in my mind. It's an experience I shall certainly never forget.

Later, on the way back to our C.P., we encountered some commotion at a crossroads. Colonel Downard was lying in the road being attended by some medics. I understand that he had been personally taking the prisoner we found back to the Aid Station, when they came under some fire, and the jeep cracked up. I never saw the Colonel again until 45 years later when I attended my first Rainbow Division Reunion in 1988 in Denver. Of course, we reminisced about that scene at the railroad car in Dachau and at the site of his accident. The last time he had seen the poor guy we had saved was at the Aid Station. He was lying on a litter next to Downard and seemed to be O.K. Through the years, the Colonel had tried to gain some news about that inmate of the Camp, but to no avail. We were all so saddened by the news that Downard had passed over the Rainbow. I pray that the man we saved is still living and well. It would be a most happy and emotional scene to re-unite with him.

I'm sure that a lot of other things must have happened that day, both before and after the train—which is what really sticks out in my memory—but you must realize there's a lot I have tried to forget.[8]

We are American soldiers, and you are Free! Free!

Staff Sergeant Joseph L. Balaban, HQ Company, 222d Regiment

Joe Balaban was twenty-three years old when he came to Dachau, and he set down his experience forty-nine years later. Before entering the service, he worked for the Bulova Watch Company. After he was discharged he returned and stayed with Bulova for fifty years. He partially retired in 1968. Since then he has been retained as a consultant in sales training.

In 1946 he married May, his childhood sweetheart. They have a son, but lost a daughter. He and his wife have celebrated their fiftieth anniversary. He moved to Florida in 1991 and is enjoying the wonderful weather and new friendships.

Joe says, "The years in the 222d Regiment of the Rainbow are a part of my life that sometimes I believe happened to me—and sometimes they are another lifetime—or, perhaps, a picture that I saw on TV."

About that twenty-ninth day of April—there are some incidents that I remember very clearly—and then, some "blanks." According to some of the reports I have seen about what happened at Dachau, I just don't remember them, at all.

I was Chief of Radio Section, Regimental Headquarters, 222d Infantry. That morning, Tony Cardinale and I were driving along a road which, I later found out, was on the outskirts of Munich. Suddenly, we found ourselves in front of a gate that said, *"Arbeit Macht Frei."* Now, no one had ever mentioned a Dachau Concentration Camp to us, so I didn't realize just where we were. We drove down this long driveway that had buildings on both sides, with garage-like doors. At the end of the driveway, we came to a Guard Tower. There were chain-link fences on either side—and there was a moat, or a canal in front of it.

All of a sudden, there was all kinds of shooting going on somewhere off in the not too far distance inside. And then, SS Troopers were coming at us with their hands on their heads; and some were holding dogs on leashes.

Since we had a radio in our jeep, an SCR 300, I told Tony to call back for help. There were no other American soldiers in that particular area at the time. Tony and I were the only ones anywhere in sight.

In Yiddish, I told those SS Troopers not to say anything to their dogs. We held them there for some ten or fifteen minutes till trucks arrived, and soon the place seemed flooded with our G.I.'s.

Tony and I then proceeded to walk along the railroad tracks until we arrived at the site of those boxcars which Tony has already told about. Tony spotted the feebly waving hand. He stopped and called out to Colonel Downard who was just ahead of us, "Hey, Colonel! Here's a live one!" Then the Colonel and the TD officer handed the survivor down to Tony and me. He kept asking, "Frei . . ? Frei . . . ?" Tony and I kept saying to him, "We are American soldiers and you are frei . . . frei . . . ."

Now, who, exactly placed that survivor in whose jeep, I cannot recall. I do remember that the jeep did get into an accident on the way to the Aid Station. I have a lapse of memory after that—and the next thing I do recall is being in a large square in Munich where our CP was set up.

We saw some inmates, who had been released from the Camp. They came crowding into the square. German civilians came out of their homes with food and drink for them. One of the ex-inmates said to me, "The German soldiers used to march us through here, and the German civilians would throw stones at us. Now that you Americans are here, they are giving us food."

These are my best—and worst—memories of Dachau.[9]

Throughout, we have referred to the confused state of affairs at the points of contact with the enemy. These accounts by Tony Cardinale and Joe Balaban illustrate the fact that the distance of perhaps a few hundred yards can create situations that are entirely different. Tony and Joe entered Dachau at a point where there were no defenders. Nearby, other members of their outfit came to places where the Germans chose to fight, and they could hear the firing quite plainly. Shortly after, Tony and Joe ran into a group of German soldiers who had no appetite for combat and were eager to surrender. So much in war hinges on time and place. Had they been some die-hard Totenkopf guards (that is, SS who wore the death's head insignia), the incident might have had a different outcome. However, we do have an insight into the group Balaban and Cardinale encountered. Since some were holding dogs on leashes, we may assume that they weren't just ordinary troops. They were handlers, and probably trainers, of the vicious attack dogs that were used to tear inmates to pieces. And now they were so determined to save themselves that they yielded eagerly to two American soldiers who were all by themselves in a jeep.

Oh, they were all going to die, anyhow.

German physician to Captain Alvin A. "Doc" Weinstein, Commanding Officer, 2d Battalion Medical Detachment

Dr. Weinstein is a graduate of the Marquette University School of Medicine in 1943. He interned at Queens General Hospital in Jamaica, Long Island. He entered the service on August 1, 1944.

He was Battalion Surgeon and head of the medical detachment attached to the 2d Battalion of the 222d Infantry Regiment. In this capacity, he believes that he was the first American doctor to enter the Dachau concentration camp. He left the army in September 1946. Returning to the United States, he took a one-year fellowship at Mount Sinai Hospital in New York City. He has practiced medicine in Asbury Park, New Jersey, since 1947. Dr. Weinstein is married and has three daughters, seven grandchildren, and one great-grandchild.

Doc Weinstein was twenty-six years old at Dachau and seventy-six when he wrote this account.

I had known of Dachau prior to entering the Army. As an intern, I treated a man for meningococcus meningitis at our hospital, Queens General, in New York. This patient suffered a high fever which caused him to rant and rave in German during the early course of his disease. When he recovered, I asked him what it was all about. He told me he had been an official in a political party that had opposed the Nazis in 1933 when Hitler became Chancellor of Germany. He and other officials of this party were arrested and imprisoned for five years at a Concentration Camp in the Bavarian city of Dachau. He vividly described the horrors of this place; and told me that the Commandant of the Camp was bribed to take him and two other officials of this political party to Rotterdam in Holland, where arrangements had been made for them to enter the United States as political refugees.

Late in April of 1945, as our Battalion was proceeding south from the city of Furth, we came upon a road sign that read "5 kms nach Dachau." I told Colonel Downard that there was a political prison in that town and how I had learned of it.[10] This was later confirmed by a German civilian as we got closer to Dachau.

Inside the camp, what stood out above and beyond anything anyone could possibly imagine was the stench. There were sights—gruesome; gruesome far beyond the horrors of the worst nightmare; but nothing could hope to convey the shattering effects of that stink.

And yet, oddly enough, the bodies in that terrible death train, as some have noted before, did not have any smell at all—which testifies to the fact that they had all died very recently. I only spent a short time inside the camp, itself. Naturally, my mind could hardly make sense of the welter of images that assailed it. But one incident I can never forget.

As a doctor, I wore my Medical Insignia, the Caduceus, on my collar. A German civilian approached and introduced himself as a German physician. He told me he had worked at the Camp.

"Doing what?" I asked.

"Research," he replied. Using prisoners as subjects, he had been engaged in a series of experiments to determine how far the body temperature could be lowered without causing death. Then, gradually raising the temperature by degrees to discover how much normal physical function could be recovered; and how much would be permanently lost. His particular interest was the reproductive capacity. He very proudly produced a sheaf of "scientific studies" which demonstrated that, even when the human body was reduced to the extremely lowest limit of 30 degrees Celsius, his "patients" could experience a full physical recovery . . . even to the ability to have an erection. I was horrified. I asked him:

"How could you do this to human beings?"

"Oh," he answered, "they were all going to die, anyhow."[11]

Being in Dachau on that day of liberation was my "wake-up call." The rest of my life, as a University Professor of Psychology, has been informed and directed by that experience.

Lieutenant George A. Jackson, Jr., B Company, 222 Regiment

George Jackson was twenty-two years old when he experienced Dachau and seventy-three when he wrote about it. But we will see from his story that Dachau was never far from his mind. During his active service in the Rainbow he was awarded two Silver Stars, three Bronze Star Medals, and three Purple Hearts.

Returning to civilian life, he has a long list of academic, business and community service achievements. He has a B.S. in agriculture, agronomy, and animal husbandry; an M.S. in agricultural economics from the University of Illinois, and a Ph.D. in interdisciplinary studies, psychology, and philosophy from Claremont.

He had four children with his first wife, Daphne Stavroulaskis: Bruce, a businessperson in Woodside, California; Debra, a computer systems analyst; Jim, a naval officer in Vietnam, the Gulf War, and now on the USS *Constitution*; Alice, a consultant for George Jackson, Santa Rosa, California; and two grandchildren.

Over a thirty-five year academic period at the University of California at Santa Barbara and the California State Universities at Long Beach, San Francisco, and Sonoma State, he became well known for his innovative and creative teaching methods.

As a combat officer in Baker Company of the 222d Regiment, I had heard rumors of inhumane treatment by the Germans of any Americans they took prisoner; however, I never became aware of the extent and nature of the concentration camps. I assumed that Dachau would be somewhat like our prisoner camps of German soldiers [well cared for and in good health]. How mistaken I was in my perceptions.

On April 29, 1945, I was released from the hospital along with about fifteen other people from Rainbow being returned to their units. At about 10:30 in the morning we arrived at Dachau. As the only officer with the returnees, I was told to help and provide for some order and security for the camp.

As I entered the camp I noticed a group of several hundred people on one side of the compound. Going closer I observed a circle of about two hundred prisoners who were watching an action in their midst. A German soldier with full field pack and rifle who had been trying to escape from Dachau was in the middle of the circle. Two emaciated prisoners were trying to catch the German soldier. There was a complete silence. It seemed as if there was a ritual taking place, and in a real sense, it was. They were trying to grab hold of him. Finally, an inmate who couldn't have weighed more than seventy pounds, managed to catch his coattails. Another inmate grabbed his rifle and began to pound the German soldier on the head.

At that point, I realized that if I intervened, which could have been one of my duties, it would have become a very disturbing event. I turned around and walked away to another part of the camp for about fifteen minutes.

When I came back, his head had been battered away. He was dead. They had all disappeared. And that is the graphic story of my experience at Dachau. That is my part of the story. I was there. I saw what I saw. We left at noon. I joined the Spearhead. And we went on to Munich, and I became company commander of Baker [B] Company.

Later, I was working in the Provost General's Office of Upper Austria, where I was responsible for the security of many of the former prisoners of Dachau, who were interned near Salzburg and Linz from 1945 through May 1946. It was a shock to see those thousands of prisoners in such an emaciated and run-down condition. It became abundantly clear to me that the combat in which we were involved was abundantly justified.

The rest of my life has been involved in teaching and discovering ways in which people could communicate without sinking to the depths of this depravity.

When I was a professor of psychology at Sonoma State University in the 1980s, at Rohnert Park, California, I discovered that there were two other professors who had been in Dachau on that fateful day of April 29, 1945—Paul Benko and John Steiner. Benko said that on that day he and several other prisoners had been led to one side of the compound to be shot. As they were waiting, with rifles aimed at them, they heard the American tanks coming in the distance. The German soldiers ran away. He said if we had not come at that time he would have been killed. Benko was a professor of biology.

John Steiner was a professor of sociology. He said he was so near death on that day of liberation that if we had been a day later he would have died of malnutrition.

The three of us started a series on the Holocaust at SSU, which continued for many years.

The trainful of dead bodies, the kiln of burning bodies, and the group I watched who killed the German soldier inside Dachau, were graphic evidence that the people who had been and were prisoners there were subjected to unimaginable horrors. Being in Dachau on that day of liberation was my "wake-up call." The rest of my life as a university professor of psychology has been informed and directed by that experience.[12]

*When we opened the [boxcar] doors, you could see bodies
piled four and five feet deep.*

Corporal Hobart E. Lewis, 342d Field Artillery Battalion

Hobart Lewis was born in a log cabin on a farm in Gass City,
Missouri, on May 20, 1917. At Jonesboro High School he played
basketball, and upon graduation he matriculated at Tarkio College in Missouri, where he starred in the sport. He is in the Missouri Hall of Fame.

He and his wife, Annette, were married in 1939. They have
three daughters, seven grandchildren, and two great-grandchildren. He has been in the insurance business and in broadcasting. Lewis managed the NBC station, KYUM, in Yuma, Arizona.
He has lived in that city for forty-four years. He was twenty-eight
years old at Dachau and seventy-seven when he wrote about it.

Early that morning, we proceeded southeastward through
the town of Rain. We managed to get across a blown-out bridge.
We found a large farmhouse where we set up our CP [command
post]. Soon, we were pinned down by enemy artillery fire. I
called back to our own artillery for support, and instead received
more shelling from those German Eighty-Eights.[13] Finally, that
barrage ceased. Then, we realized that we must be *inside* the
German lines. We waited for a few hours, and then the Germans
withdrew.

We moved out and went on to Dachau, and arrived at the Concentration Camp area. I was in my jeep, and we were among the
first people to get there. And there were those boxcars everyone
talks about. When you opened the doors, you could see those
bodies piled four and five feet deep. Colonel Downard, of the
222d Regiment, picked up the skin and bones of the only one human being found to be alive. I walked with him to his jeep, and
the Colonel, himself, took the man to the Medics.

I then went inside that Camp. I saw the furnaces where the
dead had been incinerated. Believe me, I can vouch for The
Holocaust.

We then headed for Munich. Along the road, we passed many
freed inmates who had simply broken out of the Camp. They
were hardly more than skeletons. But they were grinning happily. Someone had "liberated" a meat factory and had loaded
them down with rings of bolognas and sausages![14]

We moved into Munich under some artillery fire. We stayed in the famous "Beer Hall" where I understand a lot of the Nazis used to meet. In one of the rooms there, I took an SS Officer prisoner. The next day we moved on to Rosenheim and Salzburg.[15]

[We saw] bodies stacked like matchstick corpses.

Lieutenant Colonel Edwin "Rusty" Rusteberg, G-2 (Intelligence), 42d Division

Edwin Rusteberg was born August 17, 1911, to a German immigrant father and a Danish immigrant mother. His father became a successful farmer in Brownsville, Texas. At home, Spanish, English, and German were spoken. When the United States entered World War I, however, German was no longer acceptable. Rusty attended West Point through an appointment by John Nance "Cactus Jack" Garner, who was F.D.R.'s vice-president from 1933 to 1941. Rusty graduated from the Point class of 1934. He tried to become an army pilot but washed out. Asked where he would like to be stationed, he replied, "Fort Warren, Wyoming, because no one will know me there." He married Margery Alice Baird, daughter of Colonel R. Baird at that post. He spent the next thirty years on active duty. He retired in 1964. He started the Junior Reserve Officer Training Corps program at the Brownsville Independent School District. He died in 1990. He is survived by a daughter, Suellen McDaniel of North Carolina, and a son, William, of Brownsville, Texas; three grandchildren, William Thomas Rusteberg, Russell Lance Rusteberg, and Marjorie Elizabeth Rusteberg. His wife, Margery Alice, died in 1984. He was thirty-four years old at Dachau.

His son, Bill, writes that in the six years before he died, Rusty wrote over 160 short stories about his life experiences. In this one about Dachau, Rusty did not want the story of Dachau to die with him. The following is from a letter he wrote to his son and daughter, Bill and Suzy: He had arrived at Colonel Downard's C.P. at daybreak of April 29. His assistant, who accompanied him, was Captain Francis H. Gregg. They had breakfast with Downard (K-rations), and then they followed Colonel Downard into the camp.

There it was on his cap, the "Death Head" of the SS Totenkopf, the most dreaded and feared of Hitler's ruthless legions. He had been killed by the inmates, along with other guards

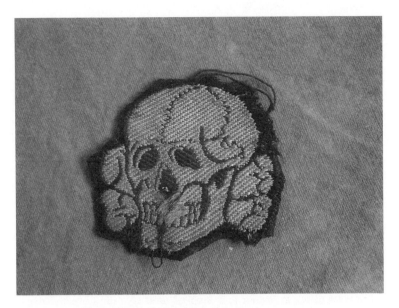

The dreaded Death's Head (Totenkopf) Insignia.

there at the Concentration Camp at Dachau, near Munich, as the Liberation Armies of the Allies approached.

I reached down and removed the cap from the head of the handsome, blond young German soldier. He and the others who had guarded the Camp lay dead in crumpled heaps nearby. I removed the Death's Head Patch, put it in my pocket, and replaced the cap on his head.

An Italian inmate assisted me and my Assistant through the Camp as it was liberated, and we saw, at first hand, all the atrocities committed there. There were thousands of inmates alive in the tiers of their bunks, with skeletonized bodies, and bobbing their shaved heads, struggling to get a glimpse of their liberators. Nearby, in heaps, bodies stacked like matchstick corpses lay forlornly, before the open doors of the incinerators.

Stunned by the experience, I sent the Death's Head Patch to Mom in California, with a description of the horrors I had just witnessed. Recently, I found the patch in a box of her mementos, and re-lived the experience once again.

The SS Totenkopf insignia, The Death Head, was witness to the scene of horror long before I retrieved it at Dachau on 29 April 1945, as the place was being liberated by our troops. In itself, it is a symbol of death, as depicted by its gruesome pattern. It relates the story of its mission of extermination of the races considered inferior to his by Adolf Hitler.[16]

I, too, can remember the smell of death.

Sergeant Earl Schabloski, H Company, 222d Regiment

Earl Schabloski was born June 6, 1921, in Oshkosh, Wisconsin. Before entering the service he attended the University of Wisconsin. In a business career spanning over thirty-two years, he was employed by Stowe-Woodward in Southboro, Massachusetts, and Mount Hope Machinery in Taunton. He was also a member of the Reserves for twenty-one years. He and his wife, Joyce, have already celebrated their golden anniversary. They had four children: twin boys, Robert and Richard, and two daughters, Earls and Lisa. He was twenty-four at Dachau and seventy-four when he wrote his account:

I, too, can remember the smell of death . . . the still-warm ovens . . . the boxcars filled with bodies . . . the sick . . . the weak . . . the dying. I shall never forget. I remember feeding some—but the new, 'rich' food only made them worse. The next day, we found some informers. They were quite dead. And so it went—a bad experience—but a lasting memory.[17]

I have a lot of memories of Dachau, but I keep
most of them to myself.

Lieutenant Dixon Rogers, H Company, 222d Regiment

Dixon Carle Rogers was born June 10, 1920, in Kahoka, Missouri. Six months later the family moved to Jefferson City and later to Fayette. In 1936, Dixon joined M Company of the Air National Guard headquartered there. Dixon attended Methodist College and was then appointed to West Point. He graduated in 1944 with a B.S. in military science and engineering. He also earned a master's degree in science and mathematics from the University of South Dakota, Vermillion. A career army officer, he served our country in World War II and Korea, where he received a Purple

Heart. He also holds the Legion of Merit, Silver Star and Bronze Star medals, and the Combat Infantryman Badge. He retired from active duty with the rank of lieutenant colonel.

He met his wife, Tommie Rogers, who served in the European and Pacific theaters as a journalist and public information officer. They were married in 1948 on her birthday. They raised a family in a series of military outposts throughout the world. They have three children, Sarah, Dixon II, and Dan. Rogers taught at Central Methodist College in Missouri and several high schools. Dixon passed over the Rainbow in 1995. He was twenty-four years old at Dachau and sixty-four when he responded about it.

I dug out some copies of Division Orders that I saved from 1945, which pertain to Dachau. The first is OI [Operating Instructions] #38 0400 hours, 28 April 1945; the second OI, 0500 hours, 29 April 1945. These OI's are issued in lieu of Operations Orders and are in overlay [a transparent sheet showing graphic matter] form. When the first one was issued, The Division was in Rain, Germany, apparently reinforced by elements of the 20th Armored. The Division also had attached to it a 692d Tank Destroyer Battalion, although it is not mentioned in the Order. But I remember that the 692d TD Bn was habitually attached to us.

Anyway, in that Order, the final objective of the Division and the 222d Regiment was to capture a line of villages that included Dachau. But since that Order was issued early in the morning of the 28th April, the Division Order on which this was to take effect, was not issued till later in the day, sometime for the 29th. Also, there were probably verbal instructions that went along with it. Most orders that were given were verbal and based on these OI's. Most Regimental Orders were verbal, and brought to the Battalions by Liaison Officers who had a boundary overlay. My function was that of Liaison Officer for the 2d Battalion. Thus, everything I say from here on about the 222d and what happened, is from memory. On the Division OI, the 45th is shown as the unit to our left [east and north]. Since Dachau is the farthest to our left in the Division Zone, I assume that some of that area is also included. All this I can confirm through the OI's. The rest is from memory.

The 222d attacked at about noon on the 29th. I rode on a TD, as I now can recall, with F Company. As we approached the town of Dachau, that vehicle was hit by a single shot from the left. I don't know whether or not it came from any of the units attached to the 42d—or from one attached to the 45th. I can only remember that we finally decided it was from "friendly" sources, and then we pushed on into the south side of the town. By this time, the Camp had become 2d Battalion's portion of the 222d's zone.

There was fighting in the north and west of the Camp, and I was instructed to look into it. I did, and found troops of both the 42d and 45th Divisions fighting around what appeared to be a Headquarters building. I reported this to Regiment, and was told to come back to the C.P.

As I was proceeding there along the railroad tracks, I saw the boxcars filled with the dead. I saw Colonel Downard pull out the one live person. I forgot to say when I arrived where the fighting was going on, I did see that General Linden was there. I did not see Colonel Fellenz or anyone I could recognize from First Battalion. This does not mean that they were not there, or that their memories of Dachau are not valid. I realize now that there was quite a good deal that I did not see and, perhaps, forgotten. I feel that eyewitness accounts after such a long time has gone by may differ, but I know that what I have said can be confirmed by the OI's and others on the scene.

I have a lot of memories of Dachau, but I keep most of them to myself. [18]

Our mission for the day was to capture a "prison"
in the next town. None of us had any suspicion of what
we would find there.

Lieutenant William E. Mayberry, H Company, 222d Regiment

Bill Mayberry of Crossville, Tennessee, was born February 24, 1922. After the war, Bill Mayberry and his wife, Sally, returned to the University of Tennessee to complete their last year of study for their B.S. degrees. He then came into the family's furniture business in Crossville. A Reserve Officer, he was called back to the Army in 1951. He spent most of 1952 in Korea as a Weapons Company Commanding Officer. He returned home and back to the family retail business. He retired in 1987. The business is operated now by his two sons.

He was twenty-three years old when he arrived at Dachau, and seventy-three when he wrote his remembrance.

Here is my memory of April 29, 1945: As Company Commander, my usual routine was to get up from whatever sleep I was able to catch at about 0300-0330, and go to the Battalion Headquarters to receive the daily attack order from Colonel Downard. While I was doing this, First Sergeant Bill Iglehart, would get the Company up, and he nearly always made sure you had a hot breakfast, and be prepared to move out in an attack at the break of day—approximately 0600.

Often, we would have our machine gun platoons attached to one or all of the three rifle companies in the Battalion, and we would move out with only the mortar platoon and our Company Headquarters Group. But, as I remember this day, we had some extra 2-1/2 ton trucks and we had our whole Company together in vehicles in a column on the road, mixed in with the rest of the Second Battalion. As I study my recently-purchased road map, I believe we spent the night before in the little town of Schabhausen, maybe 10-15 miles north of Dachau. We hadn't moved very far when traffic stopped and we just sat on the side of the road in the nice sunshine. We had been told at the Battalion Meeting earlier in the morning, that the mission for the day was to capture a "prison" in the next town. None of us had any suspicion of what we would find there.

Soon Colonel Downard came by in his jeep, and instructed me to follow him in mine. With me was my driver, Melvin Rogers, and Sergeant Knobs, our radio operator, and maybe, Kenneth Bushman, my messenger. Army Field Manuals dictate that the Weapons Company Commander is supposed to accompany the Battalion Commander in an attack situation. Once I had the Company out and moving, I would spend every day with him unless he sent me somewhere else or left me in some place with definite instructions.

The Colonel and I arrived in our two jeeps, at what I remember as the Main Entrance to the Camp. We had picked up the Tank Destroyer Lt. [Lieutenant Roy Welbourn], whose command had been attached to the 2d Battalion for several days. We left our vehicles at the Gate and went inside. It seems that we had part of one rifle company ahead of us. We were overwhelmed by the appearance and condition of hundreds, maybe thousands, of the male prisoners whom we encountered just inside the Gate.

Shortly, we came upon that railroad siding with forty to fifty freight cars loaded with human bodies in various stages of dress and undress. They appeared to have been dead for a day or two. We saw movement in one of the cars. Colonel Downard climbed up and untangled the only person who appeared to be alive, from all the other bodies. The Colonel placed the man in his jeep and went off with him to the Aid Station.

Enroute, I understand the Colonel's jeep had an accident, and he required medical attention himself. When he returned, I went with him as we walked through the Camp, past long rows of barracks, with many prisoners outside screaming, laughing, begging in all languages we didn't understand. Our trip finally led us to the Crematory Ovens, which were not in operation, but there were nude bodies piled nearby. We assumed they had been waiting to be burned.

Colonel Downard sent me out of the Camp. He instructed me to take my jeep and crew and move in the direction of Munich to see if there was enemy resistance on the way. We did encounter a small group of the enemy in the next little town; I think it was Karlsfeld. They just fired a round or two, maybe three or four. We stopped and took cover behind a building and waited them out a few minutes. Then, we drove on into town unmolested. It was getting dark by this time, so we returned to the town of Dachau. I found Battalion HQ. and reported my findings to the Colonel, and then found our Company. Lt. Naumann and Sergeant Iglehart had set up our kitchen and Company C.P. in a shoe store in downtown Dachau.

While the driver, radio operator and I were eating a belated supper, I noticed that some of our soldiers were distributing shoes from the store's inventory to some prisoners who had gotten out of the Camp.

As I recall, the rest of the night was uneventful. We moved out the next morning and headed toward Munich.

And I do recall, as I left the Camp, after touring with Colonel Downard, I met up with some officers from the 45th Division. How long they had been in the Camp, and where they had come from, was not of any interest to me. One was a Captain J. D. Goodner from my home state of Tennessee, and we knew some people in common.

And this is what I remember of that day.[19]

Doesn't somebody here need a bath?

Staff Sergeant C. Paul Rogers III, H Company, 222d Regiment

C. Paul Rogers was born in Athens, Greece. His American father, a tobacco importer who traveled extensively to the Middle

East, believed in taking his family along. When the family finally settled in Jackson Heights, in New York City, Paul spoke Greek and French; a British nanny gave him an English accent. Naturally, his schoolmates thought he "talked funny," and here is where he learned the elements of fighting. Paul attended school in Rome and London. After a stint in the export business, he settled in Detroit, where he owned and operated the two largest stevedoring firms in the city. His first wife, Betty Lee, died of cancer. He has been married to his present wife, Margaret, for fifteen years. He has four sons, Paul, Steve, Gregg, and Scott.

Rogers has a Bronze Star medal with two Oak Leaf Clusters and a V for Valor, a Silver Star, and a Purple Heart. He was twenty-one years old at Dachau, and he wrote his story at age seventy-two.

It was early in the morning—7 or 7:30 A.M.—when we, the Second Platoon of H Company, approached Dachau. We had been in or near the suburbs of Munich earlier. As we moved up in a skirmish line, we joked among ourselves about a very foul smell, and I asked if somebody here needed a bath. We were soon to learn that this horrible odor came from the Concentration Camp that we were approaching.

L. J. Rhode from Houston, Texas, was in my platoon and moving up with his squad, as well. I directed the platoon to go forward through the Gate at Dachau. I can't recall which one— there were so many. It was so very quiet, at first. We were completely unprepared for what we saw and smelled. We, of the 2d Battalion of the 222d, had been in combat a long time, and were pretty hardened, but this was unbelievable! Emaciated, dead bodies just lying around everywhere. As we moved out toward the boxcars on a siding, there were shots fired. Some were from the Guard Tower, and others from or around a building to the right of the siding. We returned the fire. Some SS Guards came out with their hands high.

There were a great many boxcars. When we opened the door to one, we found it piled two and three deep with corpses; some clothed, others naked. Subsequently, we found out that all the cars were filled with this horrible carnage.

Inmates, then, started coming toward us, crying and shouting. And by this time, other Units were moving in, and things became pretty chaotic. We gave away our own K-rations (certainly we didn't feel like eating after what we had just seen). We then spent some time trying to bring some semblance of order.

We had lost our C.O., Captain Truscott, in Furth. Bill Mayberry was our Exec. I know he was with or somewhere near then Major Downard, our Battalion C.O. [Downard had been promoted to lieutenant colonel on March 15, 1945, but many of his men still thought of him as Major], when Downard entered one of the boxcars and rescued the only living survivor of the entire train. There is a picture of Downard performing that action, which is familiar to every Rainbow Veteran.

Some of the inmates tried to grab some of the German guards and beat them, but they were really in no physical condition to do very much harm. We certainly felt no compassion for any of those German guards—but we were worried about the safety of the weakened inmates—so we separated some of those groups.

Dachau was the Main Camp. There was a number of so-called satellite Camps that were "liberated" by other Army units, and so any number of outfits style themselves as the "Liberators of Dachau." But we know better. We, in H Company, know that we were among the first troops in there early in the morning of April 29th. The Second Battalion Companies, H, G, E, and F were the point of the spearhead on the drive toward Munich, and then, Dachau. The 45th Division came into Dachau from the north, about an hour or so after we entered. It must be remembered that front-line troops did not, as a rule, wear their Division Patches or other I.D.—except for rank. Therefore, I could not identify units besides 42d Division platoons or Companies.

After months of fierce combat, we thought we had witnessed the worst horrors of war—but nothing could have prepared us for the sights and smells of Dachau that morning.

That is why we, of H Company, 2d Battalion, 222d Regiment, say: "NEVER AGAIN!"[20]

It was a day a lot of young men cried.

Sergeant Henry De Jarnette, A Company, 222d Regiment

Hank was twenty-four years old when he saw Dachau, and seventy-three when he wrote of it.

After the war, he was involved in furniture production and then went into sales. He traveled the state of Iowa for several years selling furniture. Afterward, he became an insurance agent. He also was in advertising until he took early retirement in 1983 and became involved in volunteer work in various capacities. He died November 12, 1997.

On this morning, the 29th of April, we were on the move early. No word as to where—just go! As we marched down a country road, we noticed a freight train up ahead of us. We had gone past a road sign that said Dachau, but that meant nothing to us; just another one of those German towns.

As we got closer to the train, we noticed objects lying on the ground; and a few minutes later, those objects proved to be the bodies of human beings. There were about fifty freight cars with—it must have been over 1,500 human beings. Later, we learned that only one was found to still be alive. We didn't walk the full length of the train; as we had to turn right and pass through some warehouses, I guess, and shortly, we were faced with the Camp, itself. The poor inmates were standing at the fence just yelling and waving at us. We arrived shortly after there had been a fire fight. Colonel Fellenz had gotten a hold of C Company, and they had knocked out the guards who had been firing from some of the towers. Then, Colonel Fellenz met with General Linden and Colonel Bolduc—and Fellenz was placed in charge of the Prisoners Compound part of the Camp, and a Colonel with a small unit of the 157th Infantry of the 45th Division, was put in charge of the Headquarters area.

As we stood outside, just looking at the Camp, Colonel Fellenz told us we were going inside. We were told to put our rifles on safe, and not to fire our weapons. When we got the gates opened, there's where I, and all of us who went in, were hugged and kissed by the grateful inmates—living skeletons! Those who couldn't get close, reached out bony hands just to touch us.

Our job in the camp was not to be sightseers, but to keep order. Don't let the prisoners out. Don't let any fights or rioting take place. I have no idea how many barracks I went into. Prisoners would get hold of us and take us into another barracks where fellow prisoners had a guard or a Kapo cornered, and we had to get them out of there and over to the Main Gate where we turned them over to some of our troops; and where they went from there, I don't know. Then, we would get back inside. How we reacted. Some tears and vomiting started at that train. But when we got inside, it was more common. It was a day a lot of young men cried. The filth, the stench, the disease, the death! Bodies were lying outside the barracks that had not been picked up. Bodies still in the barracks and not carried out. We were told not to give the prisoners any food, but Hell, we didn't have too much to give, anyway! By late afternoon, sightseers were coming by. The word had spread fast about what we had run into. By the next morning, the place was overrun by Rear Echelon. But the main thing these poor people needed was Medics!—and Thank God, they were arriving! We spent the night in some barracks just outside the camp fence. All night, we had to stand guard inside the Camp in case trouble arose. Thank God, again, none did! The next morning, with the Medics arriving, we had a chance to walk around and see the Main Gate, the Headquarters area, the Crematory, etc. Later, we were told we were going to move on. With a cheer just to get away from that place, we headed for Munich!

I know that on 29 April 1945, the Rainbow liberated Dachau. I have said so for fifty years. Now, it has become an important topic, as it should be. I think I can truthfully say that more school kids—Junior High, Senior High, College and University students, plus adult groups and organizations—know about the Rainbow Division, and the liberating unit, The 222d Infantry Regiment . . . . Let me express a thought I stated in an interview in 1983: "The scars of war are mental as well as physical—and the mental scar of Dachau is tremendous."[21]

[It was] a nightmare of dead and emaciated people.

Lieutenant Warren Dunn, A Company, 222d Regiment

Warren G. Dunn was twenty years old in 1945, but he has never forgotten his experiences at Dachau. He wrote this account of his memories of that day some forty-nine years later. Warren is married. He has six children, five grandchildren, and two great-grandchildren. He has had a most distinguished career as a rocket scientist, playing an important role in the unmanned spacecraft to Mars and the moon and in the Galileo projects.

I had just taken over A Company on April 27, when Lt. Powers, then the CO, was hit by shrapnel, and removed to the hospital. He was eventually sent home. A Company was part of a force called "Task Force Fellenz" [named for the battalion commander]. Early in the morning of the 29th, I was called by the Battalion CP, given orders to assemble my troops, and head for a city called "Dachau." This place I was told was the location of a large Concentration Camp—and my Company was to get there

Lt. Warren Dunn,
May, 1945.

as fast as we could in jeeps, trucks, half tracks and on tanks. We had originally been enroute to Munich, but we were re-routed to Dachau with orders to secure the Camp until relieved by Units following us, who could repatriate the Internees.

I had no idea what a Concentration Camp was. POWs? Displaced Persons? My Company headed for Dachau to do what Lt. Col. Fellenz had ordered. We arrived late in the morning of the 29th of April, and came upon a nightmare of dead and emaciated people. Our first encounter was with that trainload of boxcars. Later, I learned that one person was still alive within that horrendous mass of the dead. Apparently, they were being shipped up there to be cremated at the Dachau Crematories.

When my Company arrived at the camp, it met with no resistance, which was a bit puzzling, but I didn't mind that too much. It was my understanding that elements of our Division and the

45th had killed the remaining SS Guards. Their bodies were still in the towers and the moat.

We entered by a large gate. We were met by some of the inmates, including a Dutch officer who had been interned there. We were conducted around the camp where bodies were stacked like cordwood. They had been recently killed. We saw those emaciated people inside the Barracks; and a roomful of bodies stacked high to the ceiling in the Crematorium; an unbelievable sight.

A Company secured the Camp. The next morning, we were relieved of that assignment, and ordered to proceed to Munich.

After I had been to Dachau on that April 29th day in 1945, a significant amount of information became available which answered some questions which I harbored concerning the original events I had witnessed there. Years later, my wife and I visited Dachau. Of course, we went through the Museum which had been the original kitchen during the active Concentration Camp period. We discovered from records in the museum, that during the last stage of the war, Himmler ordered the execution of all the internees in a letter to all of his Concentration Camp Commandants. No living soul was to be found alive on the arrival of the Allied Forces. They tried to execute this order, but were unsuccessful because of the rapidity of the closure of the camps by Allied Forces. Now, I knew why our orders were modified to change our objective from the capture of Munich to instead secure the Dachau Camp.

One of the events that occurred on that day was—even in the midst of all the other horrors—a real tragedy. A significant number of the prisoners killed themselves on the electric fence which surrounded their Compound. They were so elated to see us and reach out to us, that they forgot about that fence. So, we were both Liberators and Executioners. I had forgotten this tragic episode until our most recent visit to the Camp Memorial, when upon entering through the Visitors Gate, I saw those electric wire insulators. All the trauma and horror of our discovery on April 29th came flooding back. I believe that trip in 1990 contributed to an emotional healing for me relative to the events at Dachau.[22]

They were so elated at being free—just free to walk around!

Lieutenant Burton Sides, A Company, 222d Regiment

On that morning of the 29th of April, on the highway from Rain to Munich, we had been moving rather slowly. It was stop and go because of the threat of air attacks, and German tanks block-ing the highway. They had to be "removed." During one of those "sit and wait" periods, I heard some kind of facility had been dis-covered maybe five minutes away. I decided to "take ten" and go and see for myself.

It turned out to be a large, brick building, not too far from the town of Dachau. Inside was a fairly large area, beyond which were steel bars and gates. I found out that this was The Women's Prison at Aichach. Some American troops were already there.

The prisoners were all female. Their dress was a sort of gown. They were all undernourished. To the best of my recollection, they all seemed to have black hair. I don't recall a single one with light hair.

They wanted us to be aware of their scanty food rations, which appeared to consist of the typical German small can of lard. They were so elated at being free—just to walk around—that they didn't even display a vengeful attitude toward their guards. I should have liked to stay longer and found out about them and the prison, itself, but I had to get back to A Company. The facility was under control, so I left.[23]

I was a stunned observer.

Pfc William E. Clayton, 2d Battalion, HQ Company, 222d Regiment

On April 29, Clayton was nineteen years old. When he was asked for his memories of that day at the camp, he was sixty-five. After military service, he graduated from the Rhode Island School of Design in 1951. Clayton states that he has had had an interest-ing career in advertising and graphics design. William and his wife, Joan, have been happily married for nearly fifty years. They have two children and two grandchildren. He says, "Life has been very good to me."

After the Moder River Battle, early February, 1945, I was at-tached to the 222d 2d Bn HQ Company to guard and scout a wire communications team. I stayed with them throughout the war, although I was never officially transferred from E Company. The wire team was motorized—jeep and trailer—and we operated on foot only when the terrain or battle conditions dictated. The job of our 2d Bn wire and radio teams was to stay close to Lt. Col. Downard in order to provide him with communications to the ri-fle companies. Sometimes, the hardest part of the job was to keep up with Col. Downard, who commanded the Battalion, as he was always with the lead element, especially when we were advancing. And that is how I happened to be at Dachau on the day of Liberation.

When we arrived at the Camp, I was a member of a recon patrol that went inside to determine whether the Germans were going to defend it. The patrol entered on foot. Everything inside was quiet. There was no one on the streets. There was no verbal exchange between the patrol and the inmates.

We went around several of the buildings. We didn't enter any. We could see the inmates inside, but nobody spoke. There were no shots fired. The complete silence was eerie. After a short tour, we came out and reported all was quiet. We saw no signs of defense.

Afterward, we heard about that trainload of dead bodies. We drove out there. It was quite a sight. We learned that Colonel Downard had been there but had left. We then went back into the Camp. This second time, I was there for about an hour or so—pure guess about the time. Now, the streets were filled with inmates and our troops milling about. It was quite still. The fire fight with the SS Guards at the tower must have taken place while I was at the train. There was no shooting that I can recall while I was there a second time. On this visit, I did take an extensive, walk-around tour, I saw it all—the gas chambers, the ovens, the stacks of bodies, etc., that we're aware of.

Then, we heard that 2d Battalion was moving out, so we went back out and headed for Munich.

So, you can see that my minor role on the day of liberation was mostly that of a stunned observer.[24]

It was the longest twenty-four hours of my life.

Lieutenant Donald H. Hathaway, F Company, 222d Regiment

When he entered Dachau on April 29, 1945, Donald Hathaway was thirty. When he recalled his experience, he was eighty-one. As a lieutenant, he went into the camp with General Linden and one of the officers who made the tour with Major Guiraud and the members of the IPC. He was separated from the service in 1946 and spent seven years in the reserves. Hathaway farmed in North Dakota until his retirement in 1987.

At the time, I was a Second Lieutenant, Commanding F Company. We met a lot of resistance as we approached Dachau. We engaged SS Troops who were trying to slip back through our lines. There were about twenty or twenty-five of them trying to escape the Camp. One Platoon of F Company took care of them in a gun battle on the outskirts of the town of Dachau.

We were traveling with the 692d Tank Destroyers. When we came to the Camp at Dachau, we saw those freight cars with the bodies. There was one still alive. Colonel Downard rescued him and took him to the Aid Station. General Linden arrived at just about this time, and we went into the Camp. We found an American Officer there [Lt. Guiraud] and three British Officers, who were sort of a Prisoners Committee and were now running the Camp.

F Company was there for about twenty-four hours until we were relieved and left for Munich.

It was a most horrible mess! There were inmates cheering us at the fences. Some were unconscious and lying in their feces. Others were wandering about out of their minds. I managed to get hold of a wagon and a team of horses. Some of the soldiers hauled rations from the warehouse to the prisoners.

What we found, what we saw, was hard to believe, but that's the way it was. It was the longest twenty-four hours of my life that I put in there; and what we saw made us sick.

This is what I can still recall fifty years later.[25]

In a few short hours we 'liberators,' a handful of combat kids,
. . . had truly matured. We would never again take life
and living as matters of fact.

Pfc. Norman A. Thompson, G Company, 242d Regiment

Norman A. Thompson was born in Edson, Alberta, Canada, in 1925. Both parents were dedicated outdoor lovers. His father was a hunter, trapper, trader, and author of adventure stories and novels. Norm is an artist who also was an instructor in fine arts. He studied at the University of Washington and is a graduate of the Burnley School of Fine Arts and Design, Seattle. His work has been exhibited in group and one-man shows in Washington, Oregon, and California. In addition to various business enterprises, he is a director of a family-held corporation, Service Management Group, a computer-systems consulting firm. He is presently Administrator for a HUD project that provides homes for developmentally disabled adults. He and his wife, Margy Ann, have been married for fifty-two years; they have seven sons. Norm was awarded the Bronze Star and the Purple Heart. Norm did not help liberate the main camp at Dachau. On April 29, Norm entered the Dachau satellite camp at Allach, where some 3,800 slave laborers were forced to turn out aeronautical parts and equipment. Norm was then twenty, and he was seventy-one when he gave the following account of his experience.

While I was waiting [to be reassigned for duty, following a shrapnel injury], an Officer identified the Rainbow troops present. He asked us to volunteer as "Liberators" of, and witnesses for, some displaced persons in a nearby Concentration Camp. We mustered outside the barracks, were issued M-1 rifles and carbines, and after a short orientation, were joined with more Rainbow. We were close to twenty in all. I felt an eerie mind-set about what we were to share and witness that Sunday morning, and that the experience would most likely remain forever indelible in our minds.

In recall and retrospect, the road sign Allach strangely stood out as we approached the town "as skirmishers" [soldiers spread out in extended order for an attack]. We left the road, and continued to our left out into open fields, guiding along a wagon trail toward some drab, unpainted structures, barely visible some 1,500 yards in the distance. As we approached, unmanned towers separate from the main buildings took shape on the horizon. They were fixed at regular intervals close to 200 feet apart. A ten-foot high fencing topped with barbed wire, and visible to us only from our frontal approach, stretched around the perimeter.

From the right, double rail lines skirted the outside of the compound and seemed to disappear to the rear. Three or four smoke-stained, weathered Forty and Eights sat ominously on the track. From the distance I could see something heaped on the far side of each car. Bodies, stacked alongside the tracks as cordwood, soon became discernible. Directly in front of us, the graven images of inmates appeared. They clung to the fences with arms outstretched, and fingers entwined in the meshed wire. Muffled cries in many languages permeated the air. Single words, such as *cigarette, American,* and thick-tongued *thank yous* were detectable. Some were dressed in the infamous striped blue, gray, and dirty white. Others were dressed in nothing more than rags. Many were barefoot with shaven heads. Only now, fifty years later, do I realize I can only recall men and boys. There were no women within our view.

All seemed pathetically lost. It was difficult to determine if they were capable of appreciating, or even recognizing, "liberation." They made no attempt to get out of the compound, even though their captors had apparently fled at our approach. Although they were free, they literally had no place to go. They were in varying degrees of health. Some, although certainly not sound, were well enough to move around, somewhat erect, and were probably a current work force. Others were physically unable to greet us. Others hovered about the billet doorways, seemingly unaware of us.

And then there were the dead and the dying. They lay about everywhere, propped grotesquely against the walls, lying in the doorways and inside the wood frame buildings.

Our detail leader hand-signaled me to the right toward a small outbuilding. I approached at an angle and sidled up alongside an open window. I have a recollection of a torn blanket hanging from the sill. An antiseptic odor was commingled with the stench of death. Inexplicably, it seemed I was looking into a vacated infirmary. There, on a reasonably clean slab floor, lying stretched out on a pallet, was the lone abandoned form of a young man. It was impossible to determine his age; he seemed anywhere between his teens and thirty. He probably weighed less than eighty pounds. Had he been able to stand, he would have been less than average height. He wore what looked like a diaper covering only his loins. The sunken cavity where his stomach should have been was edged by ribs that jutted out from the tight peel of skin that covered them. Ashen skin was drawn tight over distended joints; swollen knees and elbows. His shaved head had a light tinge of red. There was more tight skin over gaunt facial features; bones protruding from hollowed cheeks and sunken orbits. His great, round eyes were a light blue-gray, and they smiled. I managed a smile back.

Soon, support troops arrived. Communication lines were strung. A field kitchen arrived with portable latrines and showers. Our job was done.

In a few short hours, we "liberators," a handful of combat kids, who had formerly been bent on "Cowboys and Indians," had, without heroics, truly matured. We would never again take life and living as matters of fact. The reason for our being there at Allach had certainly been defined. I shall never forget the lone body in the infirmary. I drew this sketch several years afterward.

Did he survive—or were we too late? I like to think that we were not—and that sometimes—just as often as I think of him—he also thinks of me.[26]

The very first Rainbow soldiers who approached Dachau had absolutely no idea of what the place was like. But, as the hours passed, the shocking news was spread:

"Corpses piled up like cordwood!"

"Human skeletons with no flesh on their bones!"

"You won't be able to stand the stink!"

But being prepared for the worst did nothing to lessen the trauma. Regardless of when one entered the camp, there was the same disbelief, bewilderment, shock, anger, and pity. As the day wore on, hundreds of people kept pouring into Dachau. Officers from higher headquarters, correspondents, photographers, and, thankfully, the all-important medics and other support units who swiftly began the awesome task of saving lives. At least there was not an uneasy feeling of being alone in the house of death.

On Sunday morning, so many inmates were dazed and uncomprehending—unaware of what had taken place. But soon they began to understand that there had been a miracle. More and more of them started to show signs of life. They somehow were able to summon the strength to shout their thanks, demonstrate their gratitude, crowd about their liberators and attempt to embrace them.

Most of the morning troops were with units, or sections of units, that were ordered to proceed immediately to Munich, as were many afternoon soldiers. But a greater number of the latter were able to spend more time in the camp. Some, although not many, were able to establish a personal contact with the inmates, as did Morris Eisenstein, James Dorris, and Russell McFarland. For most, it was rather difficult because of the many language barriers, for one; and actually, we had been warned to be careful. Typhus was widespread through the camp.

But early or late—whenever one entered Dachau—it introduced a general feeling of melancholy: This is what has been allowed to happen in the world.

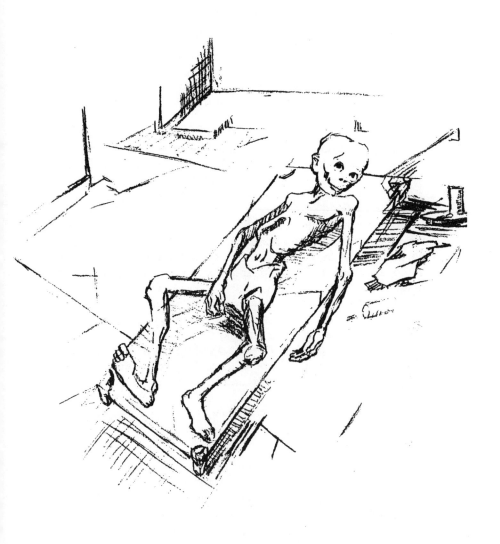

"His great, round eyes were a light blue-gray and they smiled. I managed to smile back," Norman Thompson recalls of one prisoner he encountered and sketched 29 April 1945 at the Dachau satellite camp at Allach. Courtesy Norman Thompson.

Naked bodies were stacked up like cordwood.

Lieutenant Colonel Robert B. Sherrard Jr., G-3 HQ, 42d Infantry Division

As I recall, my jeep driver and I made a short visit to Dachau the day it was "liberated." We were on our way to our new forward Division C.P. near Munich. As Asst. Chief of Staff, G-3, I was fully aware that we had overrun the Concentration Camp, but not the details of the event.

I remember vividly that my driver and I were astounded when we first came upon the railroad gondolas [open dump cars] with over a hundred dead bodies in each of the several we climbed upon to see. Then, we came to the buildings where naked, emaciated bodies were stacked up like cordwood in the Crematorium in an adjoining room.

Next, we drove along and saw hundreds of inmates along the high fence on the other side of the moat. They were waving to us, elated that they were being liberated. I did not tarry at the camp, as it was getting late, and I wanted to reach the new CP before dark.

We did hear a few shots being fired in the distance while we were traveling along the moat, but thought nothing of it as it was not an uncommon thing at the time. I do know that [Brigadier General] Linden had been at the Camp earlier in the day. I also heard that some members of the 45th had overrun it, also. However, what I have written above is what I saw.[27]

One prisoner had cut off his own leg, which was gangrenous.

Captain Buster C. Hart, S-1, 222d Regiment

Buster Hart was released from active duty in September 1946. He earned his B.A. from the University of Iowa and graduated from Harvard Law School in 1950. He clerked for Minnesota Supreme Court Justice Clarence Wagner for seven months. He was recalled to active duty in 1951 and served as staff judge advocate of the First Student Brigade in Fort Benning, Georgia, until 1952.

Since then, Buster has devoted himself to the practice of law. He has been president of a series of law firms. He is now an active member of Fabyanske, Svoboda, Westra, Davis and Hart. His wife, Jean, is a deputy director of the St. Paul Foundation, a large, community-based organization. They have four children. Nannette is a clinical psychologist; Charles, a computer sales manager;

Charlotte, an attorney who specializes in Chinese law; and Kyle, a member of Buster's firm.

Buster was twenty-two at Dachau. He sent us his reactions when he was seventy-three.

Unfortunately, I do not have a very complete recollection of the events at Dachau even though the memories I do have are unforgettable. I arrived at Dachau within an hour after it was captured and occupied. I do still have vivid memories of the following:

Emaciated bodies still on the railroad cars outside the Compound Gates. One prisoner had cut off his own leg, which was gangrenous.

Naked bodies which were stacked or had crawled up on top of one another in one of the gas chambers.

A young SS deserter had both of his legs broken and had been left leaning against a concrete wall. He was apparently grateful to be captured.

I recall seeing large German shepherd police dogs either shot or with their throats cut and thrown into the moat.

The prisoners were so gaunt and emaciated, that many of them seemed dazed and uncomprehending. I was told later that most of them could not eat and retain the food we gave them.[28]

I noticed that there were many Slavic inmates and a number of German Catholic priests.

Sergeant William A. Darmofal, A Company, 222d Regiment

William Darmofal was born September 12, 1922, in New Bedford, Massachusetts. He was twenty-two at Dachau and seventy-three when he contributed his account. After leaving the army, he entered Northeastern University in Boston. He graduated in 1952 with a B.S. in electrical engineering.

William was married in 1947. He has two children and four grandchildren. In 1952, he was employed by RCA in Camden and remained there for twenty years. He also holds a master's degree in statistics and quality control from Villanova University.

For ten years he worked for the Naval Air Development Center in Warminster, Pennsylvania. He retired in 1988 and now lives in Somerdale, New Jersey.

I remember the ovens and the stacked bodies. I noted that there were many Slavic inmates and a number of German Catholic Priests. I remember just outside the Main Gate, there was a shepherd dog. I was warned about those dogs. My "Partner" Joe—a Polish displaced person who accompanied me through a number of German villages—had to shoot the dog. Joe was about forty years old and could speak Polish and German. I can speak Polish and Joe interrogated my German prisoners. He had been picked up by another Polish-speaking G.I., who got wounded, and so he transferred himself to me. He had a G.I. helmet and carried an M-1 Rifle. He stayed with us to fight Germans. He left us at the end of the war, got on a motorcycle, and headed home to Poland.

I remember there were four civilians who were trying to get into the Camp and mingle with the prisoners. But it was discovered that they were SS Troopers who were trying to disguise themselves. It didn't help. They were arrested.

Yes, I saw it all, including that train with all the bodies.

We left the next morning. A G.I. picked up a small piano accordion in one of the SS barracks and gave it to me. Later, I played the Beer Barrel Polka and the Helena Polka at a Regimental Show in a Salzburg concert hall.

There are articles in the press which say that "Elements of the 42d and 45th Divisions arrived simultaneously" at Dachau. I know we were there. But, of course, G.I.s in line outfits don't wear their Division patches.[29]

We just gazed in disbelief.

Pfc Russell W. McFarland, F Company, 222d Regiment

I will report only what I remember, and what I actually witnessed. As you know, a Pfc in the Infantry was not briefed on plans and tactics.

I think we arrived at the Main Gate of the Camp between 3 and 4 P.M. I don't recall going through the town of Dachau. We were in Army trucks. Before we got there, the enemy fired on our truck convoy. One Lieutenant, some 2d Battalion Rangers, some soldiers, including me, went up a hill to eliminate the firing. After surrounding the enemy, 17 SS troops surrendered to us. This was the first time I had ever seen SS troops surrender.

Mine was not the lead squad that entered Dachau. I don't know how many of our troops were ahead of us. We were pinned down before the Main Gate. Across from where we were lying behind a concrete wall, we saw those freight cars with the dead bodies. Because of enemy fire, we didn't have time to investigate. Finally, we were able to go inside the Camp.

Again, we were not briefed as to what to expect. But after seeing four or five hundred people dead near the Gate, it was pretty obvious to me that the Camp itself would be no better. That huge wire enclosure with those sick and starving individuals roaming around, was a sickening sight, and that smell in the Camp was horrible. There were some dead German troops lying inside the Compound. They had been beaten and stoned by the starving inmates. It was apparent that the defenders of the Camp were more interested in fleeing than in fighting.

We were the ones selected to guard the Compound on the first night of the Liberation. We were billeted in the SS Barracks for the night. My duty started at midnight. There were no people stirring when we manned an elevated Guard House. Being a nineteen-year-old "punk kid," I asked a friend of mine later to accompany me inside the Camp. I just could not believe what I had seen and wanted a closer look. We crawled down and entered the Camp. We first visited one of the inmates' barracks. We saw a pile of about one hundred bodies in a heap in the latrine. We were told by the inmates that this was the number of people who had died in just the past twenty-four hours. We just walked and gazed in disbelief at the Gas Chamber, the furnaces, and the mass burial plots. There were a few people who spoke some English, so we had a small conversation with them.

The stench from the Camp stayed in my lungs for about three days after leaving. We got there on the afternoon of the 29th, and left on the afternoon of the 30th. We left the Camp and moved toward Munich.[30]

> *Why did mankind have to be so inhuman*
> *to their fellow human beings?*

Pfc Howard Margol, 392d Field Artillery Battalion

After his discharge from the Army in 1946, Margol returned to the University of Florida to complete his education. He graduated in 1948 and was married the same year.

He started a retail furniture business with his two brothers. He retired in 1993 to spend more time with his family and to engage in many other activities. Howard is president of the Jewish Genealogical Society of Georgia; on the board of directors of

117

the International Association of Jewish Genealogical Societies; secretary of the American Fund for Lithuanian-Latvian Jews, Inc.; and president of the Mt. Paran Parkway Neighborhood Association.

Howard Margol was twenty-one years old in 1945. He was sixty-five when he wrote the material about Dachau. Parts of his account appeared in the *Rainbow Reveille*, June 1993.

I was a gunner on a 105mm Howitzer, part of B Battery, 392d FA Bn. We generally operated in close support of the 222d Infantry. We vacated our position at the first light of dawn that morning, and moved forward. After a short advance, we set up and fired several firing missions. As things settled down, and there was a lull, one of our jeep drivers came by and told us about a "strange camp" just a few minutes away. My twin brother and I decided to go over there and see it. We had already noticed an unusual odor in the air—but we didn't connect it with the Camp.

As we approached the main gate, we quickly realized what that strange odor was. When we were kids, our mother would briefly hold a fresh-killed chicken over the gas stove to singe off the pin feathers. Whether chicken or human flesh is burned, the odor is the same. Outside that gate and parallel to the high fence around the Camp, was that train with the boxcars. Whether the Germans had brought this trainload of Jews and others to the Camp, and left them locked up in the cars to die, or were trying to take them deeper into Germany, away from the advancing Americans, who knows? In either case, the result was the same. I stopped long enough at the first boxcar to take a quick picture with my camera and then we went inside the Camp.

We saw the thousands of inmates, the ovens, the various buildings. We had no time to help the living or the dying. That would be done by those coming in behind us who would not be directly involved in the fighting. We had to return to our gun position. A war was still going on. After a five-minute walk through the woods, we were back at the gun. And not a moment too soon. Our unit was pulling out and advancing toward the Germans.

I thought about the Camp. I tried to understand the meaning of what I had seen. Why did it exist? Were there similar camps elsewhere in The Third Reich? Why did mankind have to be so inhuman to fellow human beings? I failed to come up with the answer.

Later, many people have failed to understand why Dachau was not a gut-wrenching experience for me at the time. The answer is simple. I could not comprehend the full meaning of what I was seeing.[31] I had been completely ignorant of the fact that these Concentration Camps even existed. After all, we were there to beat the Germans and save the world from Nazism. That was our goal, not the liberation of the Camps and the saving of those Jews. It was only after the war in Europe ended nine days later that I learned the full story of Dachau—and the existence of many similar Camps. And it answered many of my questions— but not the most important one: Why?[32]

I tried to make myself feel that it was a very bad dream.

Pfc Neil O. Frey, F Company, 222d Regiment

Neil Frey was born in Red Cloud, Nebraska. Neil worked on the family farm until he entered the service. When he was discharged, he returned to farm. He and his wife, Leona, have three sons and a daughter, two grandsons and one granddaughter. He still lives in Red Cloud and is enjoying his retirement.

I was a member of the Weapons Platoon, F Company. Sergeant Merrick, Youngstown, Ohio, was our Section Leader. Sergeant Woods had my squad, Chesterfield Ten. Sales was gunner, and I was assistant. I can't recall the town of Dachau. The Camp, yes. We entered a "walk in" door on the right of the Main Gate. This was at midday, I think, because I had no watch. We saw these boxcars on the siding with bodies who had been starved to death. On further were the "remains" of living inmates trying to cheer our arrival. The rest of the crowd pushed the ones in front up against the fence which was electrified. Unfortunately, some were killed.

We searched through sheds filled with the dead. I recall the whole ball of wax—the Gas Chambers, the Crematory, the open burial pits, all of it.

Sales and I spent the night in the first Guard Tower. I can recall the sign that said "Work Will Make You Free." We left on the morning of the 30th.

Words cannot express the feelings you felt. I have tried to make myself feel that it was a very bad dream, and it didn't happen. But there are times at night, when you wake up and see those striped, flimsy suits, those sunken eyes in those live skeletons, wandering around, pushed into corners like crazed animals. I guess I've never tried to let this out before. Yes, I was there.[33]

*The people who lived in the town of Dachau—
they had to know!*

Pfc Kenneth R. Ivey, F Company

Ivey was twenty-one years old at Dachau. He is another Rainbow soldier who "celebrated" part of his birthday, April 29, at the camp. He set down his recollections of the day fifty years later.

He left the service in 1946, worked at the post office, then was employed as an assistant manager of a grocery. Afterward, he became an administrative assistant for the National Guard. He returned to active duty in 1950 and was in an artillery unit in Korea. He then had three tours of duty at Fort Sill, Oklahoma; one at Fort Story, Virginia; and another tour with allied forces in southern Europe. His final duty tour was in Vietnam. Ivey retired from the military in 1968. He worked for fifteen years as a purchasing agent for a heavy construction company. He is now fully retired.

We left early in a convoy with TDs up front, and our men from F Company riding with the men from Battery B, 392d F.A. I was in a jeep with Frank Bulkly, our C.O., Harold Benton, and Jake Kizerian. We were stopped once by a roadblock. B Battery pulled a couple of 105s off the road and fired eight or nine rounds at it.

We arrived at the outskirts of the town of Dachau at around noon. We received some small arms fire from some men on a ridge to our left. Everyone got out of the vehicles, and F Company's 60 Millimeter mortar fired some covering rounds while a squad went up and wiped them out. I may have been turned around—but I think we were going southeast. Anyhow, we proceeded into the town where we stopped and dismounted.

We left the street from which we had entered, and went toward what we later learned was the Concentration Camp. The TD that had accompanied us broke through a culvert, a short way from the Camp, and we had to wait for it to get out. A bit farther on, we came to that train. It was on our left. It was filled with dead people; some were under the cars, or a few feet away from where they had crawled and died. The Main Gate to the Camp was now in sight. This is the one with the big eagle on top. General Linden, Colonel Downard, and eight or ten others were standing outside this gate.

I wasn't one of the first to enter the Camp. Our rifle platoons were already inside. The first thing I saw was a couple of our men guarding three or four German soldiers; and inmates wandering around like Zombies. There was no one else except F Company men in that part of the Camp at that time.

Soon, we heard some small arms fire, and someone said it was the 45th coming down from the back side (that would be the northeast, I think). F Company spent the night in the Camp. We utilized the Camp Administration Staff quarters.

The 45th was there—but I never saw any Black Tankers or anyone else from any other unit.

We left the Camp the next day (30 April) around noon, and we spent that next night in Munich. The following day, we moved out toward Wasserburg.

The shock of what we saw at Dachau will remain with us forever. We could not understand how the people who lived in the town of Dachau could not have known what was going on in there. They had to know!

I pity those who insist such places did not exist. They were not with us.[34]

This is surely what Hell looks like.

Pfc James F. Dorris Jr., A Company, 222d Regiment

After his discharge, Dorris graduated from the University of Chattanooga with a B.S. in engineering in 1949. That year, he married Charlotte Marie Snow. Dorris worked for the Copperhill Company in Copperhill, Tennessee. They later moved to Chattanooga, where he was employed at the Simplicity Systems Company designing and selling asphalt mixing plants. He later joined the Estee Manufacturing Company in 1967. He was in charge of engineering and sales of baghouses for air pollution control and equipment for asphalt plants. Later, he bought the company. He is now retired, and three of his sons run the company.

Dorris and his wife are blessed with five sons and two daughters. They enjoy their sixteen grandchildren. He and Charlotte own a small home outside of Cleveland, Tennessee. They travel extensively here and abroad. They are active in their church, Our Lady of Perptual Help. Charlotte is eucharistic minister and does charity work. James is eucharistic minister and lecturer. He says

God has been good to them and gave them the strength to survive the loss of their oldest daughter, who was killed in an automobile accident at the age of twenty.

James was twenty in 1945. He was seventy when he wrote his story of Dachau.

As a Pfc in a Rifle Company, I had no way of knowing where we were going or why we were going there until we arrived. Reasons or overall plans were never explained to an Infantryman. We simply did what we were told.

I remember approaching the Concentration Camp at Dachau down a wide street. Blocks before we arrived, the strong, sickening odor of burnt flesh enveloped us.

On a railroad track, in front of the Main Gate, were some forty boxcars loaded with the starved bodies of prisoners sent from other camps. Upon arrival at Dachau the car doors had been opened, and some of the bodies had fallen out. We found one man still alive on one of the cars.

Taking the Camp was fairly easy, since most of the guards had fled before we got there. Large, ferocious German Shepherd dogs, chained to the gate, lunged at us. They had to be shot.

Inside the Camp, the sight of rows of starved, naked bodies just outside the Crematory, a dead guard sprawled where he fell, dozens of inmates running aimlessly in confusion made me think this is surely what Hell looks like!

With the Camp secured, my job was to walk guard between the high outer wall and the inner wire fence that surrounded the prisoners. The fence had been previously charged with electricity, which was now turned off. We were to keep the prisoners inside until doctors could examine and treat them before their release.

While walking my post, a prisoner came to the fence to talk to me. Others stood back watching. He asked if I had a cigarette. Fearing that I might start a riot because I didn't have enough for everybody, I said, "No."

He said, "Wait a minute!"

He turned and ran as fast as he could, until I lost sight of him between some buildings.

I stood there for a few minutes. Then I resumed walking my Post. I thought I'd never see him again.

On my second or third round, the prisoner returned, out of breath, with a small rusty can which he handed to me through the wire fence. Inside was a small cigarette butt, which must have been hidden under conditions beyond imagining. He shook my hand and said, "This is in thanks for saving us."

With deep humility and tears in my eyes, I accepted his gift of probably the greatest treasure he possessed.[35]

Man's inhumanity to man continues.

Pfc Sam S. Platamone, K Company, 222d Regiment

When we asked the Rainbow veterans for some personal information about themselves, we received this letter Sam Platamone. It is dated November 29, 1996. We present it here in its entirety:

I was just three months past my nineteenth birthday when Dachau was liberated. My Holocaust story was printed in The Badge [the magazine of the 222d Infantry Regiment of the Rainbow] in March of 1986, ultimately being recycled in a number of Southern California Dailies. It was my rebuttal to those "Know-it-all Skinheads" who claimed it never happened. Indeed, the sight I witnessed at Dachau, and the trauma I shared with my brother infantrymen in rifle companies affected my postwar life immeasurably. I am certain I would have matured into a person far removed from the one I ended up being. Oh, I would have been a good person (my parents raised me with that goal in mind). But my values would have been profoundly different. Instead, I settled for a lot less than my scholastic potential indicated. I graduated among the top ten of the three-hundred and fifteen members of my high school graduating class. I was highly motivated by my loving parents; both immigrants from Sicily.

When I came home from the war, I didn't take advantage of the G.I. Bill. I tried Night School, but I could no longer glean information from the printed page as easily as before; I lacked the power of concentration. Perhaps, the trauma I shared with my friends during the almost six months I spent in the lines adversely affected my ability to learn. But I'll never use that as an excuse. I am who I am, and proud of it. I didn't become a professional person. Instead, I became a letter carrier in the U.S. Postal Service. During those post-war years, I could never dismiss from my mind the millions of horrible deaths during the War—and the fact that I had been allowed to survive—for whatever reason. I felt an obligation to Almighty God for my extended gift of life. In gratitude, I've spent my entire life doing as much for others as I possibly can. In my daily existence, I helped raise my five siblings. I was the oldest son. I supported my parents until I married at twenty-seven. My wife and I raised three wonderful kids. In my role as a letter carrier, I became a member of every family on my route, serving with far above and beyond what was expected of me. After we moved to the desert, I became involved with the Eisenhower Medical Facility in Rancho Mirage, California. Most of my work is with Orthopedic Patients. Daily, I go to work joyously, looking for new ways to please God by impacting on people in a positive manner. I shall endeavor to continue in this course of action until He calls me Home to be with my friends who preceded me so many years ago.

I was 18 years old, and I had already survived the usual hardships of frontline duty, which included 33 consecutive days of combat in frigid winter. Almost four more months of fighting against a persistent enemy had led me to believe that I had seen the worst that life had to offer. But that was before I arrived at Dachau. Early on the afternoon of April 29, 1945, K Company, 3rd Battalion of the 222d, stood before Dachau, which I discovered later was Germany's oldest Death Camp. I saw sights that day that a normal person would have difficulty even fantasizing. But they are imprinted on my mind forever.

I saw, on a railroad siding, just outside the Camp, a train of some fifty boxcars and each contained about thirty dead bodies. I understand that this train has just arrived from another Death Camp called Buchenwald, near Weimar in Germany. This served as a harbinger of the hell we could expect to encounter when we entered the Camp, itself. The SS had allowed the train to remain on the siding for a number of days, without providing the prisoners with food and water. Most died of exposure, malnutrition and dehydration. Rather than allow the survivors the joy of liberation—just before we arrived, the SS mounted heavy machine guns along the siding and fired into each boxcar. Some prisoners managed to get out, but they were methodically gunned down.

The Camp numbered, I was told, some 33,000. In the buildings adjacent to the Ovens, I saw stacked up bodies. Because of the German stalled war effort, they had run out of coal to stoke the incinerators. For all those poor people, we had arrived too late.

I feel great anger whenever I pick up a newspaper quoting some "pundit" who, in many cases, wasn't even born before World War Two ended—but who insists that the Holocaust was a myth—a Zionist plot to extort reparations from Germany. Yes, man's inhumanity to man continues. Countless people are dying needlessly all over the world. Nevertheless, it's wrong to pretend that the Holocaust didn't exist.[36]

I noticed a very old man huddled in a corner. His lips were moving as though he was either in mourning or prayer.

Corporal Morris Eisenstein, H Company, 222d Regiment

The twenty-ninth day of April, 1945 saw the capture of Dachau, but it was still just another day in the war. The path of the Rainbow to the site of Dachau led through disputed territory. In a number of places, the Rainbow encountered resistance. Morris Eisenstein, an H Company machine gunner, received two stars that day. The first was of silver:

Headquarters 42d Infantry Rainbow Division
Office of the Commanding General
Citation

Award of the Silver Star

By the direction of the President, under the provisions of Army Regulations 600-445, 22 September, as amended, the Silver Star is awarded to:

MORRIS EISENSTEIN

36 709 953, Corporal, Infantry, Company H, 222d Infantry for gallantry in action on 29 April 1945, near Dachau, Germany.

When his Battalion's attacking column was pinned down during the drive against Dachau, Corporal Eisenstein, with utter disregard for the hail of enemy machine gun fire falling around him, mounted a jeep and attempted to put the vehicle's machine gun into action. After numerous attempts to fire the faulty weapon had failed, he made his way through the deadly enemy fire to the cab of an abandoned truck, and opened fire on the enemy's position with the truck's anti-aircraft machine gun. When the supply of ammunition at the gun was exhausted, he exposed himself to direct fire, and climbed over the cab to the rear of the truck for a re-supply of ammunition. He then re-loaded the machine gun and continued to lay down effective fire on the enemy emplacements. By his outstanding courage and aggressive

Cpl. Morris Eisenstein, Spring 1945, Fischbach, Germany, after crashing the Siegfried Line.

action, Corporal Eisenstein provided covering fire which enabled our troops to capture 150 of the enemy, eliminating a strong obstacle from the route of advance. Entered military service from Chicago.

Harry J. Collins
Major General, USA
Commanding

Morris Eisenstein was born in Poland. His parents brought him to America when he was one year old. They settled in Chicago. Before the war, he worked in his father's automobile agency. When he returned after he was discharged, he went into the real estate and insurance business. He and his wife, Lorrie, have three children and six grandchildren. In 1990, he was suddenly felled by a massive stroke that paralyzed him completely. He was considered to be clinically dead. His wife was advised to make funeral arrangements. But with the same courage, determination, and tenacity, he fought his way back to life and experienced an almost complete recovery. He has been active in stroke research and lectures a class for stroke victims who suffer from aphasia.

Today, the Eisensteins live in Delray Beach, Florida. He was twenty-six at Dachau and wrote about it fifty years later. The Silver Star was awarded just before he arrived at Dachau. Inside the camp, he received a second star:

It was a miserable, cold day when elements of my platoon approached the entrance to the concentration camp of Dachau. I will never forget those two stone brick pillars on each side of the road, and the wrought-iron message which said in German: "Work Means Freedom."

We entered the camp. All around us were, literally, many thousands of individuals in those grotesque, striped uniforms. They were milling about in small groups. In the background, and farther down, just outside the camp, was a railroad spur with many boxcars on the tracks. Later, we learned that those cars contained over a thousand dead bodies.

We were approached by many of the prisoners who begged us for guns so that they could kill some of the remaining guards. Many of us carried extra weapons and gave them out. Unfortunately, those guards upon whom they exacted vengeance were not the officers or other big-shots because the most notorious of the SS criminals had already melted away.

While I was walking about, just trying to get a handle on this nightmare situation, I noticed a very old man huddled in a corner. His lips were moving as though he were either in mourning or prayer. I walked over to him. He finally looked up at me and asked me who I was. He spoke Yiddish. I replied in Yiddish that I was an American Jewish soldier. But the poor soul kept bobbing and weaving and repeating in Yiddish: "Alles Kaputt." Everything is gone! I tried to explain to him that he must remain where

The Second Star. Photo by Morris Eisenstein.

he was, because rescue units were right behind us and that they would take care of him.

Then, I happened to place my hand in my pocket. I remembered that the night before, we had fought and killed some SS troops. We searched them, and I had in my combat jacket some 15,000 marks. I took out this money and attempted to place it in the pocket of his ragged uniform. He saw the money, and then he looked at me. He shook his head and said to me, "I cannot accept this gift. It is not proper. I have nothing to give you in return."

He had, pinned to his threadbare clothing, that yellow Star of David, which all the Jews had been compelled to wear. I told him that, in exchange, I would take the Star, safety pin and all. It has been in my possession all the years since.

As a combat infantry soldier, I endured many experiences with dead and dying people. But I can tell you that when that emaciated, lost soul told me that he could not accept my gift because he had nothing to give me, I broke down completely. This moment of emotional expression and behavior will remain the highlight of my life. I have always hoped that, perhaps, my gift was instrumental in giving this human being another chance in life—perhaps, in Israel—where he might live normally once again. I have encased this Star of David in lucite and intend to contribute it to the Jewish War Veterans Museum in Washington, D.C.

A postscript to the story: When I took the Star of David to a lucite company to have it encased—and then came back for it when it was ready—the man in charge inquired how I came to have it. When I briefly related the story, he refused to charge me for the work and material he put into it. He was not Jewish.[37]

I felt I was the most fortunate of people to be on the outside coming in—instead of being on the inside hoping and praying to be liberated.

Pfc Robert Perelman, HQ 2d Battalion, 222d Regiment

Robert Perelman was born in Omaha in 1921. He graduated from the University of Omaha. Upon discharge, he went into the grocery business. After twenty years, he went to work for Dean Witter. Later, he opened the first discount brokerage in Omaha. He retired for some five years and then decided to open another brokerage. Before he went overseas, he met and married his wife, Betty Lou. They have celebrated their fiftieth anniversary. Although he has had two bypass operations, he still feels young and is determined to keep working. Since the seventies, he has been giving information concerning the Holocaust to various museums.

You could actually smell Dachau from a mile away. To me, it was reminiscent of the stench of the packing houses in Omaha. Only worse. The German civilians we encountered insisted they couldn't account for it. Even now, all these years later, I can still smell it. When we arrived, the fighting was just about all over. There was a freight train alongside the Camp—boxcars and flat cars. You could see the bodies inside. Some were covered with snow [editor's note: Perelman must have arrived 30 April or 1 May; it did not snow 29 April]. It was bitter cold. All they were wearing was those thin pajama-like uniforms. Inside the camp, it was worse. So many were sick and dying. One inmate had tried to cut off his leg, which was gangrenous. The incinerators were still hot. Piles of bodies were lying about waiting their turn to be burned away. They were so much like skeletons it was hard to tell the men from the women.

Prisoners who could walk were milling about. Some had formed groups. Somehow they had made banners to identify their nationalities. They were a League of Nations.

Everyone should have seen that place. It could provide a lesson in life. It made me a stronger person because I knew I could go home to normal life, and cope with whatever came my way. It made me feel that I was the most fortunate of people to be on the outside coming in—instead of being on the inside and hoping to be liberated!

How could those people do what they did to the human beings who were in there?[38]

I couldn't have spent more than ten minutes in the camp itself—but I saw quite enough.

Captain Carlyle Woelfer, K Company, 222d Regiment

Woelfer was born in Rockford, Iowa, in 1915. He was graduated from Kansas State University, earned a master's degree and then a doctorate from North Carolina State University. He is a career officer. After World War II, he served in Korea and Vietnam. He and his wife, Helen, are the parents of two sons and two daughters. He was thirty years old at Dachau and eighty-one when he wrote this account.

As lead unit of the Third Battalion of the 222d, we moved out on a street in the city itself [Dachau] that resulted in our movement being blocked by a large facility which was surrounded by a large, heavy wall constructed of a red sandstone about ten feet high. I reported our situation to Third Battalion Commander— and then I walked around the wall to a main gate. The situation we encountered was rather grim. We saw the train that had all those dead bodies in it. And among my men was the general feeling that all this was one of the reasons we were there [in the war], to cause that type of treatment of people to be terminated. I recall my men were quite perturbed, and I wouldn't say that their approach to the Germans for some time afterward was what you would call the most friendly.

As I look back on it, I couldn't have spent more than ten minutes in the camp itself—but I saw quite enough.

I was in the camp again after the war—about 1954, while stationed in Heidelberg, with HQ. U.S. Army Europe. By then, it was cleaned up.[39]

I can forgive . . . but you should never forget.

Pfc Fred Peterson, H Company, 222d Regiment

Fred Peterson was born in 1926. He was barely eighteen when he entered the service. When he came home from the war, he worked as a tool and diemaker. Fred and his wife, Rita, were married for forty-eight years. They have three sons. Fred was quite active in veterans' affairs. He was a past commander of his American Legion post.

In his spare time, Fred raised tropical fish. He "passed over the rainbow" in 1996. He was just nineteen at Dachau and sixty-eight when he wrote his account.

Thinking back 50 years to when we all came home, finally, I wasn't too proud of being in the Infantry. Not because of anything that we did wrong—but because there were a lot of people who thought that only "the dumb ones" were in the Infantry. It took a while, but now I can say, with great pride, that I was an Infantry soldier. No one can ever take that away from any of us. I see that people have changed their minds over the years—and now they look up to them as men who have done a splendid job.

I did get into Dachau on April 29th. I don't know why we went there. I thought we were headed directly to Munich. But I was told that some escaped prisoners told Colonel Downard about the camp, and he changed our route. But after all, I was low man on the totem pole, and someone else usually told me where to go and what to do.

Even before we actually went inside the place, it smelled awful. We entered through the front gate; at least I think that's what it was. Then, we went through a few of the Inmate Barracks. After seeing the first couple, I didn't want to see any more. Maybe that was a mistake, but that's how I felt at the time. I did go into the Crematory building. In one room I remember the dead stacked like railroad ties. It's hard to remember what you did see because so much of it was so unbelievable that your mind couldn't take all of it and hold it.

I do remember a pile of knives and other junk just outside the Camp. These could be used as weapons. Some of the prisoners were helping themselves. I remember I did see Colonel Downard lift that lone, living survivor from that death train because I was outside the camp, just walking around at the time. I remember seeing a few raw potatoes in one of the cars.

I don't believe I ever talked about Dachau the first 25 years or so that I was home. But now, so many people are talking about the Holocaust. But I do get a little upset when I hear about some outfits claiming that they were there. I read where one tank driver said he knocked down the Main Gate. Is that a fact? It was still in place when we finally got there.

I really didn't do anything important. And I just could not believe what I saw. Before that day, I didn't know what a Concentration Camp really was. I hated the Germans for what I saw in Dachau. All of them. Now I believe that they were not all to blame. You can forgive—but you should never forget.[40]

I think it's horrible that one man can do that to another man.

Pfc Herbert A. Butt, A Company, 222d Regiment

Herb Butt was twenty years old when he was inducted in Kansas City, Missouri. Before that he was working as a hydraulic leadman at North American Aviation on a deferment. He went through some Air Force basic training and at twenty-one was assigned to the Rainbow.

After discharge, he studied at Kansas City Junior College and earned an associate degree. He took a number of business courses, including shop management and training. He worked in sales for Pitman Manufacturing, leaving to take a job with one of their local dealers and then for a competitor. The business was mainly truck cranes and aerial devices for the utility industry. At age sixty-three, he retired.

He married Lora, a girl from his church, who was studying for her medical technologist license, in 1949. She died of a heart attack in 1986. They adopted a boy and a girl, and now Herb has seven grandchildren. Herb is a most active member of the Rainbow Division Veterans Association (RDVA). He has held most offices of the MO-KAN Chapter. He is now National Secretary of RDVA. He was twenty-two at Dachau and seventy-two when he put his feelings into words.

For the record, my memory of combat times is very slim. I can recall certain times and conditions—but to say when this or that happened, and when—I can't do it.

I was with the First Platoon, A Company, 222d, when we went into Dachau. I would say we were down to maybe twenty or twenty-five men.[41]

We had a Tech as Platoon Leader, and maybe a Staff Sergeant or two for Squad Leaders; maybe a Buck Sergeant. Most of us were just Pfcs or Privates. We had picked up replacements just once, I guess. I seemingly ended with Glenn Olsen from Duluth and Harry [?] Seebold, I think, from Pennsylvania.

We were on trucks and we were driven up to the gate at Dachau. We de-trucked nearest the freight cars with all those bodies. I guess by that time death, and especially in that number, was still a sorry sight to see. But I wasn't that up on the world's events just yet to recognize just what we were getting into. I don't know whether I resented the enemy more because of the train or because I had lost two of my closest buddies before we arrived at Dachau.

As I look back, we were not really restricted as to where we were allowed to wander. We were told to stay out of the prison proper—an order that wasn't too difficult to follow as we knew we had to be careful of lice and diseases.

We ran across stacks of bodies, and a Crematory—that's what it was—with piled up bodies. It wasn't the most happy area to have gone through. I think it's horrible that a man can do those things to another man. Awful![42]

It was like walking into the Twilight Zone.

Pfc Clifford J. Barrett, H Company, 222d Regiment

Cliff Barrett was born in 1927. After his war service, he entered the printing business in 1946. He worked at the *New York Sun* until it folded in 1950. For the next twenty-five years, he was with a printing firm in New York's Wall Street area. When it went out of business, he was fortunate, at middle age, to join a press clipping bureau in New Jersey. After twenty-one years there, he retired. His wife, a professor at Seton Hall University, retired at the same time. As he says, "It was time to stop and smell the roses."

Through the years, he has pursued a most interesting and unusual hobby. In 1967, he started to write letters to famous people asking them how they heard of, and what was their reaction to, the news of Pearl Harbor. Captain Eddie Rickenbacker was the first to reply, and this encouraged him to write to other celebrities. Presidents Bush and Ford sent very warm responses. His favorite is a very warm letter from Lady Bird Johnson. He has replies from military leaders, movie stars, athletes, and other notables. He has been interviewed by several newspapers, including the *New York Times*. Seton Hall University had an exhibit of his letters in 1991 to commemorate the fiftieth anniversary of Pearl Harbor.

Cliff was eighteen when he was at Dachau and sixty-eight when he told us his story.

Combat tends to harden an infantry soldier—you have seen so much death and destruction all around you. You learn how to react to each situation that you and your buddies must face. But I know none of us were prepared for what we saw at Dachau. Eighteen-year-old boys, like me, can age fast. It was like walking into The Twilight Zone.

An altogether different world was in front of us. Everywhere were sights which filled us with horror. Human beings, in the shape of walking skeletons, were dropping dead at our feet. That is one of my lasting memories. The dying, lying on the ground looking at us, and you wondered if they knew they were now free. They stretch out hands, and we pass them our rations, which unfortunately, was a mistake—but at that moment, we were overcome with sympathy and compassion—we didn't believe that it wasn't the right thing to do. Some of them died as a result, the doctors said later, from all that food at one time.

Now, fifty years later, the horror of that April day is still fresh in my memory. It is a fact that all of us who entered Dachau came out as totally different men. We just couldn't accept the fact that human beings could do all this to other human beings because of religious or political differences. We saw the Hell, but the inmates were the ones who had to live in it. And die there.

When I was taking Basic in Florida, they showed us films called, "Why We Fight." They showed the brutalities of the Nazis and Japanese. However, I'm sure that when training was finished and we left for overseas, we all forgot those films.

But on April twenty-ninth, in Dachau, we all, indeed, know "Why We Fight!"[43]

My own reaction, and seemingly that of the others,
was mainly outrage rather than overwhelming horror.
It's incredible that some still deny it.

Pfc Cliff E. Lohs, Security Platoon, 222d Regiment

Cliff Lohs was born in 1919.

After the war ended in Europe, and occupation duty in Salzburg and Vienna, he returned to his job as a newspaper photographer. Cliff eventually completed fifty years in the field. He is now retired, doing freelance photography.

He married his wife, Peggy, earlier during the war. They have three children and celebrated their golden wedding anniversary in 1994. Cliff was twenty-six when he entered Dachau, and he wrote this recollection when he was seventy-seven.

I joined the Rainbow rather late in the game as a replacement. I was caught up in the demand for more foot soldiers. Apparently, my photographic experience was noted, and I was temporarily assigned to the Regimental Security Platoon. It was a very lucky break, indeed. My two and a half years in the Air Corps had done nothing to prepare me for duty as a rifleman in immediate combat.

But my early days in Europe found me often confused and unaware of just where we were during the rapid movement of that period—a time which included the liberation of Dachau. In those days, I served in the non-Table of Organization position of Photographer.[44]

With my good friend, Joe Lill, I walked into the Camp. We were completely on our own. We had no official instructions or assistance. In addition to my full Infantry gear, I carried the standard 4x5 Speed Graphic filmpacks and flashbulbs.

Joe, much better informed than me, told me a little about the reported Concentration Camps during our walk, but I'm sure we were both unprepared for what we found there.

We first encountered that death train and its cargo of over 1,500 bodies.[45] I wish I had made those great photos of Colonel Downard with the Survivor! The worshipful look in that prisoner's eyes!

Those impressive gates masked the appalling scenes within. Shocking scenes, of course—but probably less so at that time when we were all in a combat frame of mind. My own reaction and seemingly that of the others, was mainly outrage rather than overwhelming horror.

Our troops were in charge, but the prisoners wandered at will. Those physically able were pathetically grateful to their rescuers. A touching memory recalls a couple of those living skeletons offering us some of their home-made cigarettes. We tried to respond warmly to these advances, but with a bit of worry about typhus or other possible diseases.

As I mentioned before, I'm not quite sure of the time of the day when we arrived, although, I do recall some concern as we walked "home" along the top of the railroad embankment, silhouetted against an early twilight sky. So, I expect we might have come on the scene shortly after the noon hour. And I do remember eating a hearty supper after an extra thorough handwashing.

Certainly, that day is the most memorable of my three-and-a-half-year hitch. I am glad to have had this small part in witnessing and confirming that the Holocaust really happened. It is incredible that some still deny it.

I was—and am—proud to have worn the Rainbow Patch in even so short, and comparatively minor, role.[46]

I . . . saw enough to be repulsed by the inhumane actions of the Germans.

Lieutenant Quentin F. Naumann, H Company, 222d Regiment

Naumann was twenty-five years old when he saw Dachau. He was born in Houston and served with the Rainbow throughout the war. He married Joyce Evelyn Cain in 1943. They have three daughters, Sharon, Carol, and Patricia, and two grandchildren, Sarah and Nathan Sawyer.

Quentin holds a business administration degree from Texas A&M. He had a thirty-five-year career with Humble Oil, now Exxon. His commentary, though brief, succinctly captures the feeling of many Rainbow soldiers:

I took no part in the military action—but I did go into the Camp later—and saw enough to be repulsed by the inhumane actions of the Germans. Such sights, had we seen them early in the war, would have had a very strong motivational incentive for our fighting.[47]

*That whole scene at Dachau was a very difficult day
and night to go through. I do not believe that the men involved,
or I, will ever forget it.*

**Captain James B. McCahey, Jr., Senior Aide-de Camp
to Major General Harry J. Collins**

James B. McCahey, Jr., was born in 1920. After the war he returned to Chicago and became active in politics during the fifties, ending up as a campaign manager for John Kennedy. McCahey operated a lumber business in Milwaukee, was president of a railroad company in Indiana and director of several other companies, and finally moved to Cleveland. He became senior vice-president of the Chessie System Railroads (now CSX), retiring in 1985.

He and his wife, Mary Lou, have six children and nine grandchildren. James was twenty-five years old at Dachau and seventy-six when he wrote this remembrance.

As far as the camp is concerned, I participated in a very limited way that day. Gen. Collins had asked Brig. Gen. Linden to proceed, via the 222d Infantry Regiment's line of march to be present when the Camp was reached, and report back to him how things were going.

I remember it was dusk when I arrived. There was a most foul odor about the place. Several of General Linden's guards were with me as we came to a place somewhat distant from the Main Gate where a breach had been made in the fence and some of the prisoners were escaping over the shallow moat. We joined other officers and men of the 42d and 45th who were trying to contain the surge. Since I spoke German, I contributed to this action by hollering at the same time. We were successful. Those who made it beyond the wire and the ditch, agreed to return. Among them, was a man who claimed to be a Catholic priest. Later, he was permitted to speak with the prisoners by means of a speaker system we had set up.

Evidently, General Linden had already been in the Camp and made his inspection. Lt. Col. Fellenz of the 222d had the situation well in hand. Shortly after, personnel from Corps HQ arrived. My party left the area and reported back to General Collins. I regret I cannot remember more of that day, but it has been a long time.

The next day, General Collins took a group of officers and newspaper people, Red Cross Officials, and medical doctors to

"Some were just sitting around and staring."

the Camp. They inspected the ovens, the "shower rooms," and some of the barracks. Prisoners were all over the place; some just sitting around and staring. Some were beside small fires cooking what limited food they had. Most had been on such a starvation diet for some time, that caution had to be exercised for fear an expanded menu would adversely affect their systems.

That whole scene at Dachau was a very difficult night and day to go through. I do not believe that the men involved, nor I, will ever forget it.[48]

It was beyond anything anybody could have dreamed of.

Sergeant Darrell D. Martin, G Company, 242d Regiment

Martin was twenty-four years old at Dachau. He recorded his story fifty years later. When he returned from the service, he went back to driving for Greyhound. He worked for them all of his life. When we spoke with him late in 1996, he told us: "I was never able to talk to anyone about the war. It was too terrible. It was all too emotional. I could not talk to my father or my brother about it. Dachau was like a nightmare—worse than war. I could never talk to my wife about Dachau and the war. I would have nightmares and sweat so much that my pajamas would be wringing wet. These nightmares were worse than the war—in Dachau, for I would lie on my back paralyzed—could not move. It was terrible, terrifying. My wife would shake me and wake me up. When I awoke, I knew I had had a nightmare, as my heart would be pounding."

Now, on the twenty-ninth Day of April, we came upon a place that one cannot imagine—not being told, or knowing what we were getting into. It was called Dachau, a Concentration Camp. It was surrounded by a high fence and a moat. The SS Guards were shot right there at the spot and dumped in this moat, and there were a lot of guards underwater when I got there.

When we went inside, you could see dead people there. They had starved to death. You could see how guys with wheelbarrows would haul the bodies to this one building and dump them through a window like they were delivering coal by just pouring it into a cellar. They'd just drop them down there through the window. And it was a big room. When I saw it, I called my Section Sergeant over, Sergeant Schenefield, and I said to him, "Shenny, look at this." And he looked in, and just from the smell and how it looked, he got sick.

On further inspections, we went around to see what had happened. From here, they'd take the clothes off, cut and save the hair, pull the teeth that had gold in them, bring in the bodies and stack them next to the Incinerators. Then, they'd put 'em head to foot, maybe five at a time, into these Incinerators, and burn them up. I know that when I went in there that stack of bodies was damn near high as my chest. Somebody had taken the Commandant of the Camp, I believe—he was a stocky German officer. I don't know what his rank was, but he had a red band down the leg of his pants. They had thrown him on top of all those people.

And then, we moved on to where the "hospital" was. The only bedding I saw was, like, burlap sacks. The people had hardly room to stretch out or even turn over. They were nothing but skin and bones; but somewhere in the back, somebody would call: "God Bless the Americans!" A voice that I heard that I could make out, said that he had a sister in Chicago, Illinois! Chicago, Illinois! Chicago! He'd just keep saying that over and over!

We left there and went into the Railyards. I don't know how many boxcars there were; they weren't boxcars, they were cattle cars. And the ones that hadn't starved or frozen to death, had bullet holes. In all those cars, there was only one person left alive.

It was something you wouldn't think man could be capable [of doing]. This was beyond anything anybody could have dreamed of, and we didn't know a thing about it until we were there. It just doesn't seem right that you have to be a witness to such—man's inhumanity to man. But it was certainly there. I hope to God that things like that never happen again![49]

It seems that I had experienced a bad dream—yet, I know it happened. I was there in the midst of it.

Lieutenant Jack E. Westbrook, Anti-Tank Company, 222d Regiment

Jack Ellis Westbrook was born July 8, 1924. He was not quite twenty-one years old at Dachau. He was seventy-two when he wrote his memoir. Jack holds a B.S. degree from Texas A&M. He is a registered engineer and is recognized as a corrosion specialist by the National Association of Corrosion Engineers. He is chief engineer for Sun Pipeline Company in Tulsa. He is a member of Piperliners Club, Tulsa, and the National Association of Corrosion Engineers, and he has written technical articles and taught in industry schools.

He was awarded the Bronze Star Medal with V for Valor, an Oak Leaf Cluster, and a Purple Heart. Today, Jack is an elder of St. Andrews Presbyterian Church, Tulsa. He is married and is the father of three daughters. He enjoys tennis, swimming, snow skiing, and writing.

The fullness of the meaning in President Roosevelt's "a day in infamy" did not come to bear on me until in these later years, when I have had ample time to think about the Concentration Camp at Dachau, Germany.

Up until April 29, 1945, the majority of us in my unit were not aware of the Nazi efforts to exterminate the Jews—certainly not its scope, nor its effect on the world; and certainly none of us were aware of the Dachau Concentration Camp. We had been briefed Stateside on the unjust imprisonment of large numbers of people by the Germans, and their being forced into a kind of slavery. But nothing could have prepared me for what was to unfold in that small dorf north and west of Munich in Bavarian Germany.

I had just returned late on April 27th, to my Anti-Tank Company, and was not restored to the Rolls. This, because I had hitched a ride from the Hospital in Epinal, France, thus bypassing the Replacement Depot, through which I was to have been routinely sent. But with my orders cut I, luckily, had no trouble getting a hot-shot jeep to Seventh Army Headquarters, and then, with a friendly messenger and a little bit of "politicking," on to my Company.

During my absence, I had been replaced as Second Platoon Leader—so, on a temporary basis, was assigned to a Liaison capacity by the Company Commander. Nonetheless, I was interested in my old platoon—hopeful of getting back to being its Leader. I had been reunited with the platoon, glad to see them, and looking forward to being in their midst again. They were a great bunch. We had all been together in training at Camp Gruber, Oklahoma.

As my memory serves, we were told nothing of the scope, nor of the importance of what lay ahead. I believe I remember our being briefed that there was an objective of importance north of Munich; but no more than that—we had no idea what we would encounter. I am inclined to believe that Regimental Staff was not aware of the Camp.

On April 29th, I was instructed by our Company Commander to check with Lt. Colonel Downard about the disposition of our 2d Platoon—it had been placed under his command. Its three guns were situated in defensive positions just east of the Concentration Camp. There was considerable concern—always—about a counter-attack by German tanks. I proceeded from the 2d Platoon's positions—probably about a quarter mile—to the Camp, going fairly directly to the only evident entry to the facility, which was a long walkway lined with beautiful trees framing an equally beautiful entry with a wrought-iron gate. Upon getting to the Main Gate, and identifying myself to the attending guards, and explaining my mission to see Lt. Col. Downard, I was permitted to enter the newly-liberated Camp.

I recall that it was rather like going from the rather picturesque entryway into a dungeon-like atmosphere. It was what I had come to expect as typically German, or European—old and musty. Now, I know that the Dachau Camp, built on the site of an old munitions plant, would be converted in 1933 as a Political Detainee Concentration Camp. I am sure that what I have learned since then has influenced my thinking at that time.

Dachau 29 April 1945

It must have been around 1300 hours, or thereabouts. Also, I assumed that the soldiers, who seemed to be in charge of the situation, were Rainbowers. At that time, we were not wearing our Division identifying patches. I understand now that some of them might have been members of the 45th Division. I just did not know, at the time, and certainly have no recollection at this date.

In fact, so much of my memory has been lost with the passage of time, that the whole happening seems to be something I experienced in a bad dream. Yet—I know it did happen. I was there in the midst of it all. I do not pretend to have full recollection of the occasion, because I made a conscious effort to eliminate it from my memory. I do know that the guards knew Lt. Col. Downard [who had only recently been promoted from Major], and this confirms my belief that the preponderance of the troops there were 42d Division. Also, I want to stress that I went in there after the fact. Troops were already in the Camp; so I was not in the vanguard which opened the Camp. I was under the impression that troops had been in there only an hour or so. Why that impression lingers with me, I cannot explain.

I had not recognized the stench, which became very pronounced a good distance from the installation. Finally, I recognized it for what it was, and it dawned on me just as I was entering the labyrinth of facilities. Having heard shots being fired, as I approached the Compound, I was concerned as to what I was getting into—and was cautious in that situation. This was by no means a routine matter—and I was now in a position which was completely out of the ordinary for me. I was especially "touchy" having just returned from the hospital where I recovered from wounds received in an earlier action. I immediately recognized the existing confusion and returned to the G.I. guards so that I might perform my assigned mission—which was to find Col. Downard. But they didn't know where he was, and I had to go find him myself.

It was this search for the Colonel that opened the horrors of what had been in existence here. I observed the stacks of bodies at various points in the facility. I knew when I got to the Crematorium building what must have gone on there. The ovens were cold—I do remember that. I did not witness the notorious "shower rooms"—although, I am sure they existed. Mainly, I saw the administrative offices; the crematorium [one of several], the rail sidings, the service area, and the Detainee Compound.

This Compound area stands out in my memory. Those masses of humanity, in their tattered and unkempt garb; filthy, hanging from their skeletal bodies—staring out of blank eyes, crying, screaming, reaching through the fencing, only wanting to touch us. I could not understand the language. They were all screaming at once. I did recognize one voice speaking English. He was a detainee from Chicago. I had a short exchange with him. I can't remember it precisely. But I do remember he asked me why he wasn't allowed to get out! Such a mass of humanity! The question of nationality didn't come to my mind. I don't remember seeing the distinguishing Stars of David. I do understand that the majority of the inmates were Russian and Polish, which confirms my memory of the voices and languages. My initial reaction was to give the two or three K-Rations in my pocket to the inmates. Later, as I passed that point coming back, I saw one inmate regurgitate—the food was just too rich for him.[50] Another inmate picked up his vomit. But I do not remember if he ate it.

Standing out in my memory was the extent and massiveness of the Camp. But now I know that most of the area was occupied by various service facilities. The Compound, itself, was pitifully overcrowded—far too small for the thirty-thousand pitiful pieces of humanity that were said to have been there. What stands out are those electrified fences, the guard towers, the moats, the guard dogs. And, of course, that rail siding which held those "forty and eight" type boxcars, coal cars and flat cars—some forty in number.

Yes, and the civilians, residents of Dachau, riding bicycles down the streets outside the Camp—rags tied over their noses and mouths to keep out the stench. Probably some of those very same people later told us that they did not know what was going on in the camp—that it "was a Political Detainee Lager." This has to be one of the most ridiculous postures ever devised.

When I found Lt. Col. Downard, he was at a railway siding. He was viewing the bodies stacked in a boxcar—some like cordwood, some in disarray. At one point, my resistance gave way. I vomited. Even though I had just been released from the hospital, my strength was not back to normal. Neither was my stamina. Col. Downard was somewhat amused by my reaction to the sights and the stench—I can't remember what overpowered me more. But he stood by my side in case I should have to vomit again. After briefing him on our defensive situation, he advised me to move to the south and east with Munich as our target. Orders for return of the Platoon to Company control would be forthcoming from his S-2. Other details of our conversation escape me now. Some time later, I learned that Col. Downard had pulled a live body from that 40 and 8 boxcar. After the war, I saw that picture of him doing it. It made the Nation's newspapers.

If my memory serves me right, Col. Downard also told me that First Battalion was in the Camp, too, but I don't remember seeing any of them whom I recognized.

After going back through a part of the Compound, taking advantage of the moment to see what I could—thinking, perhaps, that this might not be an historic moment, but to test my credulity as to what was happening around me. But nothing I saw on the way outside stands out in my memory. My sensitivity had already been strained to the nth degree. Again, as I returned to my jeep, it continued to sink into me—the enormity, the bestiality, the tragedy of what was happening here—of man's inhumanity to man. This had to be the most depressing, distressing moment for me, even though I had seen so much before to harden my sensitivities. I now think that had we known about this sooner, we would have had even a greater sense of destiny than what we had developed earlier on.[51]

MONDAY, APRIL 30

Generals Dwight D. Eisenhower, Omar Bradley, and George Patton visited the Ohrdruf concentration camp shortly after it was captured. They were appalled by what they saw. General Eisenhower cabled President Truman and asked him to fly a delegation of U.S. senators and congressmen to the site in order that they might personally witness the true horrors of the war. He also happened to remark that it would be appropriate for many American soldiers to become witnesses as well.

We are not aware that he issued an official order to that effect. However, usually a general's "suggestion" carried the same weight. Evidently, our General Collins felt the same way. He saw this as a most dramatic occasion to educate the troops as far as the true meaning of the war was concerned.

But the Rainbow was still very much in the war. Most of the division had already moved to Munich and Salzburg. Only a few units remained in Dachau for guard duty and to await further orders. General Collins made sure that as many men who could be spared would be sent into the camp. There, of course, they received a lesson in human—or inhuman—behavior they would remember for the rest of their lives.

Unlike the troops who had arrived in the morning and the afternoon of the first day and had to hurry through it, or were on their own and could leave when they could take no more of it, the men who were sent to Dachau for the purpose of seeing it were on a tour, and they saw all of it.

Never again!

Pfc Robert J. Calongne, HQ Company, 222d Regiment

Robert Calongne was born in New Orleans on December 21, 1921. He is a graduate of Louisiana State University. During the war, he served as a cryptographer for Headquarters Company of the 222d Regiment.

He received his bachelor's degree in mechanical engineering from LSU and has held important positions as a consulting engineer. Calongne married Rose Pasternostro, and they have two sons and two daughters. Bob, Jr., is an attorney; Daniel, an electrical engineer; Susan, a civil engineer; and Katherine, an Alexandria town representative.

I was a cryptographer for the 222d Regiment. My job was to code and decode messages for the Commanding Officer. I wasn't there at Dachau on the first day, but the men in the companies told me that thousands of weakened prisoners came out of those barracks as best they could; emaciated and hollow-eyed. They were in a frenzy—but they couldn't celebrate because they didn't have the strength. Hundreds, if not thousands of others, were waiting to be killed, but our guys got there in time to save their lives.

Later, I did go into the Camp because our Commanding Officer wanted as many men as possible to see the devastation wrought against fellow human beings at Dachau.

I saw the boxcars that were still filled with the dead bodies. We were told by the surviving prisoners that if the inmates tried to get out of those cars, the Germans would shoot them. Not fed, the prisoners progressively starved.

To me, it looked like the last one alive grouped the family together—father, mother, children. We all wondered how human beings could do this to other human beings.

What refreshed my memory about all this—some forty-seven years later, was a Memorial Service organized by our Rainbow Division and held in Dachau for the unveiling of a plaque commemorating The Rainbow's liberation of the Camp. I attended, along with some forty other Rainbowers, and about four hundred Jewish and other survivors. A former inmate hugged me and said, "Thank you for my life!" I could do nothing but cry. Our members were declared Honorary Members of the Comité Internationale de Dachau, a group comprised of Dachau survivors and their families. Each of us who attended was given a ribbon. It was blue and white—and striped like the prisoners uniforms at the Camp.

On the ribbon, written in four languages, were the words "Never Again!"[52]

I can only hope that never again will I, or anyone else of this earth, have a similar experience.

Pfc J. William "Bill" Keithan, H Company, 232d Regiment

Bill Keithan was born in Earthwalk, Pennsylvania, in 1925. Before volunteering for the army he was a student confectioner. He served in the war as a mortar gunner and a student cook and baker. With the arrival of peace, he studied at "Rainbow U" (see note 3) and took advantage of furloughs to travel to much of western Europe. At home, he worked at a number of restaurant jobs and attended Cornell University. After thirty-three years with Westin Hotels, he retired, but remains active as a consultant, teacher, author, historian, archivist, and at least a score of other interesting pursuits. He and his wife, Faye, have two children, Karen and John.

Bill was twenty at Dachau. He set down his observations almost fifty years later.

I was in H Company, 232d Regiment. I was a cook, but since our rolling kitchens were not in use, my assignments were ammunition carrier for the .30 Caliber heavy machine guns, or the 81 mm mortar squads.

Early in the morning of April 29, I arrived at Dachau with a rifle company that was moving some distance away to Dasing. The rifle Company CO released me from my duties, and I began to make my way back to my own company, when somebody told me of the existence of a prison camp. On my own, I decided to see what it was like. Thus, I heard about it early on the morning of the 30th. I had no idea what I expected to see. I approached unaccompanied.

My feelings after so great a time span are difficult to describe. I was repulsed; horrified. I came upon the Camp from the Dachau Railroad Station, following the tracks. Just outside was that trainload of "emancipated" dead, which had been delivered there, but had not yet been run over to the Crematorium.

There were no guards present when I arrived. But there were a number of German uniformed dead at various locations. One, in particular was lying face down in one of the moats that surrounded the compound.

There were German civilians outside the Camp. I saw none of them tour the place, nor attempt to bury the German dead soldiers. Their reaction was one of great physical concern for their own well-being. I can remember going through a number of homes beside the Camp and meeting civilians who urged me to stand guard over them because they feared retribution from freed inmates. But I was not ordered to protect them, nor did I in response to their requests. I remember one woman telling me she had lived in Chicago for a number of years. She spoke English quite well.

I spent that night in the Camp Commandant's own quarters. I took a small camera and some of his medals. The camera has been sent to the Rainbow Division's Memorial Museum in Kansas City. The medals are still in my possession.

In a house nearby, someone had found it necessary to shoot a very large and vicious dog. From the house, I took a 1936 Olympic Program. It had signatures of the winners of Gold Medals. Among them were those of Jesse Owens, Margie Destree, and others of foreign origin.

It was all an experience that I had no way of coping with. I did not relieve my tension in any way, nor did I have a strong reaction to what I saw, other than complete disgust for individuals responsible.

An interesting sidelight: Subsequent to victory in Europe, VE Day—and during the month of June, I was given a pass to Nancy, France. It was my first real opportunity to listen to some radio, and eat some foods long absent in Army rations. One afternoon, while I was on a Nancy street, I saw a parade of people dressed in concentration camp garb. They were carrying a large Cross, and were headed for the cathedral. It appeared to be a memorial service for deceased prisoners. Several members of that group noticed the Rainbow Patch on my shoulder. They asked me to participate in the service. I marched with them for some ten blocks, and then took part in their memorial ceremony. This sums up my experience on the liberation of Dachau. I can only hope that, never again, will I, or anyone on this earth, have a similar experience.[53]

We were sent back to Dachau to become living witnesses to a Hell on earth!

Staff Sergeant Bill Kenny, G Company, 242d Regiment

Bill Kenny was born November 12, 1925, in Orange, New Jersey. He attended the LaSalle Military Academy and was a 1953 graduate of Seton Hall University with a B.S. in marketing. Bill went overseas with the Rainbow and served until the end of the war as a machine gunner.

Kenny was in the printing business. He operated the Kenny Press in Newark, New Jersey, until he retired in 1992. Today, he is very active in the RDVA. He is a member of several sales and advertising clubs. He was elected to the Knights of Malta in Washington, D.C. He was president of the Parish Council of Christ, the King Roman Catholic Church in New Vernon, New Jersey, and continues as a trustee of the parish.

Bill Kenny married Mary A. Crecca in 1949. They have nine children and fifteen grandchildren. He was twenty years old that day at Dachau, and he set down his memories fifty years later.

I was a member of G Company, 242d Regiment of the Rainbow Division. We had been fighting since December of 1944, and we had taken severe casualties. Most of the men I was serving with were in their late teens and early twenties. When we left The States, we were just boys, but those of us who were still fighting by April, had become men. We had all seen many of our best friends either killed or severely wounded. I offer this as background to set a mental picture of how we felt that morning when we arrived at that Hell called Dachau.

My machine gun section was riding on tanks and heading for an airfield on the outskirts of Munich. Our primary objective was to capture that airfield as soon as possible.

The first sign of something different came when we started seeing people in tattered, striped uniforms along the side of the road begging for food. We couldn't stop, but we started throwing our rations to those skeletal, starved human beings. We passed by one of the gates at Dachau, without stopping. That afternoon, we secured the airbase.

The next morning, my Company Commander called me and said I was to go on a special detail with three other men from my company. That "special detail" was to be one I will never forget, nor truly comprehend as long as I live. At a National Reunion of the Rainbow Division in Louisville a half century later, I asked my former Company Commander, Jim Campbell, how he had come to choose four men for that morning, and he said, "The word had come down from some general that as many men as possible should bear witness to this terrible scene because one day people will not believe such atrocities took place."

Yes, we were sent back to Dachau to become living witnesses to a Hell on earth. I believe it was best described by my Platoon Sergeant, Darrell D. Martin.[54]

Inmates . . . they were very thin, skin and bones . . . arms reaching out . . . reaching for anything . . .

T-5 Robert W. Russ, K Company, 222d Regiment

Our Unit arrived at the town of Dachau the night of April 29. We were billeted in a home there. I was sound asleep, being very tired. That morning, at daybreak, we received word that if we wished to go "somewhere" a truck would be down in front of the meat market at ten o'clock and we should meet there. It was a chilly grey morning spitting a fine rain. After a short ride on the truck, we were left off at a rail siding. I couldn't imagine or know what I was going to see or view in the next possibly two hours.

We walked along the side of the railroad boxcars. The large side doors were open and piles of corpses could be seen in each car. I became numbed with silence—it was a different and sudden experience. We neared a high barbed wire fence. On the outside, there was a water-filled moat. I could see a dead German guard lying in the bottom. From outside the fence, we could see a crowd of prisoners—very surprised and happy to see us—at long last, relief.

We wandered further into the area—walking through several low-ceilinged barracks. I thought they looked like chicken houses. Inmates were lying in their rough, wooden cots—platforms;

they were very thin, skin and bones. Arms were reaching out—it seemed like they were reaching for anything. I think we passed on to them all the chocolate bars and cigarettes that we carried with us.

Many were talking—but not knowing foreign languages, I couldn't understand them. I think I was studying their facial expressions. Leaving the barracks, we walked out into the yard again, through the crowd. Soon, we came to the crematory. There was a small room where there was a pile of clothing heaped on the floor In the next room, a mound of naked human bodies. In the next room, were three or four furnaces with their doors open where the bodies were to be fed in to be cremated.

We then went out into the yard again, wandering through the liberated crowd, to find our truck, to return to our billet. A day—an unbelievable experience, I will always remember.[55]

For years I just didn't want to talk about it, even think about it.

Pfc Daniel Cogar, G Company, 232d Regiment

Daniel Cogar was born in Webster Springs, West Virginia, in 1925. His father was in construction. He was twenty years old at Dachau and sixty-nine when he set down his observations. Daniel has worked at a series of construction jobs. He was married in 1951. The Cogars have a son and a daughter, three granddaughters, and one grandson. The Cogars are now enjoying their retirement in St. Petersburg, Florida.

I went in as a replacement. I joined the Rainbow in January in France. We started at Alsace, and went all the way across Germany. Just before we got to Munich, we came to Dachau. I never heard of Concentration Camps. I never even knew they existed like they did. By the time I got there, Dachau had already been liberated. They took us on a tour of the Camp. We saw the bodies, and where they had burned them, and just about everything else.

I was only 19 years old. I didn't know what was going on. I mean . . . I think I felt worse about it years afterward than I did at the time. Back then, we were all hardened. We expected to see just about anything, and in this case, we did.

I remember the prisoners. They were all as skinny as skeletons, and their heads were shaved. There wasn't one who had any flesh on him—or her. It was a terrible scene, I can tell you.

But they were so happy to see us. They just couldn't believe we had come. They kept shouting, "Ami! Ami!"

When I got out of the service, I tried to put it all behind me. I know of guys who wound up in the nuthouse. So, for years, I just didn't want to talk about it, even think about it. I didn't, and I still don't, tell my wife. The only time she ever hears anything is when we get together at reunions and things. I feel I can only talk about it with somebody who was there, who knows something about it. Because so many other people would say, "Oh, he's bragging"—or "He don't know what he's talking about." You can get disgusted.

I think this should all be taught in the schools and in religious classes. It would be a great help to people.[56]

I will never, never forget what we saw!

T-5 Martin Arterburn, Anti-Tank Company, 242d Regiment

Martin Arterburn was born June 3, 1925, in Renfrow, Oklahoma. He served with the Rainbow from 1943 until 1946. Under the G. I. Bill, he studied at the Spartan School of Aeronautics. He was a licensed pilot as well as a mechanic. He was employed at the American Airlines maintenance and engineering center in Tulsa from 1949 through 1981. He married LaVerna M. Knapp. Their lovely daughter, Montee Sue, is now deceased.

Arterburn arrived at Dachau three days before his twentieth birthday and drew a map to fix Dachau in his mind. He claims that he can still see the grim building behind each of the simple line drawings, which bear his captions.[57]

Dachau Legend

1. Main Gate (Arbeit Macht Frei)
2. Where we parked jeep.
3. Large warehouse full of suitcases, shoes, and clothes.
4. Dead guards, beaten to death; eyeballs knocked out, arms and legs twisted; facial features like hamburger.
5. Dead guards floating in the water. Shot by inmates who had been given guns by soldiers.
6. Guard tower.
7. Inmate barracks (many, many).
8. Gas chamber.
9. Crematorium.
10. Numerous bodies of dead inmates.
11. Dog pens. Dogs had been killed.
12. Remains from crematorium.
13. Killing mound: a pile of dirt about two feet high; bullets that had passed through bodies were in the mound.
14. Coal bunkers with bodies of guards.
15. Inmates came to fence, crying and trying to touch us. We gave them all our cigarettes and candy.
16. Railroad.
17. Stone wall.
18. Just buildings—don't know what they were for.

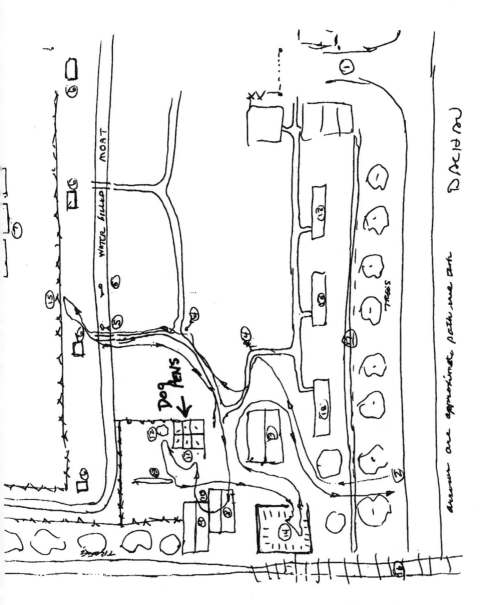

Hand-drawn map of KZ Dachau by T-5 Martin Arterburn 29 April 1945.

THE CHAPLAINS

It has been said
There are no Atheists in foxholes.
That is just not so.
When all hope is gone,
No answering artillery,
No tanks,
No advance,
No retreat.
Just the crash of shells,
The rip of machine guns
And cries for Medics,
Who are themselves casualties.
Totally abandoned,
And ruthlessly punished—
That is the time for Atheistic lapses
And new conversions.

> from "The Day of the Eighty-Eights"
> Dee Eberhart

Father (Maj.) Charles G. Erb, SVD, and Rabbi (Captain) Eli A. Bohnen were two of the fifteen chaplains assigned to the Rainbow Division. Of that number, ten were Protestant; four, Catholic; and one, Jewish. There was one chaplain for approximately every thousand men.

Although religious services of all three denominations were held whenever possible and were well attended, there were times when a chaplain of one's particular faith would not be at hand when urgently needed. All the chaplains, therefore, were prepared to cross religious lines and fill in for one another. They did so on many occasions.

Father (Maj.) Charles G. Erb, SVD, May 1945, with Fr. Hyacinth Kubicka (left) and Fr. Dominic (center).

The chaplains were with the troops from the time the division went into combat, a total of some 114 days. They shared many of the perils. One, Father (later Monsignor) Heide, was taken prisoner.

They were dealing with men who had left their homes behind, but not their problems. There were still the basic anxieties over families, money and the future. "My wife writes that she isn't getting her allotment." "Grandma is sick and needs to be put in a home." "What do you do if you're in the army and can't meet the mortgage payments?" "With my brother and myself away, how can Dad get help to run the store?" And on a seemingly trivial level (seemingly, because no worries are trivial to soldiers far from home), "How can I be sure my girl isn't stepping out on me?" And all of these concerns were intensified by the uncertainties of what the next day, even the next hour, of combat would bring.

And underlying every question was, Why? Spoken or silent, "Why is the Lord allowing all this to happen?" In trying to find the answer, our chaplains and so many of the soldiers they counseled found a renewal and a strengthening of their faith.

In the days that followed,
I was often asked, "How could they stand it, Padre?"

Father Charles G. Erb, SVD, Chaplain

Father Erb was born August 3, 1906, in Rochester. He had led a long, busy, and varied life. He was ordained in 1933 at St. Gabriel Seminary near Vienna. He entered the service in 1942, serving with the air force and the engineers in Alaska and the Aleutians. In 1944, he left for Marseilles with the Rainbow and was with them until he was separated in 1946. He earned a Bronze Star Medal and two Battle Stars. For forty-two years he was a missionary in Ghana. Reassigned to the United States, he produced a series of mission and other vocational films including *Anthropos,* which featured SVD (Society of the Divine Word) contributions to anthropology and linguistics. In 1983 he celebrated his jubilee—fifty years in the priesthood. He received the papal award *Pro Ecclesia et Pontifice* in 1987. He is living at the Divine Word Missionaries, Bordentown, New Jersey. He also serves as chaplain to the local VFW chapter and helps neighboring parishes in the ministry as priest. He was thirty-nine at Dachau, and eighty-nine when he relived that experience.

May 5th, 1945, we were driving along the Autobahn from Dachau to Salzburg, happily singing as loudly as we could. Little birds were fluttering all around us. Two Polish priests recently liberated, Joseph Dominic and Hyacinth Kubica, sat in the back of the jeep. Cpl. James Vincent Magee, my driver, and I were taking the two men, "Dachau Graduates," to the Bishop of Salzburg. He would buy them new suits and restore them to the "civilized" world.

A week before, on April 29, James Vincent Magee, my driver, and an Aide, brought me to Dachau. Just before we arrived, there had been some excitement about the possibility of the Nazis blowing up the place. I came to the barracks which held the Catholic and Protestant Clergymen. Later, we learned the statistic—1,200 priests, brothers; and 400 other Christian clerics. It was a shock when I found 15 of my own Order. One was Father Hyacinth Kubica, Polish, who had ordained me in Vienna in 1933, while I was an exchange student studying anthropology and theology at our SVD seminary in Austria. I was able to take him and the oldest priest, Father Dominic, out of that awful place.

Dachau 29 April 1945

Throughout the whole heartbreaking event, I must say that the victims I met there could only express great joy at being liberated. They were grateful—but hatred? I can't say that there was any considerable amount of anger or hatred. Everyone was just too anxious to get out of the place. Later, there had to be a round-up of the prisoners to get them back for registration and dismissal. There were so many stories of how the victims tried to help one another; it transcended all political and religious differences—the communists, especially praising the clerics helping their unfortunate mates, praying and taking counsel together.

In the days that followed, I was often asked by our men, "How could they stand it, Padre?" How could they? This place which stank of death and disease—this hole which lacked the ordinary requirements for decent living? These men, beaten, abused, humiliated, without any hope of relief, or return to their families? It must have been a veritable hell. One could imagine the infighting that must have taken place for space, for food. But I heard good stories later of heroism and charity. One of them tells of Karl Leisner, a young seminarian, who got into trouble with the Gestapo, and was sent to Dachau.

He was so good to everyone—Christian and Jew alike, that his brother clergymen decided he deserved ordination. A French Bishop secretly ordained him. Lutheran ministers gave out of their meager rations so that their Catholic brothers could celebrate properly this wonderful event. Karl died in Munich after the Liberation.[1]

And what did our soldiers say after Dachau? "Padre, I guess I griped often about our coming here to help them fight their wars," one stated. "But seeing this, I guess we just had to come to stop the horror."

Victor Frankl, the psychiatrist, himself a victim and survivor of the Holocaust, wrote in *Man's Search for Meaning,* "Our generation is realistic, for we have come to know man as he really is. After all, man is the being who invented the Gas Chamber. However, he is also the being who has entered the Gas Chamber upright, with The Lord's Prayer, or the Shema Yisroel on his lips."

Yes, if you visit Dachau today, you will find tourists from all over the world. You might be able to talk with former victims. The Museum contains Rainbow photos of the events of those days of Liberation. At the other end of the Camp, Carmelite Nuns pray day and night in their Chapel.

Yes. There is still a great need—in this world—for prayer and sacrifice; for pardon, peace and justice.[2]

I seek my brothers.

Rabbi Eli A. Bohnen, Chaplain

Rabbi Eli Bohnen was born in Toronto on September 9, 1909. He earned his B.A. in Semitic studies from the University of Toronto in 1931. He was ordained at the Jewish Theological Seminary in 1935. From 1939 to 1948 he was rabbi at Temple Emanu-El, Providence. From 1943 through 1946, he served as an assistant chaplain in the Rainbow, with the rank of major. He earned the Bronze Star and the army commendation ribbon. Immediately after the war, he worked with Jewish displaced persons in Salzburg and Bad Gastein, Austria. When he came home, he resumed his post at Temple Emanu-El in Providence as senior rabbi and then rabbi emeritus when he retired in 1973.

Rabbi Bohnen was active in many religious organizations and was awarded the National Bronze Brotherhood Award of the National Conference of Christians and Jews. He also holds honorary degrees from Brown University and Roger Williams College. In 1939, he married Eleanor Rosenthal of Ellenville, New York. They have a son, Michael J. Bohnen; a daughter, Mrs. Mayer Levitt; and five grandchildren. He set down his Dachau experience in a letter he wrote to his wife May 1, 1945:

Our Division had just taken Dachau. It is difficult to describe the emotions which my Assistant, Corporal Heimberg, and I felt as we approached the Concentration Camp in our jeep. The area had been sealed off as soon as the shooting was over, probably to avoid contamination and infection from the diseased inmates. A G.I., on guard, directed us to a harried Colonel who might give us a pass.

"State your purpose in wanting to enter the Camp, Chaplain. This isn't exactly an exhibition, you know!"

As I thought about it later, I was somewhat embarrassed by my answer. I had blurted out the first words which came to mind—the words of Joseph in the Bible: "I seek my brothers." I had not meant to be melodramatic. But all that I had heard about Dachau made me lose myself in emotion.

Our first encounter with the Camp almost made me wish the Colonel had not let us through. Nothing that I can hope to put in words could adequately describe the sights. Sometimes, the human mind refuses to believe what the eyes see. All those stories of Nazi horrors are underestimated rather than exaggerated.

The dead were piled everywhere; but there were still thousands still alive. Of all the inmates, the Jews were the worst off. Their plight was indescribable. They looked worse than the dead. They cried when they saw us; I spoke to a large group. I can't remember what I said, but Heimberg [chaplain's assistant Eli Heimberg] says they cried as I spoke. Some cried all the time we were there. They were emaciated, diseased, beaten, miserable caricatures of human beings. I didn't know how they all didn't go mad. There were thousands and thousands of prisoners in that Camp. Some didn't look too bad. But most looked terrible. And, as I said, the Jews were the worst off. Even the other prisoners who suffered miseries themselves, couldn't get over the unspeakable treatment meted out to the Jews. When I got back I couldn't eat. I couldn't even muster up enough energy to write you this letter.

We had been a fighting Division. We had seen death at close range every day for months. But this was different. For some reason, which I find difficult to convey, I did not at the moment think of the victims of this ceaseless massacre which had become a matter of routine to the Nazis. I thought of the Executioners. I recall turning to my assistant and telling him that I felt like apologizing to our dog, who was with us, for the fact that we belonged to the human race. And as we went further into the Camp and beheld the skin-covered skeletons that were its prisoners, and saw the paraphernalia which made it an Extermination Center, I felt increasingly inferior to the dog. As a human being, I was kin to those who were responsible for Dachau.

But my faith in man was partially restored a few days later. I was conducting Services for our troops in an open field a few miles east of Dachau. I noticed three young civilians standing behind the last row of soldiers; apparently joining in the Hebrew portions of the Service. Jewish civilians in Germany during the war were something of an anomaly, so it was natural for me to be curious.

Afterward, I introduced myself. They were in their late teens or early twenties. They told me they had been prisoners in Dachau. With the liberation of the Camp, they joined a group of prisoners who roamed through the countryside stealing food from the farms, and clothing themselves in whatever they had been able to find. They met with no opposition. The terrified Germans did not dare oppose these former inmates of the Camp.

About an hour before coming upon our Service, the boys had been raiding a nearby farm together with their companions. The

Band they told me was made up of Poles, Russians, Hungarians, Czechs and themselves. As they entered the barn, in the dim light, they saw a man dressed in the typical peasant garb of the district, cowering in obvious terror in one of the stalls.

It's Mueller! It's Mueller! the men cried as if with one voice. Immediately, those closest to him began to pummel him and tear at his hair.

In Dachau where cruelty was normal, Mueller had been one of the more sadistic of the SS guards.[3] He had obviously been happy with his fate which made him keeper of these doomed and helpless prisoners. While his cruelties were numerous, there was one, in particular, for which he was notorious throughout the Camp. He would seize a prisoner who had displeased him—and it was not very difficult to incur his displeasure—and would tie one end of a rope around the hapless inmate, and the other end to a huge anvil which stood out in the open. Taking a whip in hand, he would order his victim to drag the anvil around the prison yard. Obviously, it was impossible for the starved and emaciated unfortunate even to budge the anvil. The lash whistled through the air over and over again, as screams resounded through the area. No one knew how many of Mueller's victims had died under his whip.

When we saw Mueller in that barn, all of us had the same thought, the boy went on. Now the shoe was now on the other foot. We were the Captors. Mueller was now in our power. We found a rope hanging from a peg in the barn. We tied one end around Mueller's waist. There was nothing comparable with the anvil in the barn, so we dragged Mueller outside. He was crazy with fear. He was begging for mercy. His lips were covered with foam.

The boy stopped for a moment. There was a faraway look in his eyes. I could sense that he was visualizing that terrible scene. One of the other boys then took up the story.

The only thing we could find heavy enough was a boulder lying just outside the barn. Then, we managed to secure the free end of the rope around this huge rock. Each of us had grabbed whatever we could find to use as a club. There were ax handles, lengths of chain; whatever else could serve the purpose. The three of us were the only Jews in the group. We were always together. Like the others, we also took hold of whatever we could use to strike Mueller. Like the others, we relished the anticipation of doing to Mueller what he had done to so many of our friends.

This was all said in a matter-of-fact tone. I marveled that there was no indication of satisfaction on their faces; nor of exultation in their voices. They spoke of looking forward to repaying the Nazi in his own coin.

The boy continued. Those nearest Mueller began to strike him as the others closed in on him. We could see him straining at the rope. Horrible screams came from his throat. The three of us stood there waiting for our turn to strike at Mueller. Suddenly, we looked at each other. Without a word, we threw down our clubs and ran. We kept running until we could no longer hear the anguished cries of that tortured man. It was then that we came upon this service and heard the familiar Hebrew words that made us stop here.[4]

Rabbi Bohnen died December 1, 1992.

But for the Grace of God, had not my parents left Europe in the early 1900s, I would be dead, or in a place like Dachau.

Corporal Eli Heimberg, Chaplain's Assistant

Heimberg was born in Chelsea, Massachusetts, in 1917. He has an MBA from the University of Massachusetts, Dartmouth. He was, until retirement, president of Cameo Curtains, North Bedford, Massachusetts. During the Korean War his company made parachutes. He married Frances Levy. They have three children, Ellen, Paul, and William. He is active in community work—Scouts, Junior Achievement, United Way. He served four years in the army. Eli Heimberg was twenty-eight years old at Dachau. He recalled the day some fifty years later. He has been doing extensive research on Dachau and the Holocaust.

The day, April 29th, was a clear one. But as we all knew—being in an Infantry Division—one could never know how that day would end.

When I picked up Chaplain Bohnen, he told me he had information that the Dachau Concentration Camp was liberated that morning by our 222d Infantry Regiment and surely it should be secured by the afternoon. Since Dachau was in the path of our mission, The Chaplain recognized the importance of visiting the Concentration Camp to assure the living victims that they were no longer alone—that there were those who care.

We left the environs of Unter-Baar, a town south of Rain, and took the Autobahn south. Dachau would be on our left. As usual, my dog, Hundt, a Chesapeake Retriever, rode with us, sitting ramrod straight in the back seat of our jeep. I had picked Hundt up about a month earlier. He was lying wounded in a ditch. I nursed him back to health. He adopted me. Later I brought him home to the States.

As we came within a half mile of the Camp, we encountered a stench which permeated the air. It might be described as a combination of burning garbage and singed chicken feathers. It was a clear day, the kind of weather where all you would need was a jacket. We had just finished a winter of sleeping in encampments, and so any sunshine was welcome. I drove the jeep on a narrow bridge over a moat. It is difficult to depict our inner thoughts and agitation as we approached the Camp.

As soon as it had been secured (at about 4 or 5 P.M.), it had been sealed off; probably to avoid contamination and disease from the Camp's victims, and to maintain order within and outside.

After we had been given our pass to enter, we went inside. We saw a pyramid of shoes and mounds of clothing piled about fifteen feet high. Obviously, the victims' belongings. We saw the long train of boxcars filled with the dead. We were told this train had been sent to Dachau from Camps in the east to avoid the Russian advance. These unfortunate souls had agonized for 21 days with scant food or water in the cold April weather. They wore only those thin, striped uniforms. In their final moments, those who died with their eyes wide open, stared at you, as if to appeal—why?

I had heard that there were Concentration Camps in Germany, but I thought they would be similar to the Internment Camps the United States provided to incarcerate Japanese-American civilians. I never expected to see what I saw in Dachau.

Not far away from the boxcars lay the bodies of SS guards who had been killed in the battle for the Camp. Driving further inside, we asked directions to the Jewish Barracks. When we entered, the Chaplain and I, with the dog behind us, we saw emaciated, undernourished human beings, whose skin clung so closely to their bones it appeared as if a silk stocking had been pulled over their heads. Some were sitting lethargically on the ground with a far away, glazed look. Others were lying in their bunks, which were three tiers high with slats of wood as their mattresses.

Chaplain Bohnen announced in Yiddish, "Ich bin an Amerikaner Rabbiner" (I am an American Rabbi). At that moment, it was as if all the pent-up emotions of all the years in misery and agony were unleashed in that room. There was a burst of wailing and crying. We tried for a moment, unsuccessfully, to control our own feelings, as the victims, who were able to, surged forward to kiss our feet and hug our hands. I felt humble and uncomfortable, for it seemed that I should have been hugging and kissing them.

I did not take any pictures in that barracks. Who could be so heartless to take pictures of people in such misery and in the depths of their degradation and humiliation.

After this initial reaction, some became apprehensive about Hundt. After all, they were conditioned to see the SS guards use dogs as instruments of torture and terror. The Nazis tormented the inmates and had used German Shepherd dogs to tear them apart. I assured them that they had nothing to fear from Hundt. They asked me,

"Why do you call him Hundt? It means dog in German."

I answered, "Because he would probably call me Man if he could speak." It was so good to see a flicker of a smile on their faces.

For a long time, we took their names and messages to send to their families in the United States. It was heart-breaking, because in so many cases, they gave us the name of a city, but no address. Imagine someone saying to you, "I have a relative who lives in New York. His name is Sam Cohen."

We would ask, "But where does he live in New York?"

"Don't worry. You'll find him. You'll find him."

But we took all the names in the hope that the local newspapers would publish them.

Finally, in the memory of those who had not survived, Chaplain Bohnen recited the *El Moleh Rochamim*, the Memorial prayer for the dead. I wept unashamedly. Before leaving, our one thought was to assure our brethren that they were not forgotten and that aid was on the way.

Outside the Camp, after we had crossed the bridge into that peaceful little community of Dachau, we asked the good burghers, "Didn't you know? Couldn't you tell from the stench?"

"Nein," they replied.

It was late in the afternoon when we left. I felt I had just been aroused from a nightmare. I had seen with horror, I had felt with anger, but until now, my mind was numb. I started to think. But for the Grace of God—had the circumstances been different—had not my parents left Europe in the early 1900s, I would be dead or in a Camp like Dachau. I was so depressed. After a silence, I said to the Chaplain, "Given all the trials, tribulations and vicissitudes of life, why live?"

Deep in his own sadness, he answered, the best way he could, "Life must go on."

I believe it.[5]

DACHAU FROM WITHOUT

Many Rainbow soldiers were at or very near the Dachau enclosure but did not enter the camp itself. The division was moving ahead, and their presence was needed elsewhere. But even if they could not see within, there was that awful, inescapable, all-pervasive stench: so many rotting corpses, so much human waste and filth created by so many human beings crammed into dirty, overcrowded living quarters, where there was not even the most primitive means of maintaining sanitation and cleanliness.

In the theater there is a device called aesthetic distance. It sets up an act of violence but does not allow the audience to witness it. We will see the preparations for it. We know it will happen, as it must. But when it finally does, it will take place offstage. We may hear it or even glimpse a small part of it, but the actual deed is left to our imagination. And what we imagine may create a more vivid and terrifying image than what we see.

Many who were confronted by the actuality of Dachau within the gates were benumbed by it. But those who could only imagine what must have gone on in there, who only had a partial picture—a distant view of the train, a sight of some of the inmates—were emotionally compelled to complete the picture for themselves. We turn now to the recollections of those men who did.

It looked like a University from the front.

Sergeant Roy W. Dodd, G Company, 222d Infantry Regiment

I went into the Army when I was 18 years old. We were in Hawaii during Pearl Harbor. We came back in 1943, and formed the

Rainbow Division. We went to Europe in 1944. My outfit was one of the first to get into, or liberate, Dachau. Of course, I was not there on the first day. As far as my memory serves me, it was either the second or the third day. And it was an experience, if you want to call it an experience. I can't really say it was an experience. It's just something I wish I hadn't seen, and I hope that I never see it again. Unless you see something like that—it's unbelievable!

We didn't know what we were going into. Well—I had an idea because a fellow from either First or Third Battalion had already seen it. But I'm sure that when they went in at first, they didn't know what they were going to see, either.

Actually, I never really got inside the Camp, itself, Dachau. But I did see the railway cars with the bodies still in and around them. They still hadn't removed those bodies. By the time I got there, our soldiers had already removed all German Guards and the dogs.

As I said, I never got into the prison proper. It looked to me—to describe it—it looked like a University from the front. Oh, it was beautiful, if you could use that word. I certainly wouldn't use it now—but at the time—well, that was the outside appearance.

Everybody in my outfit was very angry about what had been going on in there. If we could have gotten to them, the German guards, we would have done to them the same as they did to the inmates. I mean, that's just my opinion. But from what I saw—and I say I didn't see half of what the first men who got in there saw—it was a horrible experience. I just hope I never have to see anything like that again![1]

What did they know—and when did they know it?

Staff Sergeant Theodore A. "Ted" Johnson, H Company, 232d Regiment

Ted Johnson was born in Fayette, Iowa, in 1924. He has a law degree from the University of Iowa and an honorary doctorate in business administration from Upper Iowa University. He has worked for, owned, and operated several electronics firms. He was a founder, chairman, and president of J-TEC Associates, Inc., in Cedar Rapids. He is active in community affairs and politics. In 1986, he was appointed by the president as a delegate to the White House Conference on Small Business. Ted is the senior past national president of the Rainbow Division Veterans

Association, having served in 1964-65; chairman of the Rainbow Division Veterans Memorial Foundation, Inc.; master of ceremonies for the "champagne hour" held annually in the Division memorial service; and judge advocate of the association. He spent three years in the army, earning a Silver Star, a Bronze Star, and three Battle Stars.

He and his wife, Shirley, have been married for forty-nine years. They have two sons, two daughters, and ten grandchildren.

Ted was twenty at Dachau and seventy when he wrote the piece for this book. But, as he says, "I have written it variously a hundred times before."

In the latter days of combat in World War II, our Rainbow Division had been on the line almost constantly from the crossing of the Rhine, the Main and the Danube, and was on the road to Munich. We had captured major cities like Schweinfurt, Wurzburg, and Furth/Nuremberg; and had cleared hundreds of town and hills and holes along the way.

On a clear day as we headed for Munich, we thought we could see peaks of the German Alps, and what we thought would be our final mission, to blast Hitler out of his Eagle's Nest Redoubt.[2] Toward the end of April, there were even times when you felt like dropping off in one of those endless little towns and let the rest of the world go by. Then, on the 29th of April as we approached the next town, the road sign read: "Dachau."

I remember a set of buildings well off to the side of the road that looked like a seminary or a school. Since we were the reserve regiment, we paid no attention to it.

When we entered Dachau and started our usual house-to-house, we sensed no presence of German resistance. As we paused for new instructions, we worked a few houses. We came on a big house with a screened-in porch. The porch was piled high with articles of clothing that reminded me of the rummage sales back home during the Depression when people donated their old clothes to the Ladies Professorship Association for the benefit of programs at the College. (I thought this was an outlet where they sold the belongings of the inmates of the Camp.)

While we were there waiting to move forward, word came that there was a large Concentration Camp just a kilometer or two away. I didn't know when we would be moving forward, so I didn't go. The reports being brought back by those that were in the Camp spread like wildfire. The stories were so awful you could feel the anger and the hatred build up, until we literally became a body of enraged enemies. No more carrying the facade of goodwill that we had shown in so many of those little towns. No more "haben kein angst" [We're not angry]. No more respectful treatment of civilians or listening to "*Mier Nicht Nazi*" [I'm no Nazi!]. There was only a grim determination to get this abominable war over with now, no matter what it took . . . .

There was nothing in the town to suggest that anyone was shielding some deep, dark secret. Yet, how could these things not have been known? Thirty-five years later, my company filed patents in Germany. We retained a Munich patent attorney. When he visited us in the 1980s, I invited him to our home when we were having the Family Reunion on the 4th of July. I suggested we go downstairs for a little Schnapps. I warned him that he should know that I was a G.I. in World War II, and that he would find our Family room had a lot of souvenirs from the war. He then told me he was the son of a doctor who was a Dentist and an Officer at the Dachau Camp, and that he was there when the Americans captured the town. He said he remembered it well; the vehicles, the soldiers, the tanks. He said that he had lived in Dachau as an "Army Brat," and because of his father's job, he was forbidden to play with other children. He was then about eight years old. He said that only on rare occasions had he been by the area. He had no idea what was going on in the Camp. Because of his age and what his family did to shield him, I tend to believe him. But the town was so small, and the Camp so close, there is no way anyone wouldn't know what was going on in there. Yet, everybody claimed that they knew nothing about it in spite of all the evidence that they were exposed to.

The question always remains: What did they know, and when did they know it? The Deniers and Revisionists should ask themselves that same question today.[3]

There were 20 pounds of explosives under the back seat.

Pfc Howard J. Hughes, I & R Platoon, 222d Infantry Regiment

On April 29, 1945, Hughes was twenty years old. When he wrote about his experiences that day he was seventy. After the war, he finished college and then worked in the research department of a raw-materials supplier in the print, plastics, and rubber industries. During this time he was married and unmarried. Hughes has two sons and two grandsons.

Here's what I remember about the day the Regiment moved on toward Dachau. It was the 29th of April, 1945. The night before, the I&R was told we would have three German volunteers to go on ahead and show us where the mines were. That next morning, I picked up the three of them. They were a driver, an assistant driver, and a radio operator. I put them in our "worst" jeep. I didn't tell them that there were 20 pounds of explosives underneath the rear seat. Then, I got back into my own jeep, which was driven by Don Armstrong. Don Sewell was in the other front seat, and manned the heavy .30 Caliber machine gun. Sid Shafner was in the back seat with me—and was on the radio to talk with the Germans who were riding ahead of us. We moved out, followed by the rest of the I&R and a TD. The Germans did show us where the road had been mined—but the local civilians had already removed them. There was no way to return the Germans to the POW Camp, so they had to remain in the column with us. We went ahead, and luckily, we suffered no casualties. But we did take a few prisoners. Toward the end of that day, we ran into a little resistance around some buildings. A Panzerfaust hit just beside the TD. Then, a captured Sherman tank appeared over the next hill. The TD fired its 90 mm, and the tank was no longer a threat.[4]

The Germans in the immediate area were taken with no serious resistance. We moved into the town of Dachau. We spent the night, cleaned our weapons, and prepared for the next day which was our grand entry into Munich. Cheering crowds lined the streets. Although we didn't know it at the time, all we had to do for the rest of the war was to receive the surrender of the German units which were trying to avoid the Russians.[5]

The impact of what we had seen did not sink in until some time later.

Pfc Harry D. Gruel, B Battery, 392d Field Artillery

Gruel was born in 1923. After the war, he was employed in the Baltimore branch of Parke Davis. Starting as an assistant cashier, he eventually worked his way up to office manager.

Later, he took a job with the National Bank of Baltimore as stock transfer officer.

Harry has many interests. He is a member of Delta Sigma Pi, a business administration fraternity. He is active in his church and his community association.

He was married in 1949. He and his wife are the proud parents of two daughters. He is a sports fan and roots for the Baltimore Orioles and the University of Maryland. He is also an avid gardener. His specialty is vegetables.

Harry Gruel was twenty-two years old at Dachau and seventy-two when he wrote about his impressions of the day.

Concerning my recollection of my experiences at Dachau, I am trying to recall what I saw and did on that historic day. I must confess that my memory of the event is rather vague. One might ask, "How can that be? You witnessed one of the most horrible incidents in world history, and your recollection is sketchy?" I'm looking for an explanation. I now believe there are two reasons: First, we were on the outskirts of Munich, a city where the Nazi movement had strong roots. The Nazis did not make a determined stand at Nuremberg. Therefore, we expected a last ditch effort to hold the line at Dachau. The probability of a bloody, bitter-end battle had been on our minds for several days, and we were thinking more of the immediate future than the present. Second, the human mind has a tendency to block out the worst and most horrifying happenings.

I believe those are the reasons why my recall of the events at Dachau are not as vivid as some of my other wartime experiences. But here is what I do recall:

I was a member of a Forward Observer Team from B Battery, 392d F A Bn. We were attached to an infantry company (I don't remember which). We were moving along a street in the town of Dachau, near Munich, getting into position to engage the enemy should they decide to defend the city. Our F.O. Team was in a jeep. The infantry company was on foot. We came by the Camp area at approximately ten in the morning. The street ran parallel to the high fence at the edge of the Camp. There were hundreds of cheering inmates inside the fence as we went by. We kept stopping briefly to observe the pandemonium. It was the most startling, horrifying sight one could imagine. To see the joy and—at the same time—also witness the pitiful physical condition of those inmates. Our orders were to keep moving to the staging area for entry into Munich. Therefore, we couldn't leave the jeeps and go inside the Camp. I estimate that we were in the vicinity for about thirty minutes. But the impact of what we had seen did not sink in until some time later.

I returned to Dachau a few years ago, when the Rainbow Division placed a memorial plaque at the camp. It was with a deep feeling of pride that I was privileged to participate in that memorial dedication.[6]

I had now experienced what war was all about.

Corporal Harold Collum, B Battery, 392d Field Artillery

Harold Collum was born in 1924. He served with the division from 1943 through 1946. After the war, he went home to Wichita and to a job as a grocery clerk. In 1947, he married Margaret Doherty. They had forty-six years together. He has five children—three girls and two boys—and four grandchildren. In 1951, he was called back for service in Korea, where he saw action as an artilleryman. On his return, he worked ten years for the Safeway Grocery Company. He became a full-time labor organizer and then took the position on the AFL-CIO staff for community services. He was active there until 1989. He is presently enjoying his retirement.

On April 29, 1945, Harold Collum was twenty-one. His Dachau story was written when he was seventy-one.

I was a Forward Observer [a member of an artillery battery who is sent ahead to radio fire corrections] assigned to F Company, 222d. We had a four-man team. The jeep driver, two radio men, and the man who would direct the firing—in this case, me. On the radio, we heard that they had found a soft spot in the line, and we loaded up. Later on, as Olin Hawkins said, we ran into some stiff resistance, and there was a fire fight with artillery and everything else. From where I could see, around a curve in the hill, there were some snipers. But we moved up there and got rid of them.

Later on, we stopped because we saw some inmates. They looked like walking skeletons. I remember I passed out some doughnuts. I had some Red Cross doughnuts left over from breakfast. They all got down on their knees and thanked me just as if I were a God, just for those doughnuts! I remember that! How could anybody do that? They were starving!

A bit farther on, we heard some firing. It was from a Browning Automatic Rifle, and we came across ten dead SS lying along the road. And then, some lady came by. She had a veil over her face. We stopped to look at her. She lifted the veil. Her face was like a human skeleton. It was as if someone had burned her face off—leaving just the eyes, nose and mouth. But then, General Collins's order came over the radio. It told us to get to Munich fast! I never did get into the Camp. But we did pass by it. And even then, I could tell something horrible had gone on in there. And I knew I had now experienced what war was all about.[7]

They were just skin and bones.

Pfc Robert Jecklin, Battery B, 232d Field Artillery

At Dachau, Bob Jecklin was one of "the older guys" in his outfit. He was twenty-eight; the others mostly ranged between eighteen and twenty-five. He met his future wife just four weeks before the division left Camp Gruber, Oklahoma, for Europe. January 1997 saw the celebration of fifty happy years of married life. The two Jecklin sons are doing very well in their careers.

Bob participated in the dedication of the Holocaust Museum, April 22, 1993. He represented the twenty U.S. army divisions that took part in the liberation of the wartime concentration camps. He says:

That was the high point of my life—to be on stage with President Clinton, Vice-President Gore, the President of Israel, and other notables. I'll never forget that cold, windy day. The wind blew so hard and made so much noise. It seemed to sound like people shouting. I looked at it as if it were the voices of people who were lost in the Holocaust, shouting praises of joy to be remembered by this dedication of the museum—so that people would not forget the terrible things that happened in those years of Hitler's rule. I wish I were a writer so that I could make a story of it . . . .

On April 29, 1945, I stood at the Gates of Dachau. I became a witness to a part of history's worst atrocities. I was an Artillery truck driver. We were headed toward Munich on that day when we "stumbled" on Dachau. That's how it appeared to me. We weren't told about it. We didn't know about it—and then, suddenly, we were *there*! We'd heard about "Concentration Camps," but we weren't prepared for what we saw. We thought, perhaps, in a "Camp," you might have several hundred, or so, prisoners—but in that place, there were over 30,000! So many of them couldn't move. They were just skin and bones. And so many more were dead, and just lying around. The sight of all this just builds up the anger inside you. But now, we knew why we were fighting—to liberate these people. I was never able to forget the Holocaust. Last year, in an Army newsletter, I read that there was going to be a Memorial Dedication at The Holocaust Museum. I wrote to ask for information. They asked me if I had been there. When I told them, yes—they invited me to come to the Ceremony, as the representative of the thousands of American G.I.'s who had liberated the Camp.

It was a most impressive event. The President and Mrs. Clinton were there, as were Vice-President and Mrs. Gore. Also, political figures from Europe and celebrities from all walks of life.

But on a personal note, I was excited to meet a man named Bill Lowenberg, a Dachau survivor. He and I were together on the dais. Bill made a most moving speech, and then asked me to join him at the podium. Because I represented all of our troops, he said, and I will never forget his words, "There are no words to express our gratitude, no gift we can give you nearly as precious as the gift you gave us. What I can give you is a photo of my wife, my children and my grandchildren. They are everything in the world to me. They have made my life worth living."[8]

Many of the prisoners said, "We're lousy,
so don't get close to us."

Pfc Elwin W. Davis, B Battery, 232d Field Artillery

In April of 1945, Elwin Davis was twenty-one years old; he was seventy-two when he sent in his account. Following the war, he married in 1946. He was a farmer and rancher until his retirement at sixty-five.

What I can remember of Dachau is that our four trucks arrived with some infantry on board. I do recall those gondola railroad cars full of the dead. I took pictures of some of it while still on the truck. But after I came home, I burned them. But that didn't burn away the memory.

We went to the gates and gave the prisoners K-Rations, cigarettes and candy. I don't remember if we heated the water or they did. But I do know that there were bonfires.

Many of the prisoners said, "We're lousy, so don't get close to us." But some of them wanted to get to Munich, so we helped them get on the trucks, anyhow.[9]

*It was as much of a shock as if the whole world
had caved in on us.*

Corporal Charles Rheault, B Battery, 232d Field Artillery

Charles Rheault was born June 12, 1924, in Boston. After the
war, Charles attended Harvard. He spent his business career in
printing and bookbinding with the Riverside Press. He and his
wife, Maud have two sons and four grandchildren. Although officially retired, he still keeps busy in the printing business.

I well remember Dachau because our Battery had to cross
that very muddy, soft Dachau Airport, and our trucks with the
guns kept getting stuck. At the same time, the German 88s at
the far corner of the airport were firing phosphorous shells. It
looked, for sure, as if we were all going to be sitting ducks.
Quickly, we all jumped out of our truck and tried to get it, and the
gun, moving.

Finally, we got going again, and were on firmer ground. Now,
suddenly, there was a swarm of strange-looking humans. They
climbed up and over the truck. One of them kept crying, "Mangiare! Mangiare!" He kept making gestures as if he wanted something to eat. He was an Italian inmate of the Concentration
Camp. However, at the time, I didn't have the slightest inkling of
what was going on—even though this kind of food would probably kill starving people. But how could we refuse them? That is
about as much as I can recall, because our gun crew never got off
and went into the Camp. It wasn't till later in the evening that
we learned what really happened there. It was as much of a
shock as if a part of the world had caved in on us.[10]

*For me, the twenty-ninth Day of April, 1945, was a standout.
Dachau was liberated—and Hitler ended his life the next day!*

Lieutenant Charles G. Paine, G Company, 242d Infantry Regiment

Charles Paine was nineteen years old when the Rainbow entered Dachau. He was sixty-nine when he placed his thoughts on
paper. He had planned to become a teacher in the high schools,
but his experiences in the war changed his career goals. Paine
felt that it was of vital importance to find better ways to resolve
troubles and quarrels than by fighting. He went into administration in order to work with teachers, who would help present these

A ten minute break en route to Dachau. Three members of G Company, 242d Regiment. Left to right: Pfc. Tom Tewell, squad leader; S. Sgt. Wirt Glover, platoon sgt.; Lt. Charles Paine, platoon leader.

methods to students. His career has been spent in the Bridgewater, Connecticut school system. Paine also has been active in seminars and memorial meetings concerning Dachau.

Charles and his wife, Irene, have five children and seven grandchildren. The Paines are now retired and are living in Pinehurst, North Carolina. He is still active in Rainbow Division veterans' affairs.

I was among those who were supposed to have gone back to Dachau—so that we could say later that, yes, it did happen. But when I turned up, I had missed the truck that was to take us there—and so, I didn't get to go. From the reactions of those who did make the trip, I have often thought that I was lucky to have missed it. The day before, on that twenty-ninth day, we started moving out in a southerly direction along a blacktop road. We could see the tall buildings in the center of Augsburg. How great it would be to stay in a city with all the amenities. But that dream fell to the wayside when a sharp, left turn onto the Autobahn headed us toward Munich.

In the fields on the south side of the Autobahn, we could see low structures with three sides and completely open to the front. Some had Me [Messerschmitt] 109 fighter planes inside. At this point, it became clear why the median of the Autobahn had been painted green to simulate grass. It was, in truth, a landing strip, a small airfield. Whether it fooled our planes overhead, I don't know.

A number of tanks came along. We were on foot, and we shouted for them to give us a ride. They told us they didn't have time, as they had to hurry to pick up some troops ahead. Quite some time, and many tired feet later, we swung left across the Autobahn and we met up with those same tanks. We were the troops they were supposed to meet. And they had roared through us before because they were in a rush to get to us on time.

Better late than never, we mounted the tanks, and the part of the day I remember best was rolling down that Autobahn and sitting over the bow gun on the right front of the tank, and in such a position that the gunner couldn't see if he had to shoot. We were on our way to Munich to occupy a large German Airfield near Dachau.

Then, we pulled into the city of Munich, itself. The sidewalks were quite crowded with people who were quietly watching us. Then, we saw a gap between some buildings, and a five- or six-story structure beyond it. Soon men came pouring out. They were mostly American POWs. The guys kept crowding right up to the tanks. There was great happiness and excitement on all sides. Chocolates, cigarettes, K-rations—everything we had, filled the air.

We picked up speed and headed for the Airfield. This one didn't have a plane in it. Suddenly, a volley of fire, with tracers, passed about six feet over my head. I knew it had to come from one of our light machine guns. I could tell by the rate of fire. I looked out to see where those shots had come from—and off in the distance were those very same tanks that had brought us here.[11] Soon they must have realized who we were, because that was the end of the shooting.

Another complication: word came back that we were now on hold as far as the official surrender of the Airfield was concerned. The German Colonel would not turn over his sword and the field to our Company Commander, a Captain. So, Captain Jim

Campbell radio'd back to Lt. Col. Reynolds, our Battalion Commander. On his arrival, the Airfield changed hands.

The fighting war was over for me—and the only shots in my direction that day had been "friendly." Looking back in memory, I have come to see April 29, 1945, as a standout. First, the "friendly fire" had missed me. Second, our Rainbow had liberated Dachau. Third, American and British POWs had been freed. And finally, it was the day before Hitler had ended his life in that bunker under the Reichschancellery in Berlin. A great day all around!

Looking back at it, all that most of the members of my unit knew about Dachau was practically by osmosis. Those who went inside the Camp to examine it, went off by themselves. They simply wouldn't talk—which made it worse. Dachau was clearly beyond what they could put into words at that time, and in many cases, even now.[12]

In vivid contrast to the desolation of the nearby Camp of human misery, was the attractiveness and apparent prosperity of the host town, itself.

Pfc Dee R. Eberhart, I Company, 242d Infantry Regiment

Dee Eberhart was born in Los Angeles in 1924 and received his public school education in Toppenish, Washington. As an undergraduate, he attended Rainbow University and the University of Washington; as a graduate student, Northwestern University. He taught geography at Ohio State University and East Tennessee State College and was named a distinguished professor and professor emeritus at Central Washington University. He was a partner in an international real estate consulting firm and has been involved in a number of his own real estate ventures. He is now a partner/stockholder in five family-run farm and orchard companies near Ellensburg, Washington. Like many Rainbow veterans, he plays an active part in the affairs of his community and in the Rainbow Veterans Association and its Memorial Foundation.

In 1953, he married Barbara C. Boulton in Seattle. They have four daughters, three sons, and eight grandchildren. Dee is also a poet, carrying on a Rainbow tradition: in World War I, we had Joyce Kilmer. Some of Dee's poems appear in this book. He was twenty years old at Dachau and seventy when he set down his thoughts for this book.

Pfc Dee R. Eberhart, I Company, 242 Regiment, on the morning of 3 May 1945, after the liberation of Dachau and the capture of Munich, just before crossing the Inn River in assault boats.

The morning of April 29, 1945, was indeed a dawning of an eventful day. We were motorized and alternated riding in 6 × 6 trucks and on Tanks or Tank Destroyers accompanying us. The Bavarian Alps glistened white to the south, but our attack convoy had veered southeastward somewhere in the vicinity of Augsburg. Heavy one-way traffic on the Autobahn, but there were pauses, one alongside a German jet with its tail section damaged by a strafing attack.

It was at another of these stops that I lost my prized SS belt buckle (but still have the belt). It was prized because I wore two pair of pants—wool O.D. [olive drab]—and an outer pair of combat pants, but the army had only issued me one belt. It was also prized because I had acquired it after a vicious battle around our Platoon CP on January 24 and 25 against 10th SS Panzer Division troops at the eastern edge of Haguenau, France. We had killed, wounded and captured more of the enemy than we had in our own, entire, and badly depleted Platoon. I wore that SS buckle with a certain amount of bravado, especially where German prisoners and civilians could see it as inscribed *MEIN EHRE HEIST TREU* [My Honor is Loyalty]. The Germans all knew what it meant. However, after I heard that a captured American soldier who had been wearing a German Army belt had been found dead with three of those detachable belt buckles jammed down his throat, I would leave my SS belt behind with my other gear when we went out on patrols. Shortly before we liberated Dachau, I lost my SS belt buckle, which was appropriate considering the event of that day.

Our 3rd Platoon had recently been attached to the 1st Battalion, 222d Infantry, which accounted for our presence at Dachau on April 29th. In the afternoon, the day gradually lost its brightness to a thin, gray overcast sky. We detrucked. In the near distance were numerous factory-type buildings. We spread out in open formation and moved toward them over a grassy area. Our Assistant Squad Leader, Sgt. Jack Parry, with several other men, went forward and returned a short time later, stating that there was a large enclosure behind a moat in which "the prisoners were beating up the guards." He had reported to an American officer who told him that everything was under control and to head for Munich. Instead of following that advice, our 3rd Platoon changed direction and entered the town of Dachau where we took over several houses as billets for the night.

Before reaching the town, we encountered numerous liberated prisoners in their blue and gray striped uniforms, some of whom rushed to embrace us. Almost instantaneously, the stories by our men of the prisoners—living, dying and dead—circulated among us. The woman in the house where my squad was billeted, said she didn't know anything about the Camp.

In vivid contrast to the desolation of the nearby camp of human misery, was the attractiveness and apparent prosperity of the host town, itself. How could the nearby presence of such a place of depravity not have assailed the senses of everyone in that town?

Early the next morning, April 30th, we left that accursed place, past the death train, nursing a new, ratcheted-up hatred for the Nazis. Of the many vivid scenes and events in our sweep toward Munich on that cold, gray, winter-like day, was my view from the top of a lead tank as we moved forward through a depressing, working-class suburb. About a block ahead of us, we saw a German soldier running away. Close behind him, also running, was a man in the blue and gray vertically striped Concentration Camp uniform. The pursuit was over in a moment, and by the time our tank had clattered past, the former victim had kicked to death his oppressor. Any one of us could have easily saved this newest "victim," but no one raised a hand or a rifle to protect him.

Killing in the German War was nearly over. Another week and it had ended, but the dying at Dachau continued.[13]

We became very angry when we learned about conditions in the camp.

T-5 Jack Summers, HQ Company, 222d Infantry Regiment

Jack Summers was born and raised in California. His hometown was Santa Cruz. He entered the Army in 1943 and served until 1946. He joined the Rainbow in 1944, assigned as a radio operator. He returned to civilian life and received a degree in electrical engineering from Stanford University in 1951. He was employed in the electronics industry in California. He is married and has three grown sons and has resided in the Los Altos area since the mid-fifties.

During that particular time, my assignment was to run the Regimental Radio Base Station. We located this Base Station in the village of Dachau. We were billeted in a fair-sized house with all of our radio gear. We only remained there 24 hours, plus or minus a bit. My duties did not take me into the Concentration Camp itself. However, upon leaving the village, enroute to Munich, we did drive by the Camp, and noticed the boxcars, but we were too far away to see the details.

My duties in the 42d Division were those of a radio operator in Regimental HQ Company, 222d Infantry. There were 17 of us in the radio section, and our duties were rotated frequently. Sometimes, we were assigned to the Base Station, and other times we were assigned to a radio jeep and provided radio communication for an officer or a Company group.

In Dachau village, we ran the radio in shifts 24 hours a day. As I can recall, we didn't see any Germans in or around the house, or even the neighborhood. I do recall that the last time we experienced shelling from enemy artillery was when we were in this village at Dachau. Fortunately, there was no damage done in our immediate area.

I remember we became very angry when we learned about the conditions in the Camp. So, in the interests of freedom, we released all the rabbits that were located in about a dozen cages that were situated in the backyard of the house we were in! The rabbits thought this was great, and they all mingled together in the yard!

Well, I had all but forgotten this rather minor—but amusing— event until one day, while serving on jury duty in San Jose, California. I had picked up a copy of the New Yorker Magazine during one of our long waiting periods between trial activity. Turned out the magazine had a lengthy and interesting article on the history of Dachau—before, during and after the war. The article stated that, in recent times, the town of Dachau has become quite famous for its rabbit breeding industry.

Well, I laughed like crazy when I read this and thought that maybe it was our action of releasing all those rabbits back in April, 1945, that led to the unique breeds they now have in Dachau.[14]

Something has arisen from the ashes of Dachau.

Pfc Sid Shafner, I & R Platoon, 222d Infantry Regiment

Sid was born in Philadelphia on September 14, 1921. He was educated at Temple University. When he entered the service, Sid was sent to study engineering at Regis College in Denver. In that city he met his future wife, Esther. In 1944, he was transferred to the Rainbow Division at Camp Gruber, Oklahoma. Home again in 1946, he married, and the couple celebrated their golden anniversary in 1996. The Shafners have three children—a daughter, who teaches school; a son in real estate; and a second son who is a lawyer. Sid is in real estate and also in the furniture business. He was twenty-four at Dachau and seventy four when he set down this account.

My experience is more in the nature of a human interest story that continues to this day. Our I & R Platoon, consisting of seven jeeps and twenty-eight men, were patrolling the road to Munich. It was a narrow, rural roadway, and the village of Dachau was just another "Dorf" [town], and on the map, it appeared just like any other German "Dorf." We didn't think too much of it, but when the tall church steeple in the center of town came into view, we had our jeep-mounted .30 Caliber machine guns at the ready. On previous occasions, we had discovered that the Germans would place snipers in those steeples.

As we approached the outskirts of the town late that morning, we encountered a couple of fifteen-year-old kids, two boys who flagged us down. They wore black and white striped clothes, and quite frankly, at first glance we were quite startled and surprised.

They asked if anyone could speak Greek or Spanish or German. I had learned Yiddish from my Grandparents, which is similar to German. I became the Interpreter.

They told us we must come quickly because there was a trainload of dead Concentration Camp prisoners on a railroad siding, just outside the town.

I told those kids, since they wore strange-looking clothes, not to play games with us. We were American soldiers; and if they were with a Circus or Carnival, we had no time for pranks! But they kept insisting they were serious and were telling us the truth! I got on my SCR 300 Radio and notified Lt. Short in the Headquarters jeep, two jeeps behind us, and told him what we had just heard. Lt. Short then radio'd the information to Regimental Headquarters—and the rest is history.

Now, for the human interest part of my story. We took the two kids with us. They told us they were part of a Greek-Jewish family in Salonika, Greece. The Germans came to the city, killed their families and shipped the able-bodied to work in the Concentration Camps.

The inmates of Dachau, after the Liberation, were put into D.P. [displaced persons] Camps. But I & R Platoon kept those two kids with us. Up till now, we had hired German civilians to do our K.P. work. But from here on, we had the boys do it. They were happy to work for their food. We gave them some old O.D. [olive drab] uniforms, without insignia, and decent shoes. They did a good job, and everyone liked them. They rode with us when we took Munich that next day; and on into Salzburg, where we were told of the German surrender. The boys remained with us when we went to Linz, and on to Vienna. They took care of all the kitchen work, and were considered almost like a part of the outfit.

When April, 1946, arrived, it was time for me to go home and be discharged. But the boys, who were now 16, had never been registered at any D.P. Camp. I took them to the Allied Joint Distribution Office in Vienna, which had set up shop there a few months earlier. The kids explained their story, and I recounted how our outfit had picked them up.

One of them, Joe Salas, had met a young Viennese girl, and decided to remain there. The other lad, Marcel Levy, said he had an uncle in Israel, which at the time was Palestine. The Joint Distribution Committee arranged for him to go there and, at least, be united with a part of his family.

We have been in touch with each other over all these years. Marcel met and married a Greek-Jewish girl in Israel. They have two daughters and are now proud grandparents. As a result of Marcel's kitchen work with us, he became a cook in the Israeli Army and served in the various wars that Israel has fought.

In 1970, my wife and I were invited by an organization in Holland to participate in the Twenty-fifth Anniversary Celebration of that group's liberation from Dachau. I remember that veterans from the 45th Division were also invited. We were wined and dined and appeared on TV and in the newspapers. These people had resisted the German Occupation Forces, and hid Dutch Jews, in a manner similar to the Anne Frank Story.

Afterward, my wife and I decided to go to Israel to visit Marcel Levy and his family. We met in Tel Aviv, in the lobby of our hotel. They had been waiting for us all day. Marcel and I recognized each other, we embraced and burst into tears. We introduced the wives and then we just talked and talked and talked for hours and hours and hours.

We are very close. Whenever any of my family or friends visit Israel, they always look up Marcel and his wife. And all of us, here and in Israel, are looking forward to my granddaughter's Bat Mitzvah, which will be held in Israel in June 1995.

I'm sure that many of my Rainbow Buddies have adequately and accurately described the horrors of Dachau. But I feel that this human interest story—this closeness between Shafners and the Levys will continue long after Marcel and I are gone.[15] At least, something has arisen from the ashes of Dachau.[16]

JUST OUTSIDE OF DACHAU

There were two Dachaus. One was the concentration camp; the other was an open field next to it that served as a temporary, makeshift holding area for British and American prisoners of war. They were not part of the Dachau concentration camp system. They were being driven back by the German army, which was in retreat from the American advance toward Munich. Many of the prisoners had been captured months before, in Alsace. Thus, they had been forced to travel across Germany. The field outside of the concentration camp would be the last stop they would make.

Although many of our Rainbow buddies claim to be the first to enter the Dachau area, a dispute that is generally goodnatured, the fact is that the first member of the Rainbow in the vicinity was Walter A. Brophy of E Company, 222d Infantry Regiment, a POW who came there around April 9, thus settling the question for all time. Brophy's story is more than the telling of an individual experience. It is part of one of the proudest achievements of the Rainbow Division.

Brophy had been taken prisoner three months earlier, at Schweighausen in eastern Alsace-Lorraine. This epic battle represented Adolf Hitler's last desperate gamble to thrust the Allies back to the sea and reverse the tide of the war. It culminated in what has come to be known as the Battle of the Bulge, in which the heroic American stand at Bastogne in Belgium forever destroyed Hitler's dream of conquest. However, that Nazi offensive was a two-pronged attack, starting with a strike in the north. It made an impressive initial penetration. Therefore, men, equipment, and ammunition were stripped from Seventh Army units positioned in what seemed to be a relatively quiet front in Alsace and sent north. The Seventh Army had also been ordered to occupy Third Army positions when General Patton wheeled north to relieve Bastogne. This stretched and thinned our own defensive positions. Taking advantage of this situation, the Germans thrust a powerful second prong of the attack against the Seventh Army in what became known as the Ardennes-Alsace campaign.

The Rainbow was directly in their path. We had been overseas for hardly more than a month. For most, this would be our very first combat. Military experts and strategists write in their impersonal treatises about the advisability of "blooding fresh troops." This calls for that ideal situation in which untested infantrymen are placed in a relatively quiet sector. Here they may receive their "baptism by fire" at the cost of relatively few casualties. But the Rainbow was not accorded that luxury. It is completely accurate to state that we weren't "blooded," we were hemorrhaged. And yet, although we were outnumbered by the veteran 21st Panzer and the 25th Panzer Grenadier Divisions, and later by the SS 10th Panzer Division and the 47th Volksgrenadier Division, our three Rainbow infantry regiments outfought a more experienced enemy. We not only stopped him, we threw him back.

But the Rainbow paid the price. The snows of Hatten, Haguenau, Kaltenhouse, Schweighausen, and Ohlungen were red with American blood.

E Company's 222d Regiment Weapons Platoon fought valiantly and suffered many casualties.[1] Finally, surrounded and with ammunition exhausted, they were compelled to surrender. Walter A. Brophy was a survivor of that battle.

All we were given to eat was a little bit of soup once a day.

Sergeant Walter A. Brophy, E Company, 222d Infantry Regiment, Prisoner ID # 099866

Walter A. Brophy was born February 19, 1921, in Colorado Springs, Colorado. He has spent most of his life in Portland, Oregon. He retired in 1983 after working for Langendorf & Franz Bakeries. In 1947, he married Esther Gardner. They have four children, Walter, Kenneth, Ruth, and Yvonne; twelve grandchildren; and three great-grandchildren. His hobbies are family, camping, hunting, and fishing. He is a member of the Rainbow Division's 222d Infantry and Northwest chapter, the Disabled American Veterans, and a number of ex-POW organizations.

He was twenty-four years old on April 29, 1945, and seventy-four when he wrote of his experience.

It was January 25, 1945. We were trying to hold a small knoll just above the Moder River. We found ourselves completely surrounded by Germans. We were cut off. They pounded us with mortars and artillery; everything they had. And then, we ran out of ammunition. We just couldn't hold them off any longer. I, myself, was wounded. Sixteen of us were taken prisoner. There was a lot of confusion. We became separated from one another. I was put on a truck with other G.I. prisoners and taken to the city of Worms in Germany. I recall most of us were wounded. There our wounds were treated, and we were interrogated. Then, we were sent to some Camp which didn't seem to have a name. That was the beginning of a whole series of moves because the Germans were retreating. We went to a place called Hammelsburg. I understand that General Patton had sent in some tanks to try to get his son-in-law out of there. I don't know how that all came out. We were put on a train to Nuremberg. Then, they shipped us to Moasburg. Then, finally, to Dachau. There were close to two hundred Americans and a hundred British.

The Camp was a fenced-in, open area, with just some tents. It was close by to the Concentration Camp. We couldn't see what was going on in there. All we were given to eat was a little bit of soup once a day. Now and then, we would get a piece of bread. We received no medical attention. We had to take care of our own wounds.

For the most part, we were disregarded. There was always a great deal of confusion. Since they had to know they were losing the war, I believe they thought of us as hostages.

Fortunately, we were there for only three weeks. And then, on the morning of April 29, we heard the sound of shelling. This was soon followed by small arms fire. The German guards ran away and escaped.

Now, American G.I.s came in. And they were led by my own outfit, E Company, 222d! What a great moment that was! And the very first one in was Corporal Akins! We had some reunion.

Akins was the only one I can remember. E Company had taken casualties the day I left, and after three more months of heavy fighting was now filled with replacements.

Very soon after, I was flown to Le Havre and taken to Southhampton in England. From there, I was put on a Hospital Ship which sailed for Camp Kilmer in New Jersey.

I'm so sorry I never saw many of my old buddies again.[2]

The prisoners appeared to be sick, weak and starving.

Sergeant Lester E. Bruns, E Company, 222d Infantry Regiment, 42d Rainbow Division

Les Bruns was born in 1925. After the war he was on occupation duty in Austria until May 1946. He settled in western Nebraska, marrying Geraldine Cech in 1948. They have four children. He was a farmer and rancher until he retired in 1988. He spends winters in the south and comes north for the summer.

He was twenty years old at Dachau and was over seventy when he told us about it.

On the morning of the twenty-ninth, we entered that POW enclosure. However, the Germans had fled during the night. We only went in a short distance. The prisoners appeared to be sick, weak and starving. I understand that Walter Brophy, a member of E Company was one of the prisoners there, but I didn't know it at the time—and in the condition he must have been in, I probably wouldn't have recognized him. But we were there for only a very short time. We were told that rear echelon troops who were following us would soon be there to take care of the prisoners.

We were in Munich later that same day. There, we also liberated a large number of American POWs.[3]

STORIES FROM BEHIND THE WIRE

The Rainbow soldiers and the others who made their way into concentration camp Dachau on the twenty-ninth day of April, 1945, did not actually see Dachau. Oh, yes—they saw the death, the despair, the misery, the unspeakable degradation. But in witnessing these things, they saw only the end products of Dachau. They did not see (indeed, how could they) Dachau in operation, the sadistic murderous routine that ground away or suddenly shattered uncounted thousands of lives.

Most of what the Rainbow soldiers knew about Dachau was what was there on their arrival. Obviously, the place was hell. But, like Dante's Inferno, there were a number of rings, divisions, and subdivisions. While none of the inmates had an easy time of it in Dachau, some had it much worse than others.[1] All were there because they had "committed crimes against the state." For the Jews, their crime consisted of being born. Others had been sent there because they were common criminals—thieves and murderers. These were folk who did not realize that one could rob and murder with impunity only as a member of the National Socialist Party. Some were there because they were "deviates": homosexuals. Some were listed as "politicals"; they had spoken and worked against the regime. It was a catchall group that included Communists, socialists, Catholic priests, Protestant ministers, liberals, former government officials, and conservatives who were opposed to the Nazis. Another group was the "antisocials," those denounced by neighbors, coworkers, spies, and even members of their own families for some violation of the norms of national socialism.

Members of each group wore a cloth badge on their prison uniforms. These were colored for immediate identification. Politicals wore red; criminals, green; antisocials, black; Jehovah's

Dachau 29 April 1945

Liberated prisoners pulling cart filled with rations taken from SS stores by Rainbow soldiers.

Witnesses, violet; homosexuals, pink. Jews wore a yellow Star of David. Superimposed on the badges were letters to denote nationality: F for French, P for Poles, and so on. Some of the politicals also wore the letters NN. These stood for *Nacht und Nebel*, "Night and the Fog." From the very beginning, Hitler had boasted that he would send his enemies off into eternal, enveloping darkness, where they would vanish from the face of the earth. All memory of them would be blotted out forever. The world would never know they had existed. The letters NN signified that these prisoners were destined to "disappear." Unfortunately, this process was well under way. Fortunately, we arrived at Dachau in time to prevent its completion.

Dachau "behind the wire" was known only to those who lived—or died—there. Gleb Rahr and Joseph Knoll, who arrived on the Death Train two days before Dachau fell; Ernest Seinfeld, who was there for six months; Sidney Glucksman, who somehow managed two years of survival; Steve Ross, who came to Dachau at age fourteen; and Bill Lowenberg are better qualified than anyone else to tell the true story of how it was before the Rainbow Division arrived.

I thank God and all his Angels—his Angels
from the Rainbow Division.

Gleb Rahr, Dachau survivor

After the liberation, Gleb Rahr studied at Hamburg University. He worked for a Russian emigre publishing house in Frankfurt. He was a correspondent for that institution for four years in Tokyo. Rahr was also a lecturer in Russian history and culture for the Far East Department of the University of Maryland.

In 1975, he went to work for Radio Free Europe. He is now retired but still freelances for that station.

I was born in Moscow, October 3, 1922. Before I was two years old, my family was forced to leave Russia. I grew up in Latvia. When Latvia was invaded by the Red Army, we had to run for our lives. This meant we had to go to Hitler's Germany, which was the only country willing to accept refugees.

In Germany, I joined an underground organization which was both anti-Hitler and anti-Stalin. When the Gestapo found out about us, I was arrested. I was imprisoned in a number of Concentration Camps, but you have asked about Dachau—and the Death Train.

April 1, 1945, was Easter Sunday. It was a frosty day in Langensalza, a small town in Thuringia, a region in Central Germany. I was forced to work in a former textile factory which had been transformed into a plant that produced parts for Heinkel fighter planes [used by the Luftwaffe]. I was one of about fifteen hundred prisoners, mostly Russians, Poles, Serbs, Czechs, and a group of German Socialists and Communists. Early that day, work was stopped. We were driven out to the courtyard. From far off, and for the very first time, we could hear the sounds of artillery. We were counted and then surrounded by a special SS unit that had police dogs. They led us out of the Camp, and we walked some sixty kilometers to Buchenwald, the Main Camp of which Langensalza was an outpost. It took us two days to reach Buchenwald. We spent two nights in open fields, surrounded by SS and barking dogs.

Buchenwald was already filled beyond capacity, but still groups of prisoners from other Concentration Camps were being herded into it. Finally, someone made the decision to evacuate some of us unwanted arrivals to what still remained of Hitler's Germany to the South. There, some Nazi leaders hoped to

Dachau 29 April 1945

Dachau survivor Gleb Rahr one
year after freedom.

continue resistance in the Alps Mountains—the Alpenfestung,
as they called it.

On April 5, I was one of 5,000 prisoners who had to proceed on
foot to Weimar, where 60 open boxcars were waiting for us.
About eighty prisoners were forced into each car; thirty would
have strained its capacity. Two SS soldiers were attached to
each car.

We former Langensalza prisoners were still in relatively good
shape, but at the last moment, other prisoners were distributed
among all the cars, in addition to the original eighty. They had
come from the infamous Dora V-2 rocket plants [working conditions there were intolerable]. When the plants ceased production, they were just left in the surrounding caves to starve. But
now that the Americans were approaching, the SS decided to
bring them here. Two or three were jammed into each boxcar.
All were dying of starvation, and infected with typhus. Within a

few days, every one of them had died. But the lice they had brought with them multiplied and settled on the rest of us.

Before we departed Weimar station, each prisoner was handed a "bread-brick" and told this would be our ration for the next three days. Then, the train—or I should say three trains of 30 cars each—started for Leipzig. We arrived in the early morning just after the city had been bombed by the British. We continued toward Dresden, and from there to "The Protectorate of Bohemia and Moravia"—the Nazi name of Czechoslovakia.

As time went on, the SS became increasingly nervous. It seemed no other Concentration Camp would accept us. No German Garrison Commander was willing, or able, to provide us with food. We, sitting in those open cars, also could stand it no longer. In my car, a young Russian boy named Vassily or Vasya, rose to his feet while asleep, and was immediately cut down by an SS Man's MP—Maschinen Pistole. In another car, some sort of mutiny must have taken place. The SS shot everyone in it.

We passed the city of Pilsen, world famous for its beer, and continued south, passing small towns and villages. Sometimes, we had to stop for hours, even days, in open fields because the rails in front of us had been destroyed by bombs.

After nearly two weeks, our trains crossed the mountainous Bohemian Forest and reached the outskirts of Passau [a city to the northeast of Munich near the border of Austria]. The most able-bodied of us were selected to march to the other end of the city to a military barracks to get some bread for us. But when we came back with it, the SS took it all. Two weeks had already gone by—and all we were given was that original bread-brick on the very first day!

How to describe the life—and death—on those trains! The constant, unrelenting hunger. The pain of the cramped positions—being unable to move. The stench of too many unwashed bodies lying in their own waste. Unceasing, almost casual brutalities of the SS. This became the whole world.

Finally, we arrived at a lonely place called Nammering. The rails were destroyed. We would have to stay here four or five days. The dead bodies were taken out of the trains to be burned. Whole trees were cut down to feed the fires. But, evidently, they couldn't generate heat high enough to reduce the corpses to ashes. And so we, in our badly weakened condition, were compelled to bury them.

We were becoming more and more desperate. Some tried to escape and were immediately shot down. Trigger-happy SS just shot people for any reason, or no reason, at all. And still—we were given no food, whatsoever.

On April 23rd, we moved south over the Danube, then west. Finally, on the morning of the 27th, we came to Dachau. There was the usual, interminable counting at the Camp gate. Thirteen hundred of us—all who could stand on our feet, all that remained of the original five thousand—were still alive. Another fifteen hundred or so, remained on the train. They were dead on arrival. Some two thousand others died en route. We were marched to the Quarantine Barracks on the very far end of the Camp. And, finally, some hot oat soup was brought—the first food issue of any kind—to us, the "lucky ones" who had survived that terrible journey on The Death Train.

April 28th, fighting was going on, somewhere—not too far away. We prisoners were warned to stay in our Barracks. The SS patrolled the Camp on motorcycles.

April 29th, the fighting came much closer. Now, we could hear the whistle of shells overflying the Camps. White flags appeared on the watch towers.

I was lying on my wooden bunk in a semi-conscious state. I had no mattress, no cushion. And then, at around 1800 hours, there was a sound, the like of which I had never heard in my life. It was a howling—not the howling of wolves—but of men! The first prisoners who recognized the American soldiers just outside the gate began this cry: "Aaaaaah!" Others, becoming aware of what was happening, joined them. Finally, thousands of Dachau prisoners roared, "Aaaaaah!" We broke out of our Quarantine Barracks, and joined everyone. We stormed that part of the fence where those first Americans had been sighted.

Yes! Yes! They were here! Some of them stayed outside and threw cigarettes at us. Others opened the gate and marched through our midst. I will never forget them. They must have been my own age, twenty, or maybe twenty-two, or even younger. But we had become accustomed to looking at our own faces; prematurely aged, haggard, and ravaged—compared to us, they seemed to be twelve and fourteen—just boys!

I can't remember very much about the next week or so. I had typhus. I was unconscious most of the time. And then, I remember the day when I was, at last, able to walk out of the barracks and into the open air. It was a sunny May morning. I lay down on a heap of freshly cut grass. The lovely smell permeated the air—a lovely smell for a change! I fell into a deep, dreamless, untroubled sleep. When I awoke, I realized that I was not only alive—I had been born anew! Life for me had begun again right here in Dachau. And whenever—wherever in the world, the smell of freshly cut grass reaches me, I think of my second birth at Dachau. And with all my heart—I thank God and His Angels—His Angels from the Rainbow Division![2]

Oh, how the face of a prisoner can change through hunger.

Ernest Seinfeld, Dachau survivor

Ernest Seinfeld was born in Vienna on December 17, 1924. He was fourteen at the time of the *Anschluss,* the German takeover of Austria. Seinfeld was subjected to Nazi persecution during his entire adolescent years. When he was seventeen, he was drafted into the labor service. A year later he was sent to his first concentration camp, Theresienstadt. Afterward, he managed to survive a series of notorious camps—Auschwitz, Kaufering, Landshut—until he was finally liberated at Dachau at the age of twenty-one.

After the war, Seinfeld came to the United States. He worked at several jobs and then started his own business. At the same time, he attended the College of the City of New York, where he earned his bachelor's degree magna cum laude. In 1966, he earned a master's degree from Columbia University. He later become an assistant professor at Western Connecticut State University. Seinfeld is now busily engaged in writing an historiography of Theresienstadt.

When Adolf Hitler took over Austria, my father was out of the country on business. He never returned. The persecution of the Jews began on the very first day of "The Anschluss." We had to get out of our apartment. We finally ended up in a small abandoned storefront which my mother managed to convert into living quarters.

During the first year, just one school was permitted to the Jews. I was able to go there. It was where I met the girl who would become my wife eight years later. She was able to remain in Vienna. Although she was Jewish, she was not arrested and taken away because her mother was "Aryan." According to existing regulations, Jewish children who lived with an Aryan parent would not be deported. It was quite complex, but it protected her until just before the end of the war; but, by then, it was too late for the Nazis. When they closed that school, we

Dachau 29 April 1945

Ernest Seinfeld, Dachau
survivor, one year after
liberation.

tried to continue our education by organizing private classes. I
had a granduncle in New York. My mother tried desperately to
send me to him, but by the time he was ready to help, it was
1941, and too late, since leaving by boat was no longer possible.

In May of 1941, I was drafted into Labor Service for road building. The experiences I went through here, plus all the other
abuses I had suffered since 1938, had steeled me mentally and
physically to face the shock of my first Concentration Camp—
Theresienstadt. Just short of my 18th birthday, I was sent there
with my mother in 1942. In Theresienstadt, as in all the other
Camps, one was constantly subjected to hunger, brutality,
forced labor, and disease. But it did have one advantage. It was
supposed to be a "Showplace." Here, the Nazis tried to counter
reports of atrocities and mass killings which, despite the greatest secrecy and censorship, still managed to seep out and reach
the Free World. From time to time, whenever Red Cross and
other "Investigating Commissions" would appear, the Nazis
were always prepared for them. A few streets and buildings
would be converted into a sort of benign Potemkin Village,[3]
cleaned and spruced up for the tightly controlled tours

conducted for these often gullible visitors. In that same spirit, some artistic and educational activities were permitted. Thus, I met the former Stenographer of the Austrian Parliament, Dr. Berthold Oplatek, a fellow prisoner. He taught me Gregg Shorthand. I helped him with English conversation. He died in Auschwitz.

Theresienstadt was a Transit rather than an Extermination Center; over 141,000 were sent there, 33,456 died there, 88,196 were sent to extermination camps in the East, 1,654 were released and 764 made their escape.[4]

In September, 1944, I was among 2,500 men in what turned out to be a shipment to Auschwitz, though we were told we were destined for "Labor Service in Germany." They decorated this fiction further by saying that only persons "of good characters" could be selected. They feared if the true nature of the shipment were known it might have sparked the sort of desperate resistance that led to the uprising in the Warsaw Ghetto. After I left Theresienstadt I never saw my mother again.

We were packed into freight wagons, and two days later we arrived at Auschwitz. Only half of us would survive because, right there and then, the Nazis performed an immediate "Selection." This, we learned, meant that the "selectees" were taken at once to the Gas Chambers. The shock was so great that two days later I anxiously volunteered to be sent to Germany as a "Carpenter." Anywhere would be an improvement over that Hell! And so I was chosen. After another two-day journey in an overcrowded freight car, I arrived at Kaufering, a satellite camp of Dachau. Here, we starved, we froze, we worked long backbreaking hours to construct what were intended to be new aircraft factories to replace the ones destroyed by Allied bombers. When a call came for "craftsmen" to volunteer for another Camp, I felt I had nothing to lose. I was sent to a Camp in Landshut, in lower Bavaria, another satellite camp. I landed a job in the Carpentry Shop. Fortunately for me, it was run by men from the Organization Todt—the semi-military Nazi Construction Corps. Most were from Vienna, the city of my birth. That warm workroom and the food they were able to give me, was a dramatic improvement. But this relatively snug situation did not last long. Landshut Railway Station had been bombed, and we were sent there to work. A very decent civilian gave me some bread coupons, and one of the Todt men used them to get me some bread. It was so fresh, I devoured it all at once! The next night, when returned to Camp, we helped unload some frozen carrots from a train. I managed to get some for myself. I devoured these, too.

But during the night, I was overcome by terrible cramps. There were neither medical facilities nor medicine available in this new camp, still not quite finished. The Camp Commandant, therefore, had received permission to use the facilities of the nearby military hospital for "emergencies." A fellow prisoner who was a doctor, "certified" the emergency. I was diagnosed by the Army Doctor to have a twisting of the bowels. He operated on me immediately. After a few days, the Camp Commandant sent an SS guard to fetch me. But my officer doctor refused to release me. Fortunately, he was not only an officer, but was rumored to also belong to the SS. Some days later, the Commandant sent another guard to get me, and when the guard insisted, the officer-doctor not only refused but ordered the guard to stand at attention when addressing him.[5] All this was told to me by a Medical Non-Com who worked in that hospital. He was from Vienna. He tried to help as much as possible. He sent letters from me to my future wife in Vienna. My Non-Com friend received packages, and also some money for me. He did this through the Military Mails, at considerable risk. About half the nurses were nuns. They took good care of me. They helped me not only to recover, but also to stay "sick." They never blinked when I returned the thermometer still showing a high fever. They may have known that I created those numbers by rubbing it.

But my idyllic stay at that hospital was over on February 5th. It had been decided to close down the Camp. The sick ones would go to the main camp in Dachau. This time, when the guard came, the doctor could no longer protect me. But what I feared as a misfortune turned out to be a lucky break. There were no gassings at Dachau at that time, and as incredible as it may sound, Dachau was—compared to the hell of Kaufering and Landshut—quite an improvement. In Kaufering, we lived in holes in the ground covered with boards. We slept on the always cold and wet earth. In Dachau, we lived in wooden barracks. Nevertheless, the mortality of the undernourished and the sick was high.

The situation of the Jewish and non-Jewish prisoners was not nearly comparable. Many more of the Jews were near death. One of my notes I made then read: "Every day, prisoners die. Especially Jews, mostly from typhus, and weaknesses caused by hunger. Oh, how the face of a prisoner can change through hunger! When they wrap a cloth around their heads in the morning, you think that aged women (*greisinnen*) stare at you. One feels compelled to say, God! Oh, God!"[6]

My knowledge of English helped me, possibly saved me at Dachau. Some prisoners, especially Germans and quite a few Poles actually had fairly good jobs. I had been assigned to a Block where the Secretary and his Deputy were two former Polish Army Officers [non-Jews]. They entertained a romantic notion that, somehow, they would join the Polish Corps that was fighting with the British. They wanted to learn English, and they found something for me to do in their little office. They had an English text, and I helped them translate it. I also made them a small dictionary. I managed to keep a diary, which I wrote in Gregg Shorthand.

On April 26, some 7,000 mostly Jewish, German and Russian inmates were assembled to be sent off somewhere. I was among them. I decided to try to get out of it. It was clear that the Americans were coming closer. Therefore, Dachau was the place to be. I removed my yellow Star of David, and hid in the barracks until the transport departed. This had been quite risky for me, but none of the remaining prisoners gave me away. About two-thirds of the block had been Gentile. But Jews and non-Jews lived in separate rooms. We met only in the yard. Even here, on occasion, one met active anti-Semitism. I had a fistfight with a Frenchman who had made anti-Semitic statements about Jews. I was surprised and gratified when no one in the crowd intervened on his part when I was getting the better of it.

And, then, three days later, on the 29th, white flags flew up all over the Camp. The Americans arrived. Again, my knowledge of English came in handy. When the Americans came, I spoke to them in English. I was able to get a job as an Interpreter, and, thus, I found a series of jobs with The U.S. Army until October, 1945, when I could return to Vienna. There I became the local manager of the office of the American Joint Distribution Committee.

I married my wife, Eva, in 1946. In February of 1947, with the help of my uncle in New York, we arrived in the United States on the liberty ship "Ernie Pyle" after a three-month journey, due to a sailors strike.

I had survived two of the most notorious Nazi Concentration Camps—Auschwitz and Dachau.

My mother had been sent from Theresienstadt in the last transport to Auschwitz. But she didn't live long enough to see the Day of Liberation. Four days after she arrived, the gassing installations were destroyed. But for her, it was four days too late. I had written a hopeful note in January, 1945. It had been seven years since the Anschluss [Hitler's takeover of Austria], and it said, "This will be the year the Seven Lean Years will end. I hope the Seven Good Years will follow." And surely they did. They began on the twenty-ninth day of April, 1945, when I stood at a Dachau gate and saw those first American soldiers with the Rainbow patch on their shoulders.[7]

I don't know how much longer I could have lasted.

Sidney Glucksman, Dachau survivor

"Sidney's" is an institution on Chapel Street in New Haven. It is almost as well-known as its more venerable neighbor, Yale University. Sidney Glucksman's popular, busy tailor shop has served a host of customers for over thirty years. Sidney and his wife, Libby, are on a first-name basis with practically all of them. All day long, Sidney measures, pins, and sews while Hebrew "soul music" flows through the shop and out into the street.

Kindly, smiling, cheerful Sidney and Libby. It is so hard to believe that they are survivors of the Holocaust.

I'm a fourth generation tailor. I was seven years old when they made me start to sew. You know, in Europe, the trade was passed down from generation to generation. I lived with my father, my mother, and my older sister and younger brother in the town of Chwonow, Poland.

When the Germans came and took me away, I was twelve and a half. I never saw my parents or my brother or sister again. I was put in a work camp, where I had to help build barracks for the Concentration Camps. From there, I was sent to other work camps, and finally, when I was seventeen, I came to Dachau. This was in 1944. If I thought that the other places where I had been forced to labor were bad, this was absolutely the worst![8] I had seen a great deal of death—but never so much as here. It was all over, everywhere around you. And that stink! Absolutely indescribable! There was death everywhere you looked. I believe I gave up the very first day I came there. All these people dying—how could *I* hope to survive!

How did I endure it—the beatings, the hunger, the infections, and the endless back-breaking work. I suppose it was because I was young and strong. The days, the weeks, the months, even two years, go by. You lose all track of time. I don't know how much longer I could have lasted.

And then, one day there was a rumor—the whole camp was going to be blown up! The Americans were coming and the Nazis didn't want to leave any living evidence. It was said that the explosives were all in place—but before the button could be pushed, we saw tanks. Green tanks, not German gray ones! At that moment, we realized, all of us, that we were free! I ran toward a Gate. I just had to get out! But American soldiers were standing in the way. They wouldn't let us leave. They were afraid we had typhus. Some of them could speak German; some of us could speak English, and they promised us that doctors and medicines and food were coming.

Slowly, all the other prisoners who were with me, walked back to the barracks. But I refused to go. It isn't that I didn't believe those American soldiers—it was just that I *had* to get out of there! But they didn't allow me to—so I just sat on the ground and stared at them. I don't know how long I sat there, just staring and staring at them. Finally, one of them went off somewhere and came back with some disinfecting powder. They poured it all over me. The soldier who had brought it started to talk to me in German. His mother had come to America from Poland. He wanted to find a prisoner from there who could tell me about the place. We hit it off immediately. He got me some Army clothes to wear, and arranged for me to have a bath. He treated me like one of his own buddies. And that's what we became— the closest of friends. Shortly afterward, I received a letter from him. Would I like to come to the United States? Would I? I did. After Dachau, I was at a D.P. [displaced persons] Camp where I met Libby, the girl who would become my wife. We owe our wonderful life here to that G.I., a soldier named Jerome Klein. Jerome and I remain close to this day, closer than brothers. He attends all our gatherings and celebrations—as he should— since he has become a member of the family.[9]

Neither time nor distance has eroded the friendship between Sidney Glucksman and me.

Jerome Klein, Rifleman, 48th Battalion, 14th Armored Division

Jerome Klein was not a member of the Rainbow. But since he happened to "find himself" at Dachau on the day of liberation, he

was there when we were. And since his story is so intimately connected with survivor Sidney Glucksman's, we will include it here.
Jerry Klein was born in New York City in 1925. He attended the
city's school system from kindergarten through college. His education was interrupted by the war. When he came home, he decided to change his major from engineering to literature. He took
graduate courses at the New School for Social Research. He wrote
fiction pieces for the "pulp magazines." In those days, news-
stands were filled with magazines that specialized in adventure,
the Wild West, science fiction, detective and murder, romance,
confession, etc. Writers were usually paid two cents a word. Jerry
also worked as a copywriter and later had his own public relations agency. He then became a photographer and a teacher of
photography. At present, he has homes in New York City, upper
New York State, and Cannes. He was twenty years old at Dachau
and almost seventy when he gave his account.

I regret that my contribution to the record is necessarily insignificant. To state that my outfit was in the spearhead of the drive
to liberate Dachau would be putting too broad a spin on the
facts. However, we could not have been too far behind. I was on
a foot reconnaissance mission when I found myself detached
from my squad. How I came to be separated from the others is
part of the "Wrong Way Corrigan" theme that haunted me
throughout the war.

Sidney and I met when our forces entered Dachau. I was not
in the forward element that captured the camp. By the time I arrived, most of the German soldiers, guards and SS had fled. Oh,
there was one exception: a guard who had attempted to disguise himself in prison garb. Whom did he hope to fool? His
well-fed appearance immediately gave him away, and he was
pummeled to death by the released inmates.

As Sidney says, we hit it off at once. Somehow, the right note
had been struck between us. Probably because we could communicate in German and Yiddish. I came to see Sidney, or Stas-
sek, as he was then called, several times while he was still at the
Camp. Later, he was at the D.P. Camp Reidenberg and then he
found an apartment in Munich. I had been transferred as a Li-
brarian to 20th Corps Headquarters in Tutzingam-Stranbeger
See, only a few miles away; and we were able to continue our
friendship. Soon after, I was sent home to The States and discharged. But we continued to write to each other, quite often;

and now my mother enters the picture. My mother, who had a heart for all the world, read and was touched by his letters. She had been born in Poland, then a part of Austria, in 1890. From personal experience she knew what it was like to be Jewish and poor there. And then, to suffer the anguish of the Holocaust. When she read Sidney's letters, she could sense in them a yearning to come to America. It didn't take long for her to decide to become his sponsor—and that is how Sidney Glucksman became an American Citizen. I have often said that my friendship with Sidney was one of chance; Mother's was one of choice.

As Sidney, himself, has said, we became part of each other's family. At Sidney and Libby's daughter's wedding, Bessie, my mother, was specially honored. And she is seated proudly at the center of every photo that commemorates a family celebration. Sidney lived with us in our Brooklyn home for only a few months before moving to New Haven where he has resided ever since. Neither time nor distance has eroded our friendship, which is deep and lasting.[10]

For some of us, it was the end of the world, but for others, it was the beginning. The horizon, from a distance, was glowing with Freedom.

Steve Ross, Dachau survivor

Ross was born in Poland. At the age of nine, he was swept into the death camps. He survived ten of them between 1940 and 1945 before he was liberated at Dachau at the age of fourteen. He was brought to the United States under the auspices of the U. S. Committee for Orphaned Children. He has led a most useful and productive life. Despite so many painful memories, he recovered his health, acquired an education, and raised a family.

Steve Ross earned a doctorate degree at Northeastern University. He is a licensed psychologist for the Board of Registration, Commonwealth of Massachusetts. As senior staff psychologist for the city of Boston's community schools and centers, Ross provides guidance and clinical services to inner-city youth and families. He has spent four decades on the streets of Boston in the delinquency prevention field.

I was locked up in a quarantine barrack with 1,800 prisoners. The barrack was actually built to hold about a hundred. This area of the Camp was my whole world. We were guarded day and night, so we couldn't get out to the Main Camp. From this quarantined area, the German SS Doctors, Siegmund Rascher, Prof. T. Karner and Dr. Claus Schilling, removed thirty to forty prisoners on a daily basis for experiments.[11] I can still see their faces when they spoke to me.

Food was becoming very scarce. Occasionally, we got a biscuit, hard as a rock and covered with mold . . . . Two weeks before the Liberation, we got no food at all.

Every morning, at dawn, we carried out the dead, numbering eighty to one hundred. We placed the bodies by the electrified fence. Then, they were piled on flat carts and taken to the Crematory.

One morning, we heard shooting. During this commotion, we were afraid to take out the bodies from the barrack. There was a big wooden door, but we didn't dare open it. Finally, someone on the outside pushed it open. We could see the guard was no longer there.

I saw prisoners running to the Main Gate. I was very weak and hardly able to walk, but I had to get to the gate. I walked for a while, but got dizzy and fell down. My brother didn't want me to go, but he followed me. When I fell, he picked me up and walked with me. There were hundreds of dead bodies lying everywhere. We were forced to step on some just to get by.

On the way, we saw giant soldiers carrying emaciated victims in their arms. They spoke to us, but we couldn't understand them. As we got closer, we saw many soldiers enter the Camp. There was such confusion and bedlam, the soldiers didn't know what to do first.

They immediately gave us food: crackers, canned food, chocolates. They even shared cigarettes. They were called "God's Army." I looked at them and they looked at me. I wanted to be a soldier just like them. I was so overwhelmed with joy and happiness when I saw such strong men who had saved my life. Had they arrived a few days later, I might not have survived.

So many prisoners were broken and dying. Life was no longer meaningful; there was no way to rekindle their spirits and will to live. I can still hear their cries of anguish when they were begging for their last rites.

The American soldiers did absolutely everything in their power to nurse us back to life. For some of us, it was the end of the world, but for others, it was the beginning. The horizon, from a distance, was glowing with Freedom. It was a time I can remember vividly, of shock, despair and pain. I was concerned

Years later during a visit to the camp museum at KZ Dachau, survivor Stephan Ross (left and above left) recognized himself at fourteen in the exhibit photograph above .

with finding food, but even more concerned about finding my mother. I hadn't seen her in five years. I asked my brother to take me to my mother. He had promised me, long ago, that he would find our family after the war.

I was completely unaware of the Army Unit that had actually liberated Dachau. I didn't even know that the date was April 29th. I had been isolated in quarantine for experiments since September, 1944.

Later, of course, I learned that the courageous men of the 42d and 45th Infantry Divisions of the Seventh U.S. Army, freed us from Dachau. We had been saved from Hell on earth.

Our Liberators kept us in the Camp for medical and physical reasons. After a while, we could leave from Dachau on our own, if we wished, to seek hospitalization. That was the first English word I learned.

We traveled in a group of three—my brother, his friend and myself—toward Munich. We had been walking for almost a full day, when we came upon a tank column parked on the side of the road. Soldiers were sitting on top of the tanks, eating and talking. One soldier was eating out of a can with his bayonet. When he saw me, he jumped down and gave me his unfinished can. I removed some of the food with my finger and gave the rest to my brother and his friend. Then, I fell to the ground and cried for the first time since my incarceration. He called out to his fellow soldiers for more rations, which they threw to him as if the cans were balls. He then removed a handkerchief from his pocket and gave it to me. I thought it was to wipe my eyes. And then, he moved off with his unit.

Later, I discovered that the handkerchief was a U.S. flag. I have kept it ever since as my most treasured memory of that day.

I spent six months in a hospital where I was treated for a variety of ailments, including tuberculosis. Then, I went to a displaced camp orphanage in Landsberg, Germany.

That kind-hearted American soldier who gave me the flag rekindled my spirit to go on living at a very critical period of my childhood.

In 1989, through a TV Program, "Unsolved Mysteries," which is a missing persons program, I got the opportunity to try to find my hero, who has been an important part of my life. Through research done by the Unsolved Mysteries staff, I learned that he could have been a member of the 191st Tank Battalion, which supported the 45th Infantry Division.[12]

My deepest appreciation to all American soldiers, and the Allied Forces, too, who liberated us and bore witness to the horrors that existed in the Camp. They provided hope, comfort and compassion to the surviving victims of this unspeakable tragedy. We will always remember G.I. Joe, the Liberator. And to all the sons, daughters and wives of the World War II servicemen, I pledge my most sincere appreciation, especially to those who may have lost a loved one during the most heinous war.

Even though fifty years have gone by, the trauma of my past is still haunting me. Yes, it is difficult for any of us to recall the past—but if we deny it, it could all too easily happen again.[13]

History proves that a system promoted by hatred makes the society insane, and anything and everything can happen.

Joseph Knoll, Dachau survivor

Joseph Knoll, M.D., is a distinguished professor and head of the Department of Pharmacology at the Semmelweis University of Medicine in Budapest. He is noted for his research in brain activity. He enjoys an international reputation. He has published many important papers and is a highly respected member of the international scientific community.

There was a resurgence of political anti-Semitism in my country, Hungary, when the Horthy era began in 1920.[14] Horthy's Hungary was the first country in Europe to codify the infamous Numerus Clausus Laws, which set quotas for the number of Jewish students in Universities. This was the first step in mid-Europe—in that long chain of deprivation of civil and human rights which culminated, finally, in the Holocaust. History proves that a system promoted by hatred makes the society insane, and anything and everything can happen. Those who set books on fire will necessarily arrive at the stage where they also set fire to the authors of those books. Thus, Hungarian society was not prepared by the Horthy regime to stand against "The Brown Pestilence" emanating from Hitler's Germany.

I was eight years old in 1933, when Hitler started to translate openly his exactly delineated theory published in Mein Kampf. Nine years later, I was 17, when the "Endlosung," the annihilation of millions of innocents in a never before imaginable form, reached its final formulation at Wannsee.[15] Only two years later, in June, 1944, when I had just completed my nineteenth year, I experienced the consequences of the Wannsee Conference. I was deported to the Death Camp at Auschwitz, with my parents. This was accomplished thanks to the zealous assistance of the Horthy Administration, and the absolute indifference of the overwhelming majority of the population.

I lost my parents immediately on arrival. I, myself, had a most unhappy start there. I was selected, as his next victim, by a sadistic Lithuanian SS Guard, who regularly beat inmates to death.

Dachau 29 April 1945

Joseph Knoll, M.D., six months after liberation.

Although, I was subjected to the most vicious and inhuman punishment, I, somehow, managed to survive. A Hungarian inmate who had come there earlier, was in a good position to help me recover. He was leader of a group that worked (very hard) in the bread storage. He found a place for me there, and this gave me a new chance for life.

Always, good luck was needed for survival. My father's native language was Yiddish; my mother's was German. Thus, I could speak German fluently. Because of this, I was selected to serve as batman [personal servant] to the Chief of the SS Guards. I had enough to eat; and I was in good condition when I was sent to Ohrdruf [Germany] in September of 1944. It was a long trip; we passed through many small camps before we arrived.

Ohrdruf was a cruel, forced labor camp. We would get our whole day's rations early in the morning. Then, we would have to march to and from the work-place, which required almost two and a half hours. It was a bitter cold winter. We had inadequate clothing; the work was extremely strenuous. The death toll was terrible. It was little short of a miracle (luck again) that I survived. Finally, Ohrdruf was evacuated. I cannot recall the exact date when I was brought to Buchenwald. But I recall there was a final, forced march before we got there. Many were killed during this march. In my row I was the only one who somehow (luck again) managed to survive the beatings and the shootings.

For me, Buchenwald was a transit station. I was soon placed on a train [the Death Train] for my last, unbelievable trip which ended in Dachau. We never left the wagon during this seemingly interminable journey. I believe we were deprived of food for about three weeks until we arrived in Dachau. The wagon was packed with corpses.

I had become a skeleton. I weighed 70 pounds, 37 kg; my normal weight is about 143 [65 kg]. My mind was clear, but there was scarcely a glimmer of life left within me. My hands and feet were frost-bitten. I had to learn to walk again, and I can never forget the fantastic joy I experienced as I began to walk more and more, and better and better each day.

But my over-all recovery was slow. I ate day and night. Although, by now, I was well over my normal weight, much of it was water. I was badly swollen. I had a persistent pleural edema. It had to be tapped regularly.

I finally left Dachau for Budapest in September, 1945. But it was another year before I was fully recovered. It was almost four years before my frost-bitten limbs were normal again.

In January, 1946, I started my studies in the Medical Faculty of the University of Budapest. I earned my M.D. in 1951. However, I had started to work in Research while still a student in 1949, and I have been working in my laboratory ever since.

As a Survivor, let me thank all of you for your noble fight against the Deniers and Minimizers of The Holocaust. I am happy to convey to all the Veterans of the Rainbow Division, and especially to the members of the Memorials Committee, the words of gratitude of a still-living former inmate of Auschwitz, Ohrdruf, Buchenwald and Dachau—who will never forget that he owes life to those glorious Rainbow Soldiers who captured the evil Concentration Camp of Dachau.[16]

There isn't a day that I don't thank the American soldiers who gave their lives and their energies to enable me to live with my wonderful family in the United States of America.

Bill Lowenberg, Dachau survivor

Bill Lowenberg became an American soldier himself. He served in Korea. He now lives in San Francisco, where he is in the real estate business and is active in his community.

I am a survivor of Auschwitz, and I was liberated at Dachau. I cannot recall too many details of that fateful day so long ago when our freedom was finally restored. I was thin, weak, dazed and sick. I do remember that during the final twelve hours, the camp was fired on and bombed by German anti-aircraft guns. These took a terrible toll among the prisoners. The Nazis kept slaughtering the innocent until the last possible moment. At approximately 6 A.M. we saw American tanks coming toward the Camp. We warned them not to touch the electrified high-voltage wire fence. The troops were stunned and dazed by what they saw. An American soldier offered me a cigarette, and I fainted. They realized that we were starving, and they brought us food. They also offered us a different, but no less important, sustenance—a compassionate word and a helping hand. They were so different from the other soldiers it had been our misfortune to know. The Medical Corps also arrived to help. We had so many cases of typhus. One of those soldiers was Bob Jecklin [See Jecklin's account in chapter 6]. I have been so happy to meet him again after so many years. I say again, because we may have met that day in Dachau, I was there and he was there. Is he the Rainbow soldier who offered me that cigarette? Neither of us can say for sure. I was one of thousands—he was one of hundreds.

There isn't a day that I don't thank the American soldiers who gave their lives and their energies to enable me to live with my wonderful family in The United States of America.[17]

Rahr, Seinfeld, Glucksman, Knoll, Ross, and Lowenberg—survivors all. How did they survive? Why did they survive? We have seen how tenuous and fragile was an inmate's hold on life. What other answer is there but chance. By chance they might elude death today, and tomorrow, and the day after, until that twenty-ninth day of April, 1945, the day of liberation.

And that day had arrived just in time. Because from that day forward, had there not been the rescue, any chance that they might live would have given way to the certainty that they must die. Even chance could no longer save them. Rahr had typhus and was dying of starvation. Knoll and Lowenberg were also at the point of starving to death. Glucksman did not know how much longer he could endure the conditions in the camp. What could be the life expectancy of Steve Ross, confined to the quarantine barracks to be available as a laboratory rat for two of the most notorious Nazi doctors—Schilling and Rascher? Seinfeld had been selected for transport to an extermination center. Only the confusion created by the imminent arrival of American troops enabled him to slip away.

Did these men and the others who lived through it have anything in common? We can say that they were smart and resourceful and had a powerful will to live. But the same could be said of so many of the millions who perished.

Did these survivors possess a mysterious armor to shield them against the sadism of the guards and the kapos, and all the brutalities and privations of prison life, and enabled them to fight off all the devastating diseases that were endemic in the camp? Yes. Call it chance. Consider for example, the role of chance in contracting a fatal disease. In December 1944 there was an outbreak of typhus. By January, three thousand inmates had died. This was almost ten percent of the camp. Reporter Nico Rost described the acute situation:

There was not enough room [in the hospital] for the numerous patients, and the conditions of hygiene were disastrous. There was no nutritious food, no dressings and medication either to prevent or treat the disease. Prisoners, nurses and doctors fell victim to the epidemic, as did the inmates of other work kommandos. I have asked 11 of the doctors about the mortality rate in the cases of Typhus: under the age of thirty-five, it hovers around forty percent; over the age of forty-five, and especially under the prevailing conditions, it is eighty percent. Moreover, in most cases, other diseases such as thrombosis, ear infections and paralysis complicate the situation even more.[18]

Who would live and who would die? For most, it didn't matter who they were or what their position in life might have been. To disease, they were hosts for infection; to the guards, as one of them put it so succinctly, "They're swine!" Yes. They were reduced to swine sent to the camps to be slaughtered, save for the relatively few who, by chance, escaped the butchery. Unfortunately, there was not enough favorable chance for all the millions who died in the Holocaust.

THE RAINBOW AFTER DACHAU

Dachau was more than just a shocking experience. It was a revelation. It confronted a group of mainly young soldiers with mankind at its absolutely unimaginable worst. What tortures even in Hell itself could surpass those that were perpetrated here? Many Rainbow soldiers wanted to erase all memory of it from their minds. Of course, it couldn't be done. It remained, but buried deeply.

As Ted Johnson tells it, "In the years right after we came home, we told lots of war stories among ourselves, but Dachau was not standard table conversation. At an early reunion, a Signal Corps film on the Dachau liberation was shown in a large room crowded with veterans and their wives. When it was over and the lights came on, only four were still present. The others couldn't take it—it was too terrible to watch.[1]

THE RAINBOW DIVISION'S MEMORIAL FOUNDATION

Rainbow soldiers have always considered the liberation of Dachau as one of their greatest achievements. Just as the Rainbow fought to free the camp, now the Rainbow strives to preserve the memory. And the Rainbow is also a part of the memory at Dachau. Today, on the wall of the main gate to the Dachau concentration camp is a majestic bronze plaque dedicated by the Rainbow Memorial Foundation.

The Rainbow Division Veterans Memorial Foundation, Inc. was organized in 1970, with Sam Seymour as chairman and Ted Johnson as president. It was the "brainchild" of WWI/WWII Rainbower veteran Dan Glossbrenner of Indiana. Its purpose was to perpetuate the history of Rainbow in both WWI and

WWII, the men who gave their lives, and the causes for which they fought. Purposes included preserving monuments, publishing history, establishing archives, and providing scholarships.

The first major effort was to erect an outdoor amphitheater in Muskogee, Oklahoma, near Camp Gruber, where the reactiviation of the name and colors of the 42d Rainbow Division took place on July 14, 1943. The monument fund drive to erect an outdoor amphitheater was successfully conducted by Colonel Starr West Jones. A second major effort was the establishment of a scholarship program as part of the "living memorial" portion of the Foundation. Over one hundred fifty scholarships have been awarded to date, and major funds have been established and are being expanded to ensure the scholarship program's continuation into the future.

Other Foundation missions included the support, maintenance, and upkeep of the Rainbow Division's national and international monuments. Monument refurbishing and improvements and dedication of plaques at historic sites are among the Foundation's past activities and its future obligations. Projects include Major General Harry J. Collins's land fees and gravesite in Salzburg; refurbishing of the Chicago Rainbow Park; the Montgomery memorial; the Macon memorial; the Rosedale Arch in Kansas City, Kansas; General MacArthur's grave and birthplace; and the tomb of General Henri Gouraud at Navarin Farm, near Souain-Perthes-les-Hurlus, France, along with other approved sites covering World War II battle sites in Alsace-Lorraine.

Other programs include support of historical publications. The reprinting of the division's World War II history book, a combined World War I/World War II history book; distribution of a "Year of Progress" report, published during the occupation in Austria; and the publication of *Winter Storm: Northern Alsace, November 1944-March 1945*, a book by Lise Pommois covering the Seventh Army; and now this story of Dachau's liberation.

Rainbowers have for decades been talking about the Holocaust to schools and civic groups. A close relationship exists between Rainbow and former inmates of Dachau and the Dachau Museum. In 1992, the first plaque ever erected in the former Dachau Concentration Camp acknowledging the liberators was mounted by Rainbow at the Gate in Dachau:

IN HONOR OF 42ND RAINBOW DIVISION
AND OTHER U.S. 7TH ARMY LIBERATORS
OF DACHAU CONCENTRATION CAMP
APRIL 29, 1945 AND IN EVERLASTING
MEMORY OF THE VICTIMS OF NAZI
BARBARISM, THIS TABLET IS
DEDICATED MAY 3, 1992.

EN L'HONNEUR DE LA 42ème DIVISION
"ARC-EN-CIEL" ET DES AUTRES ELEMENTS DE LA
7ème ARMEE AMERICAINE QUI ONT LIBERE LE CAMP DE
CONCENTRATION DE DACHAU LE 29 AVRIL 1945
ET A LA MEMOIRE INEFFAÇABLE DES VICTIMES DE LA BARBARIE
NAZIE CE MEMORIAL A ETE INAUGURE LE
3 MAI 1992.

ZU EHREN DER 42, REGENBOGEN - DIVISION UND ALLER
ANGEHÖRIGER DER 7.US ARMEE, DIE DAS
KONZENTRATIONSLAGER DACHAU AM 29.APRIL 1945
BEFREIT HABEN UND DEM FORTWÄHRENDEN GEDENKEN
AN DIE OPFER DER NAZI BARBAREI GEWIDMET
AM 3.MAI 1992

RAINBOW DIVISION
VETERANS MEMORIAL FOUNDATION INC.

After a good deal of soul-searching, a series of changes were effected to the constitution and bylaws of the Rainbow Division Veterans Association and its Foundation so that the organization will meld into the foundation in the year 2010. Its rights, responsibilities, assets, and functions will be taken over by a group of carefully selected permanent trustees, including Rainbow progeny, who we trust will carry our mission into perpetuity.

A CONFERENCE AT DREW UNIVERSITY

Rainbow veterans participate in meetings and conferences that disseminate information concerning the Holocaust. Typical of our activities was our presence at a large gathering at Drew University in Madison, New Jersey, in November 1994. Twenty-six Rainbow vets attended, coming from many parts of the country. Several were speakers at the event, and Richard J. "Dick" Tisch, A Battery, 392d Field Artillery Battalion, was one of the organizers. He also constructed a most moving and dramatic pictorial display.

It was an impressive meeting. Its theme was "The Liberation of Dachau—Fifty Years Later." Cosponsors were the Drew University Center for Holocaust Study and the Simon Wiesenthal Center. In the audience were many Holocaust survivors.

The opening address was given by the Honorable Thomas H. Kean, president of Drew University and former governor of New Jersey. His speech was titled "Encountering the Concentration Camps: End of Innocence in America." Governor Kean is the son of a former Congressman, Robert Kean, Republican, of New Jersey. Many recall him as the first United States Congressman who spoke out against how the Jews were being treated in Eastern Europe at that time (the early 1940s). Governor Kean carried on his father's legacy of maintaining involved interest in the Holocaust. He noted that he was the first governor in the nation to establish a statewide public school curriculum on the issue. He spent some time as the state's chief executive teaching lessons about the Holocaust to elementary school children.

In his talk at Drew, Governor Kean said:

> This was not a horror done by people who will never again be on the face of the earth. This was done by humans. It could happen again . . . I believe that our children will condemn this generation for our refusal to become involved in Bosnia. The American government had evidence of the camps during World War II and did nothing to stop the Holocaust early enough. That is a shame on our national history; that is a shame on our national character. That is why we study the Holocaust—so these things will never, never, never happen again.[2]

The keynote address was given by Barbara Distel, director of the Dachau Museum in Dachau.[3] She presented a detailed review of the history of Dachau, which is the place where the SS State began. As she spoke of the miseries endured there, there was a silence among the concentration camp "graduates" in the hall. Hearing her words, they were reliving a part of their own lives. When she described the last days of Dachau and the Nazi effort to destroy the Jews and others there, she told of how some prisoners managed to elude the last fatal transport. One of them, of course, was Ernest Seinfeld, who was sitting in the audience.

Also on the program were Attorney William D. Denson, chief prosecutor of the Dachau War Crimes Tribunal, 1945-1946; and Army Captain (Ret.) Victor Wegard, who served on the defense team at the trials. Thus, prosecutor and defender were seated on the same platform.

William Denson prosecuted the war criminals who ran Flossenberg, Dachau, Buchenwald, and Mauthausen—in all, 177 Nazi officials. Ninety-seven were hanged. He explained the challenge, which was to prove that each criminal did, in fact, commit war crimes. There were the guards, commandants, and doctors who beat, tortured, and starved to death thousands of inmates. He established credible evidence to convince the court of their guilt on a collective and individual basis.[4]

Of the forty criminals Denson prosecuted at Dachau, thirty-six received the death penalty, two were sentenced to life, and two got ten years. He scoffs at those who said they were only "doing their duty as soldiers and were obeying orders." He says, "This business that they would be shot if they didn't obey was for the birds! We had evidence of some of the doctors who declined to participate in some of the activities. They were not taken out and shot, they were just transferred to another outfit."[5]

Nazi war criminals were being brought to justice. Therefore, they were entitled to a fair trial. The task of counsel for the defense fell to a group of officers with legal training, one of whom was Captain Victor Wegard. He had served on General Patton's staff in North Africa and Sicily, 1942-44; and as an investigator with the War Crimes Investigating Team 6832 in Nuremberg during 1945-46. He had personal knowledge of the horrors of the concentration camps: his unit and the 97th Infantry liberated the Flossenberg camp, which was located near the Czech border. When the Germans realized that the liberation was imminent, the guards resorted to poisoning, gassing, shooting, and stabbing the inmates. Wegard stated that hundreds were killed just before the liberation: "The bodies were still warm as we entered the Camp. The blood was still flowing."[6] Wegard managed to take many pictures of the camp, which are now displayed in the Holocaust Museum in Washington, D.C., and the Simon Wiesenthal Center in Los Angeles.

Wegard says that the mission of the defense team was not necessarily to defend the war criminals but to make the prosecution prove its case. At the end of his talk, he turned to Denson and said, "Thank God, you won and we lost."

Just before the conference ended, Dick Tisch spoke for all Rainbow soldiers who were there: "We have come to Drew and to other places to bear witness to the persecution and to perpetrate a legacy of remembrance. We will fight to refute the growing tendency to deny the Holocaust."[7]

DACHAU RECONSIDERED

Everyone who witnessed the carnage at Dachau was staggered emotionally by a knockout blow to the psyche. Yes, feelings of fury directed at the fiends who could perpetrate these atrocities could be vented freely. But deep inside, where so many were hardly aware of it, was a faint but persistent unease. And when one decided to face up to it, there was no mistaking what it was: guilt. A feeling of guilt is a familiar one to combat soldiers. A buddy is killed, and one is overwhelmed with grief and remorse: Why him and not me? What could we have done? What should we have done? The questions are complex; the answers, even more so. Rainbow soldiers who experienced Dachau at first hand, and whose accounts of the day have appeared in this book, still wrestle with the moral issues humanity faced then, as now.

Not all of the guilty had been punished.

Pfc J. William "Bill" Keithan, H Company, 232d regiment

The euphoria, relief, and relaxation at the War's end was an unrivaled feeling. The knowledge that I had survived was a powerful and pleasant stimulus. Little reference was made to the horrors of Dachau. We, who were there, anticipated the War Crimes Trials at Nuremberg would punish the perpetrators at the highest levels of the Nazi Government; and local Military Governments would root out and punish the lesser lights who were responsible for the atrocities committed against the citizenry of Europe.

In all my letters written home at the time, there is no mention of my experiences at Dachau. Perhaps, it was denial from the shock—or, I felt it would be a useless enterprise to describe and make them understand what I had seen.

Making up for lost time as a civilian consumed most of my thoughts and energies for the next three decades. There was my college education; followed by marriage; securing a demanding job; the arrival of children; and the effort to climb the corporate ladder. All this gave little time to think of what I had seen, experienced, and felt at Dachau.

But gradually, it became evident that not all of the guilty had been punished. And there was culpability on the part of our government and the American people in not speaking against the treatment of Jews and other devastated minorities in Europe before and during World War II. And there were Revisionists afoot who contended (and still do) that the Holocaust never happened. Fortunately, a large number of people are dedicating their lives to documenting the Holocaust; writing and speaking out to silence Revisionism, seek truth, establish the concrete evidence, and establish memorials and repositories.

As people learned of my presence at Dachau, they began to ask me to participate; tell my story and attend ceremonies of commemoration.

In 1979, I provided a deposition to Emory University's Research Project, and conducted a number of talks at special events.

In 1981, I was invited to represent The State of Washington Liberators at the First International Liberators Conference held at The U.S. State Department in Washington, D.C. I also attended several events in New York City where I met Elie Wiesel. In 1992, at the opening of an Anne Frank exhibit, I met a most talented violinist, Shoney Braun, a survivor of Dachau. Yes, he survived—but how many great talents were there among the millions who were destroyed by the Holocaust?

I will continue to speak out against the great tragedy. And there is one encounter that will remain indelible in my memory. In 1981, at that Liberators Conference, a man—well dressed, perhaps about fifty, or younger, but aged by his Concentration Camp experience, approached me and said, "I remember you. You liberated me at Dachau." This was highly improbable because when I arrived there, the inmates were once again behind fences, and the celebration had given way to organization and medical treatment. In addition, I had gained thirty pounds in those thirty-plus years. I was about to deny it, but something in his eyes stopped me. I realized I must have reminded him of someone else at that great moment of Liberation. So, I said that I was pleased that he remembered me and that I was happy to see him. He saw in me a someone who had been there to free him. The light in his eyes, the joy in his face, the enthusiasm, the genuine gratitude and his opportunity to say "thanks" is a wonderful memory.

The human mind has amazing capabilities. After all these years, I can move that unwholesome experience into a separate compartment. Occasionally, a sound, a word, a picture, a smell can return to my consciousness that scene with all its shock. And then comes the sense of guilt. Perhaps, had we reached the Camp sooner, more might have survived. A National Guilt that we denied entry to so many Jewish people fleeing Germany before the war. The guilt that we didn't bomb the railways leading to the Camps—or that we didn't openly threaten more directly those responsible. And my own guilt that I should have been, and even now be, more vocal in telling the story of my direct and personal experience. May it never happen again![8]

"What could I have done?" is a question that has frustrated so many Rainbow soldiers, but it is a question of the past. Today, we face a renewed challenge—or perhaps it is the eternal one: "What can I do now?" George Jackson is a Rainbow soldier who has created for himself a "life's journey": to build awareness, in the hope of destroying the roots of any future Holocaust.

At Dachau, I wondered how a nation which called itself Christian, could participate in the terrible things that it did.

Lieutenant George A. Jackson, Jr., B Company, 222d Regiment

My experience in the liberation of Dachau in World War II was *the* major turning point in my life. Everything else was a footnote to Dachau.

One prisoner at Dachau on the 29th of April, 1945, told me later that if we had been twenty-four hours later, he would have been dead because he was so emaciated. Another prisoner there on the 29th of April also told me later that he was lined up before a firing squad about to be shot to death when the German soldiers heard us and ran away. This saved his life.

Both of these people later taught with me at Sonoma State University in California. The three of us started the Holocaust Series there, which has been going for fifteen years. I was the lead-off speaker and showed a video tape from the *Real People* television show of some of us who participated in the liberation of Dachau. This was about 1983.

Another incident deriving from Dachau was my meeting with Beatrice Hoffman in 1983 at Sonoma State University. I was an advisor to her, and we awarded her a $1,000 Rainbow Scholarship from the Rainbow Scholarship Program of the 42d Rainbow Division that liberated Dachau. I was National Chairman of the program at that time.

Beatrice was born in 1946 after World War II in Munich, Germany. When she was fourteen, her school class visited Dachau and saw the horrors of what had been perpetrated there. Upon her return home she asked her father how it happened and why it occurred. He told her it was in the past and over and she should not be concerned about it.[9]

She later discovered her father's diary in the attic. It included a letter from Hitler to her father's father commending him for his superb efficiency in establishing a spiritual basis for the creation of the SS troops and their role in exterminating the people in the concentration camps. She also discovered that her father had participated in this program of extermination by transporting prisoners from the east front to the concentration camps in the west.

Needless to say, this shattered her perception of her family and her life. Upon completion of her high school, she ran away to Paris and found her way to the United States, ending up at Sonoma State University. She wrote a graduate master's thesis on the impact of her discovery of her family's participation in the most heinous atrocities in her life, inasmuch as she was born after the war.[10]

When I presented her case to the National Rainbow Scholarship Program Committee, they voted unanimously to award her the scholarship. She was the first person to receive the scholarship from the program, which has awarded over one hundred scholarships by 1996. This means that the Rainbow Division, which liberated Dachau on the 29th of April, 1945, thought that her thesis and work were of the utmost significance in clarifying and focusing on a better understanding of the significance of Dachau.

When I returned home to Mt. Ida, Arkansas, in May of 1946, I urgently wanted to help clear the misunderstandings that led to tragic results in World War II.

At Dachau, I wondered how a nation which called itself Christian could participate in the terrible things that it did.

Dachau 29 April 1945

I was offered a position as Teaching Associate in helping start the Department of Religious Studies at UC Santa Barbara— the first such department in the UC system. Here I realized that religion itself was perhaps the major culprit in fostering misunderstandings between cultures of the world. Paradoxically, while fostering the greatest misunderstandings, it has also generated some of the greatest understandings of the world. This led me to the use of the myth, symbol, dream, metaphor, and experiential learning as a starting place for education preparation for world understanding.

The stories of the cultures of the world and their comparative literature then became my next step.

I have been a plenary speaker at the World Conference of Religion at the California Institute of Technology, and at a National Conference for Alternative Strategies for Educational Change in Higher Education sponsored by CAEL (Council for the Advancement of Experiential Learning). This led to an invitation to write for their newsletter. I was also a distinguished faculty lecturer at California State University-Pomona.

From all this activity emerged a clear understanding of my journey and what I now wanted to do:

1.) Expanding the study of the nature of language to include the interactive ways in which logic, story, tradition, and non-verbal experiential learning interact, supplement, and fulfill each other.
2.) Writing a book of some 200 stories of my journey before and since Dachau.
3.) Completing a book, *Back to the Basics-Metaphor.*
4.) Supporting scholarship endowments through the Rainbow Scholarship Endowment, The Vernon Hall 4-H Scholarship Endowment at New Mexico State University (named after my best friend who was killed on his first day of combat in World War II), the George and Daphne Jackson Almond Seekers Memorial Scholarship Endowment at Sonoma State University, and an endowment through the Methodist church in Santa Rosa, California.
5.) Fulfilling my duties as Professor Emeritus at Sonoma State University.

I have shown the connection and development of my life's journey, and how it has been an exploration of all of the ways in which people interact and try to understand each other. A continual restructuring and revisioning of the ways of going about "what is next." Finally, a crystallization of what is practically and realistically needed for the world to experience Peace, Understanding, and Brotherhood.[11]

DACHAU REVISITED

The words, thank you, thank you were repeated from their hearts in so many languages.

Bill Kenny, at Dachau fifty years later

The Rainbow Division's efforts to shed light and disseminate information on Dachau and the Holocaust are not confined to our efforts here at home. The fiftieth anniversary celebration held at Dachau was more than just a reunion of survivors and liberators. It was also an opportunity to talk with the German people. William T. "Bill" Kenny has written an essay, "Germany Revisited— Fifty Years Later," excerpted here with Bill's permission:

In 1945, when I was 19 years old, after having fought through France and Germany, my unit secured an airfield on the outskirts of Munich. The next day I was chosen by my Company Commander to be an official witness to the atrocities that had taken place at the nearby Concentration Camp in Dachau.

Fifty years later, on a pilgrimage to Dachau, I was again chosen to go to local schools in Munich and Dachau along with four other teams of three veterans each, to address the students who ranged in age from sixteen to nineteen.

The students were attentive and inquisitive. They learned little from their elders about the terrible deeds of the Nazi Era. This new generation and their teachers—who were themselves mostly children during the war—are eager to learn what happened.[12] They thirsted for knowledge about how the Americans feel about the Germans. The teachers are anxious to alert their students to the dangers of National Socialism, which caused such world-wide havoc. They warn of the threats from fringe groups and dissidents organized by leaders eager to grasp power and advance their own agendas.

Emotions ran deep, in both veterans and students. One veteran had a heart seizure and was taken to the hospital. Discussions were frank and probing. The students knowledge of current world events was remarkable. The intimacy of geography in Europe demands their attention to the events surrounding them. The sessions were very revealing as to the mindset of the current generation, and the ones in their forties and fifties. The latter were children during World War II. Almost to a person, they remember getting chocolate from the American soldiers, which was indicative of the humanity of Americans after they had won the war. In the schools, we found that people lived with great regret for what had been done in the past. They wish for a strong relationship with America. During our week's stay, we were treated as great dignitaries. We were guests of the Bavarian Government, the Lord Mayors of Salzburg, Munich, and Dachau. We were feted at one reception after another with sincerity that is seldom experienced in such proportions.

The defining moment of the journey was at the return to Dachau. The skies were grey and so was the whole camp. It was a fitting backdrop for contemplating the sights I had witnessed fifty years ago—and the intense emotions they had provoked.

This day, two thousand survivors and their families from around the world, joined their American liberators in commemoration. The gratitude they felt was demonstrated in strong embraces, and the words—Thank you! Thank you!—were repeated from their hearts in so many languages.

After the memorial ceremonies, an elegant reception followed at The Kaiseraal—The Emperor's Hall—in Munich. It was hosted by the Lord Mayor and the President of Bavaria. Here we could all mingle again on a very personal and happy level. A Czech man approached me with his daughter. He handed me a gift—a beer stein he carved from a piece of wood. A part of himself came with it, and it will always be one of my treasures.

"OUD DACHAUERS"

*The Americans with their particular way of talking we knew
so well from the movies we used to see. It all came back to us—
Tom Mix, Humphrey Bogart, Gary Cooper—our heroes from the
screen were back! In battle worn fatigues that spoke of the long
and heavy journey it had taken them to get here.*

Pim Reijntjes, Dutch survivor of Dachau

Oud Dachauers, the Dutch survivors of Dachau, are relatively
few, but their influence is great. With the help of their families
and many other supporters, including members of the royal family, they are dedicated to preserving the historical memory of the
Nazi Holocaust years. The 1996 dedication of the National Dachau
Monument in Amsterdam was a front-page headline story in the
leading Dutch newspapers, including *De Telegraaf, Nieuws van
de Dag, de Volkskrant,* and *Algemeen Dagblad.* They all described
the monument, memorialized the dead, and paid tribute to the liberators. Special mention was made of the Rainbow Division and
its representative, Dee Eberhart.

Dee has attended several Oud Dachauers reunions and memorial celebrations as a representative of the Rainbow Division. He
has formed a warm personal relationship with some of the survivors. This is the story of Dee's experiences among the Oud
Dachauers:

On the twenty-ninth day of April, 1945, I did not talk with any
of the 603 Dutch inmates still alive at Dachau, of the 2,596 who
had been sent there to die. However, on May 3, 1992, following
Dedication Ceremonies of The Liberators' Plaque installed at
Dachau's Jourhaus Gate, I had a long conversation with W. G.
[Pim] Reijntjes, Executive Committee Member of the International Dachau Committee, and a *Nacht und Nebel* survivor. He
told me about the Herbertshausen SS firing range close to Dachau, where the SS used live Russian prisoners as running targets—always with back-up shooters to preclude their survival.

In April, 1993, an invitation was extended to three of us in The
Rainbow—Ivan Wallace, 222d Infantry, Ted Johnson, 232d Infantry, me, 242d Infantry; and Bill Walsh, 157th Infantry of the
45th Division, to be the guests of the Oud Dachauers at the Rotterdam Holocaust Memorial Ceremonies. It was there that we

became well acquainted with many of the remarkable Dutch Survivors of Natzweiler, Dachau, and other Nazi Camps. Most had been assigned to oblivion under the Nacht und Nebel decree for their Resistance activities, or for attempting to escape to England to join Allied Forces there.

As Chairman of the Rainbow Division Veterans Memorial Foundation at the time, I was asked to address those present. I said:

Europe's liberation and Germany's defeat followed by only a few days the liberation of the last of the Nazi Concentration Camps. I have tried to compress the feelings of liberators into a very short poem. We dedicate it on this 24th Day of April, 1993, in Rotterdam, in the presence of Your Royal Highness, Prince Bernhard, to you, the wonderful Oud Dachauers, and to all the survivors of all the other horror camps, in memory of all the victims of Nazi barbarism:

When First We Met

Forty-eight years have passed
Since first we met.
To us, those years are nothing
You are everything.
Before we first met,
We had learned the hard lessons of war,
We had learned that battlefield glory
Was merely to survive,
And that our dead were the heroes.
When first we met,
We saw you and disbelieved.
You saw us and your joy overflowed,
As did our horror, rage and sorrow.
You, who had forgotten how to cry,
Wondered at our tears

Dedicated to all those who were there,
Former prisoners and the U.S. Army Infantry.
—Dee R. Eberhart

At the Rotterdam Commemoration, fragments of stories, and hints of ordeals overcome by the Dachau survivors emerged. The presence of family members of both liberators and liberated drew closer the bonds which were first formed on that twenty-ninth day of April, 1945.

Two years later, April 30, 1995, the Fiftieth Anniversary of the liberation of Dachau, hundreds of survivors and liberators came together at Dachau and Munich to memorialize the event. It was a wonderful opportunity to see old friends again. It was there that Sonja Holtz-Arendse, whom I had met at Rotterdam two years earlier, told me the touching story of her father, Henk Arendse, a former NN prisoner. He had been sent to Dachau in 1941, and managed to survive somehow, but was incapacitated by the brutal treatment he had received at a series of Camps— Scheveningen, Amersfoort, Buchenwald, Sachsenhausen, Natzweiler, Allach, and Dachau. In 1993, when he was dying of cancer, Sonja gave him one of the Rainbow lapel pins, emblematic of his liberation in 1945. He requested that this Rainbow pin be affixed to his clothes and be buried with him when he died. When he passed away on April 26, 1994, the family honored his request. He was cremated April 29, 1994, at 5:28 P.M., exactly 49 years after the liberation.

A year and a half later, I was invited to participate in the dedication of the National Dachau Monument in Amsterdam. It consists of a long corridor between two high hedges of Taxus (Yew) trees. The Belgian Bluestone walkway is purposely ridged in the center—resulting in an uneven surface. As Pim Reijntjes explained, at Dachau the cobblestones were uneven and difficult to walk, run, or stand on while wearing wooden shoes, or no shoes at all. On the bluestones are inscribed the names of 350 notorious Nazi Camps, most appropriately underfoot.

Among those present were Oud Dachauer officials Pim Reijntjes, Carel Steensma, Sonja Holtz-Arendse, Joop Vonderen, former NN, who lost his seven brothers to the Nazis; and Dan Bamberg, NN, born in the United States, who researched all the Camps names in the Monument's stone walkway—including Dachau, his last.

At this Dachau Dedication Monument Ceremony, Amsterdam, December 1, 1996, I was asked to speak. I delivered a brief address:

Thank you for the special invitation to be here with you today, and share in this important remembrance. My part in the liberation of Dachau on the afternoon of April 29, 1945, was insignificant. Men in my rifle platoon were spread out in an open field, preparing to attack a cluster of buildings which I thought was a factory complex, when an advance patrol from my squad returned and told us that it was a prison camp, and the guards had just surrendered to our Assistant Division Commander, Brigadier General Henning Linden.

We were embraced by a number of former prisoners who had just left the compound. We spent the night in the town of Dachau. On the following day, we captured Munich. That night, it snowed. May Day had arrived. Hitler was dead.

It is one thing to be brave with a rifle in your hands. It is quite another to confront an armed enemy with only your bare hands. There is no group of people I admire more than you survivors, and your dead comrades. You have maintained your courage and your faith, and all of you have paid a terrible price. It is you who are the true moral guardians of freedom and civilization.

All of my Rainbow Division friends, who were at Dachau on the day of the Liberation, wish that we had done more—and done it sooner.[13]

At all the reunions, memorials, and dedication ceremonies, whenever we meet with survivors, we can feel the depth of their gratitude and appreciation. A most eloquent expression of this sentiment was written by Pim Reijntjes in the December 1996 issue of *Nieuwsbrief Dachau*, to coincide with the dedication ceremonies:

DEAR AMERICANS

Dear Americans: It feels good to have old friends across the waters. People who came to our rescue in times of trouble. Who heroically slew the demons and freed us from our chains. Who helped us, fed us, dressed our wounds, cured our sick. Who gave us new hope, freedom and friendship.

Uniformed men who were kind to us; we could hardly believe it! After an eternity of being shouted and hollered at in an abominable German tongue; fit only for swearing—it seemed to us. Then, there were the Americans. Americans from all over the States, with their particular way of talking we knew so well from the movies we used to see at home. It all came back to us—Tom Mix, Humphrey Bogart, Gary Cooper. Our heroes from the screen were back! In worn battle fatigues that spoke of the long and heavy journey it had taken them to get here.

The atrocities in Dachau had become a numbing, daily routine to us. In order to survive, we had to harden ourselves, and put things in the back of our minds. But you, our American friends, who came from so far, and had seen so much misery and suffering on the way, you were deeply shocked by Dachau. You had not thought it possible for human beings to do such things to one another.

You gave us the food we needed so badly. Respect and understanding which we needed even more. And your friendship which remains to this day. Again, we thank our liberators!

The Oud Dachauers and members of the Rainbow Division Veterans Memorial Foundation have much in common. Both were together, if only briefly, at the same place and at the same emotional time on April 29, 1945. Both organizations have strong and lasting family support which assures a future beyond the lives of the last survivors, and both are unanimous in their determination that the atrocity that was Dachau will never be forgotten.

Dee Eberhart prepared another poem for the fiftieth anniversary of the liberation, but it was not presented at the ceremonies:

Dachau Return and Farewell

Drawn together by the Dachau magnet,
From throughout Europe,
From every country,
From across America,
From every state,
Those imprisoned innocents,
Those who fought
To kill the tyrant,
Met in turmoil,
Death and sorrow.

The din has ceased,
The smoke has cleared,
The uneasy place is quiet now.
The shuffling gait and
Slumping file of despair and anguish,
Are survivors lasting memories only.

Those who reached out
From inside the wire
To those who stared in disbelief,

Dachau 29 April 1945

Look now, just once more,
Deep into each others eyes,
See half-hidden there
Remembered pain
From injuries past and comrades dead,
In KZ Lagers,
On battlefields.

All victims of the
Same dark force.
A pain unending,
Despite that sunlit
Springtime moment,
When gunfire ended,
Guard towers emptied,
And life and hope
Returned once more.

Raise a glass.
Extend a hand.
Salute to all of the survivors.
Final victors uber alles.
Final victors over evil.
Santé—good friends.
Farewell!

HUMANITARIAN AID PROJECTS

Austria was a very crowded place when the war ended.
The task of unraveling all the twisted strands of humanity,
was almost staggering.

Major General Harry J. Collins, Commander of the Rainbow Division

Harry John Collins was born December 7, 1895, in Chicago. In 1917, he left the University of Chicago to attend the first officers' training camp. From 1917 until 1922 he was a company officer in the 3rd Infantry. He attended the Command and General Staff School and the Army War College. In 1941, he was sent to London as an observer and was there during the Blitz. He activated the 42d Division at Camp Gruber, Oklahoma, in 1943, and served as its commander through the war and the occupation. He was awarded the Distinguished Service Medal, the Silver Star for gallantry in action, and the Bronze Star for heroic achievement in action. Harry Collins "passed over the rainbow" on March 8, 1963, and is buried in Salzburg, Austria.

When the sun set at the end of the twenty-ninth day of April, 1945, the prisoners of Dachau were finally free. But it was not the heads-held-high, shining-smiling-faces, marching-off-to-glory, singing-an-inspirational-hymn-of-victory type of free seen in happy-ending motion pictures. Serious questions arose: free to do what, free to go where? For Jews, the problems were particularly acute. Entire families had been wiped out. Their homes no longer existed. They, like all the others, had been stripped down to skin and bones. Without means, they possessed only the striped rags on their backs. They didn't even have a country that would welcome their return. And just as important as liberation was the immediate restoration of health and spirits and, of course, food and shelter.

The World War II Rainbow successfully completed its military mission and also liberated Dachau. But the story should not end there. We should note its other great achievement; its humanitarian work to rehabilitate the victims of the Holocaust.

Because of the foresight and sensitivity of commanding officer Major General Harry J. Collins and many others in the division, hope and spirit were revived in the souls of thousands of victims. The general acted quickly and cut away yards of red tape when it was his turn to do something for the displaced persons and those fleeing from eastern Europe.

General Collins had a warm relationship with Rabbi Eli Bohnen, assistant division chaplain, and often called him Padre. He had asked Rabbi Bohnen for a list of supplies that were most needed by the former inmates. When Rabbi Bohnen submitted it, General Collins made sure they were received and distributed. He was able to provide a better food ration. With his blessing, letters were sent from the chaplain's office to religious congregations throughout the United States. People were asked to send food parcels, clothing, shoes, soap, and cosmetics. Some could not understand the need for cosmetics until it was pointed out that cosmetics would help establish a feeling of self-worth.

General Collins was a hands-on officer. He personally checked all reports. He inspected living quarters. He noted that Jews and others were housed in an installation called Camp Reidenberg. Despite the fact that all these ex-inmates were now free, they still lived in an "enclosure." The unfortunate fact was that they had to remain there until arrangements could be made for them to go home. Since most Jews had no homes, their outlook was bleak. General Collins and his officers then made and implemented a plan to remove the remaining Jewish inhabitants of Camp Reidenberg to a housing development in a suburb of Salzburg. It was a blessed undertaking. Families could now live together in real apartments. Soon, a community again emerged. The living skeletons of Dachau were once again functioning members of the human race, thanks in no small measure to General Collins and the officers and men of the Rainbow Division.[14]

I used to go into the Camp and talk to the people in Polish.
Many of them reminded me of my mother.

Captain Stanley Nowinski, HQ 42d Rainbow Division, Displaced Persons Control Officer in Salzburg, Austria

Stanley Nowinski was born in Ripon, Wisconsin, in 1911. His parents came to American from Poland in 1905. He graduated from Ripon College with majors in history and German. He entered the service in 1941, receiving his commission in 1942. Nowinski went into Dachau on April 29, 1945 at age thirty-four.

After the war, his mission, as displaced persons control officer, was to collect, house, feed, and clothe all refugees, and return all who so desired it to their homelands. In 1950 he served in Korea for two years. In 1953 he married Hazel Yacks. He retired as lieutenant colonel in 1961 and later taught German and American history at Union Grove High.

Major General Collins wrote, "Few of us are aware of the difficulties in restoring order to a conquered country which is not self-sustaining. Few of us know how the confusion is made worse by the fact Austria is at the crossroads of Europe—the remnant of a nation that once embraced 12 different nationalities in which the cross-currents of war mixed slave laborers, refugees and soldiers of every European nation."[15] Beyond the task of creating a self-sufficient, democratic nation—a job which the Rainbow and other army units helped accomplish—was the immediate problem of the refugees. For many, it was simple: all they needed was transportation back to their native lands. But many others had no desire to return, and there were the Jews, who had absolutely no place to go. These were the problems that faced Captain Stanley Nowinski when he was assigned as displaced persons control officer in Salzburg.[16]

The D.P. camp in reality consisted of a number of smaller camps for the refugees of the various nationalities. The French, Spanish, and Polish camps were emptying on schedule as thousands entrained for home. But the Italian camp was always full. Could there possibly be so many Italian D.P.s? Nowinski decided to have a close look at the camp. At the entrance, he saw a large sign that read, "International Red Cross Committee for the Repatriation of Italians and Greeks." Nowinski didn't know that there was a committee that was working with the camp, but he was glad of all the help he could get. He asked the camp's civilian commander why there were Greeks in a camp that was supposed to be for Italians. The answer was that the quickest way to get them back to Greece was through Italy. It sounded reasonable enough. Nowinski's sergeant happened to remark that those people didn't look like Italians. Well, Nowinski thought, perhaps they were Italians who had married Poles and were taking them back home to Italy. But it became increasingly evident that these were not Italians. Nowinski confronted the civilian camp commander, who was Jewish. The commander admitted that he was sending illegal Jewish immigrants to Palestine. He said that he expected another opportunity to send five hundred more very soon. Would the captain sign the order approving the shipment?

Stanley Nowinski went back to his quarters and thought about it. He could do one of three things concerning the situation. He could disregard it. He could put an end to it. He could help it in every possible way. It didn't take him long to arrive at one of the most important decisions he would ever make.

He had been to Dachau himself. He had witnessed the whole catalogue of horrors. A quiet man, a devout Catholic, he knew he had undergone an experience that would change his life. He had seen the despoiled and ravaged Jews. He knew now that their only hope for building a life lay in Palestine.

And there was something else. They were more than people who deserved pity. His mother had been an immigrant from Poland, which is where most of them had lived. So many of the women reminded him of her. He could also speak Polish. He could talk to them as one human being to another. Because of Poland, they shared a common heritage and language. Some of them knew the very town where his mother had lived.

He threw himself wholeheartedly into their cause. The camp was run by a clandestine organization called Brichach, which means "flight" in Hebrew. Its mission was to get as many Jews as possible to Palestine (this was before the state of Israel had come into existence). But international politics had become a most disturbing factor. The British, for reasons of their own, were determined to prevent a large-scale migration to the Holy Land. They suspected that the refugees were using forged documents to get out of the camp and into Italy. They protested. The CIC (Counterintelligence) investigated at their behest but arrived at the conclusion that Nowinski was doing an excellent job.

A tip from a friend in a higher headquarters warned Nowinski that he was on dangerous ground and that he could be risking his army career. But Nowinski was aware of this from the very beginning. He persisted in his humanitarian efforts, and thousands of refugees passed through the "Italian camp" and found their way to Palestine.

In 1973, Stanley Nowinski and his wife, Hazel, were invited to visit Israel. They were greeted by Israeli officials, some of whom were former members of Brichach. They visited Yad Vashem, a national shrine that houses the archives and the Mourning Light commemorating those who did not survive the Holocaust. They relighted the Mourning Light and were taken inside—a special honor. Stanley also received a Righteous Gentile medal, the highest award the Israeli Government can give to a non-Jew. He was also presented with a certificate symbolizing thirty-six trees, representing thirty-six honest and upright people—one of whom will emerge to help the Jews in times of trouble.[17] This award had also been given to him in 1947 and was one of his most prized possessions.

Aba Gefen, as a young Jewish refugee, was a member of Brichach who worked closely with Nowinski. When Nowinski was transferred home in 1947, a farewell party was held for him in Salzburg. Gefen summed up the feeling of everyone present:

> We bid farewell to Nowinski, as to a dear friend, a truly righteous person, our unfailing protector in all our troubles and mishaps, who had undergone so much, had risked his career, and endured vilification for his humanity. . . .
>
> No words of mine can adequately express the value and extent of his efforts on our behalf. Whenever we got into a tight corner, he would appear like an angel out of the blue and extract us. . . . He was always ready to lend a hand, to lighten the hardships of the refugees, and get them with

the least possible delay to where a happier life awaited them—though he was fully aware that these contacts might do him professional harm.

Nowinski expected no rewards. He considered it his duty as a human being to do his utmost for the survivors of a people that had lost six million of its sons and daughters, sadistically assassinated by the bloodthirsty German Nazis and their criminal accomplices in other lands. We remember Nowinski with overflowing love and grateful affection, and all Americans who will read these words and note my homage to Nowinski, may be proud of him and thank him for rendering a service to The United States. By helping those survivors, Nowinski was sharing with the American people the merits of his noble attitude, gallantry, friendliness and magnanimity.[18]

This great and good Rainbow soldier died of Parkinson's disease in 1993. A host of Jewish and Israeli friends attended his funeral service. Among them were displaced persons whose lives he had helped rebuild by his selfless and courageous actions. For them, he had truly been an angel of mercy.

Father Charles Conley, the celebrant, paid tribute to Stanley Nowinski's heroic and humanitarian labors to help the survivors of the death camps. He concluded his prayers for Stanley with the Hebrew blessing "Barak Ata Adonai, Elohaynu Melech Ha Olam" (Blessed Art Thou, Lord our God, King of the Universe . . .).

TWO ROADS TO DACHAU

There were two roads to Dachau. The one the Rainbow traveled crossed the heart of Germany. There was beautiful Wurzburg, with its stately castles; Schweinfurt, which turned out those vital antifriction bearings—without them, the mighty Nazi war machine would have been unable to move over the land, on the sea, and in the air; picturesque Nuremberg, which called to mind the medieval city where the dark Teutonic legends were born—and also the spiritual birthplace of the National Socialist movement. There was the fierce fighting at Furth, Neustadt, Donauworth, and so many other towns and villages (Rainbow Division records show some five hundred) whose names many of us never knew, or have long since forgotten—unless, of course, one of them happened to be the place where a buddy had fallen. It was a long, hard, hazardous road—and liberally stained with Rainbow blood.

There was also another road to Dachau. It isn't listed in atlases, nor shown on maps. It existed only in the heart, the mind, and the soul of Germany. We became aware of it when we saw—or, we should say, experienced—Dachau. We were able to divine its presence when we spoke, listened to, and questioned SS guards, Wehrmacht soldiers, and German civilians. This invisible road was a masterpiece of consummate evil. It was paved with false piety, perverted patriotism, and tortured logic. It was maintained through simple cowardice, silent lies, and chilling denial. This road not only led to but also created the killing fields of Dachau—which were planned in advance to execute National Socialism's "final solution."

What the Rainbow found most disturbing was the fact that Dachau's crimes against humanity (many felt they were also sins against God) were committed not by horrific monsters out

of science fiction fantasy but by everyday, ordinary human beings, people like ourselves. And so we asked—and to this day
keep asking—Could there be another road to Dachau? Could one
begin in our own country?

The answer is yes. Yes, because every day, everywhere in the
world, there is a never-ending battle between good and evil.
And when evil wins, as it too often does, Dachau waits.

Dachau Waits

Dachau, restless and uneasy, waits.
One day past freedom,
Snow softly fell,
But could not hide the horror here.

The chill remains
Throughout all seasons,
Felt by those who still pass through,
By those who live within the shadow,
Who wish that it would go away.

Survivors still return on pilgrimage.
When they are gone,
Who then will keep the memory?
Who then will keep eternal vigil?
Dachau, restless and uneasy waits.

(Dedicated to those who were there, former prisoners
and U.S. Army Infantrymen.)

—Dee R. Eberhart

This book is the Rainbow soldiers' own memorial to Dachau
and the Holocaust. The lives of all who entered or were near the
camp that day have been changed forever. For some, the changes
have been dramatic; for others, imperceptible—even subcon-
scious. But no one has been able to walk away from Dachau as if
nothing happened.

We Rainbow soldiers feel that we were privileged to be in the
vanguard that liberated Dachau. Privileged? Yes. Because we
were able to put a stop to atrocities the world had not even con-
ceived. It was given to us to confront, at first hand, evil beyond
all imagining. We were given an insight into how depraved, how
vicious, how inhumane human beings can be. We saw that a
great nation, a religious nation, noted for its art, science, and

philosophy, could sink to barbarism unmatched in the history of the world. Yes, fate, accident, chance—any or all of these placed us first at the Dachau gate. We now have the privilege of attesting to sights denied to millions of others. Yes, there have been pictures. We can vouch for their authenticity. But we saw the living (and dead) reality.

This privilege carries the burden of responsibility. We must keep the memory of the reality alive. We had hoped to accomplish that with this book, but we have come to realize that it cannot be accomplished or finished. For all of us, it must be always a work in progress.

NOTES

PREFACE

1. The SS (*Schutzstaffel*) was created by Hitler to serve as his personal guard. They wore special black uniforms. Each member swore an oath to be loyal to Hitler. When Heinrich Himmler was placed in charge, he soon transformed it into the nation's most powerful political force. It was able to influence every facet of life in Germany. It even had its own army divisions: the Waffen SS. One of them, The SS 10th Panzer Armored Division, attempted to penetrate the Rainbow defensive line in January 1945 but was hurled back.

2. For a detailed study of the police battalions, see Daniel Goldhagen, *Hitler's Willing Executioners* (New York: Alfred A. Knopf, 1996).The actions of Police Battalion 101 surfaced in an investigation of Captain Wolfgang Hoffman et al.

3. If these sentiments were voiced only by neo-Nazis and extremist fringe groups, they might not be taken too seriously. (It might be well to remember, however, that Adolf Hitler started out as the leader of an extremist fringe group.) Unfortunately, Holocaust revisionism is finding support among a small number of academics. Revisionists tend to fall into one of three categories: deniers, minimizers, and relativists. Among the deniers is an eminent historian and educator, Harry Elmer Barnes. His books are still being used as texts for the history of western civilization at the university level. In articles with titles such as "Zionist Fraud," Barnes insists that Roosevelt and the Allies were responsible for the war. A leading minimizer is Arthur R. Butz, professor of chemistry at Northwestern University. In *The Hoax of the Twentieth Century* (Torrance, CA: n.p., 1976), Butz states that Jews were indeed singled out, but the Nazis didn't kill six million, only one million. Finally, the relativists do not deny the horrors that were perpetrated by the Nazis, nor do they minimize them. Rather, they argue that everyone was guilty of atrocities, and that those committed by the Allies against the German people were even worse. Prominent among this group is Freda

Utley who wrote: "If imitation is the sincerest form of flattery, no one has paid a higher compliment to the Nazis than their conquerors. We affirmed the doctrine that Might Makes Right. Instead of showing the Germans that Hitler's racial theories were wrong and ridiculous, we, ourselves, assumed the role of a Master Race." *The High Cost of Vengeance* (Chicago: H. Regnery Co., 1949) p. 14.

EDITOR'S INTRODUCTION

1. Excerpted from Johannes Neuhausler, *What Was It Like in the Concentration Camp at Dachau,* trans. Father Angelus Siebert (Munich-Dillingen: Mainz Manz AG, n.d.). Neuhausler, an inmate, was auxiliary bishop of Munich. A similar item appeared March 21 in the *Volkischer Beobachter,* the official newspaper of the National Socialist Party: "On Wednesday, the first concentration camp, with a capacity of 5,000, will be established in the neighborhood of Dachau. Here all Communist party officials and as far as the security of the State requires, those of the Reichsbanner [a self-protection group of the Social Democratic party] will be interned." See Barbara Distel, *Dachau Concentration Camp* (Comite International de Dachau, privately printed, 1972), Dachau Archives, KZ Gedenkstatte.

2. The transformation of the theories of national socialism into bloody reality began in the camp at Dachau. For details on the camps' design, see Distel, *Dachau Concentration Camp,* p. 2. For information about the first commandant at Dachau see Robert Jay Lifton, *The Nazi Doctors* (New York: Basic Books, 1986).

3. Neuhausler, *What Was It Like in KZ Dachau,* p 29.

4. As of January 1943 there were 250-60 buildings in the camp. Of these, 244 were numbered. A German-language itemized listing of the usage of each of the 244 numbered buildings exists. For example, Buildings #3 and #58 were *Bekleidungswerk* (clothing workshops); #113, #213, and #236 were *Schneiderei* (tailor shops); # 50, *Waffenmeisterei,* #59, *Suhwertschmiede* (armament works); and, #224, *Waffenwerkstätte* (weapons workshops). See the archives on Dachau at the Hoover Institution, Stanford University. Inmate population counts are from the Service of Research and Documentation of the Ministry of Public Health and the Family, Brussels. The records are at the Slaski Institute, Opole.

5. Testimony at the Nuremberg trials, Doc. 3462—Exhibit #USA 528.

6. Ibid.

7. Soldiers' questions about the camp at Dachau usually led to the following types of response: "Camp? What camp?" "Oh, *that* camp!" "We had absolutely no way of knowing it was *that* bad!" When residents admitted its existence, they voiced inability to do anything about it, fearful for their own well-being. The Rainbow soldiers' experience accorded with similar findings in a study made shortly after the camp

was captured by the Intelligence Section, Seventh U.S. Army; see *Dachau* (official document in the records of the Seventh U.S. Army), National Archives, College Park, MD, hereafter cited as *Dachau*, National Archives. Investigators examined the camp and spoke with the inmates. They also interviewed the townsfolk. One inhabitant, who admitted he was a member of the Nazi Party, added hastily (as did others), "I was forced by business reasons." They also claimed that "We were lied to in every respect." When asked whether they realized that during February, March, and April 1945 a minimum of thirteen thousand men had lost their lives within a stone's throw of where they lived, they showed shocked surprise. Concerning the transport of prisoners through the streets along the railway, residents claimed to have witnessed only the last one. They insisted that most trains were sealed cars that arrived at night.

Nerin Gun, a Turkish war correspondent who had been imprisoned in Dachau for his anti-Nazi stance, wrote a book, *The Day of the Americans* (New York: Fleet Publishing, 1966), which tells a story of some attitudes in the town of Dachau: "If you go into the City of Dachau, and order a good beer in the brasserie of the Church Square, there will be a fat waiter in leather pants, who will tell you, 'The Camp is all right to tell the tourists about, but between you and me, it never really existed. It's just an invention of Communist Propaganda.'" (p. 185).

Nevertheless, several Dachauers were known to be anti-Nazi. One of them, Josef Scherrer, had come into conflict with the authorities but through friends had managed to remain free. He insists that the people of Dachau knew very well what was going on in the camp. In his opinion, they were afraid to say anything (much less do anything) because the shadow of the camp hung over them as well. People were afraid even to watch prisoner transports for fear they might be interned for mere knowledge of the crimes. *Dachau*, National Archives.

Another outspoken anti-Nazi was Josef Engelhard. When asked how far he considered his fellow townsmen responsible for the Camp, he replied (as translated), "Ninety percent are dirty and have daubed themselves with the blood of innocent human beings." *Dachau*, National Archives.

Eduard Grasal had stood up in an open meeting and said he would not join the storm troops, "Because, my dear Major, I won't." He walked out of the meeting. Weeks later, dozens of people said to him they would have refused as well, had they known it was possible. His reply (as translated), was, "Cowardly and cowards! They were all too cowardly. They really didn't want to risk anything. And that's the way it was in all Germany. The courageous can be counted on the fingers of your hands." *Dachau*, National Archives.

SIX OFFICIAL REPORTS

1. Scott Corbett, conversation with Sam Dann (transcribed), June 13, 1996.
2. Pat Donahue to Sam Dann, Racine, WI, April 5, 1995. Note: All letters and official reports cited are in the Rainbow Division archives unless noted otherwise.
3. This estimate of Dachau's inmates at that time is from the International Red Cross.
4. Excerpted from the report of General Henning Linden, in his personal files.
5. It was unusual for a young soldier like Cowling to use the term "doughboys," which had long passed from fashion. Current usage during World War II was "G.I." or "dogfaces." In General Pershing's Mexican expedition just before we entered the First World War, his men were called Adobe Boys because of the burning heat and blinding dust south of the border. (MacArthur Museum, Norfolk, Virginia.) This phrase soon became "Doughboys."
6. Excerpted from the report of William J. Cowling III.
7. William Cowling to his parents William J. Cowling Jr. and Grace Cowling, Dachau, April 28-30, 1945; collection of Barbara Cowling Cuite, reprinted by permission.
8. Excerpted from the report of Charles Y. Banfill, US Air Force.
9. Excerpted from the report of Walter J. Fellenz.
10. Walter Fellenz, from a letter to his children dated 1975—now in the Rainbow Archives.
11. *Dachau*, National Archives, May 1945, pp. 14-15.
12. Information on Rene Jean-Anare Guirard comes from Central Intelligence Agency (CIA) files, document ref. 92-0564, released by John Wright, CIA information and privacy coordinator, to Art Lee, Dec. 2, 1993, by request under the Freedom of Information Act.

THE RAINBOW DIVISION'S OFFICIAL CORRESPONDENTS

1. The army had "specialist" ratings under the heading of "technician." A Technician Fifth Grade (T-5) was equivalent in pay and grade to a corporal; a Technician Fourth Grade (T-4), to a sergeant; and a Technician Third Grade (T-3), to a staff sergeant.
2. The Nazi soldiers we captured usually referred to their prisoners in the camp as swine. This was part of the basic Nazi philosophy to justify their treatment of Jews and others as subhuman enemies of the state.
3. One museum is the world-famous Pinakothek.
4. The word "training" seems to sum up Major General Harry J. Collins's attitude toward his military mission. "Let No Boy's Soul Say, 'Had I but the proper training. . . . '" These words were inscribed on

wooden plaques displayed on the walls of every day room, orderly room, and mess hall—every division building in Camp Gruber, Oklahoma, where the Rainbow Division was preparing for combat—and we were all the better for it. After the war, and while the Rainbow was on occupation duty in Austria, the general encouraged as many men as possible to continue their education. The division set up "Rainbow U," the equivalent of a junior college. The school had six hundred graduates. In addition, schools were organized in nearly every battalion. There were twenty-five in all, with a total enrollment of some 2,792. Eight Rainbow soldiers studied with some of the finest music teachers at the Mozarteum in Salzburg. The division sent over four hundred to such schools as the Sorbonne, Oxford University, and the Universities of Florence and Geneva; and to such excellent on-the-job training activities as conducted by the French motion picture industry, and dress design industry, British farms, botanical gardens and department stores. See *A Year of Progress—The Commanding General Reviews the 42d's Occupation Job in Austria* (Salzburg: Rainbow Division, 1947); in Rainbow archives.

GENERAL LINDEN'S GROUP

1. Transcribed from videotape recorded at the Rainbow Division reunion, Louisville, July 15, 1994; Rainbow archives.

2. Regarding their possession of knitting needles, these women probably were workers in the clothing and repair shops. They were so closely guarded and watched that they couldn't possibly be a threat.

3. Harry Shaffer to Ruth Shaffer, Dachau, April 29, 1945.

4. Because of the tragic story of the five Sullivan brothers, who served on the same naval vessel earlier in the war and went down with it when it was sunk, many military commanders would try not to have brothers serve in the same units. (The Sullivan story was dramatized by the 1944 movie *The Fighting Sullivans*, starring Anne Baxter and Ward Bond.) In addition to Bill and John Veitch there were other sets of twins in the World War II Rainbow: Howard and Hilbert Margol, Floyd and Lloyd Gee, and Donald and Ronald Segel. Both Segels were taken prisoner at Hatten, in Alsace, on January 9, 1945.

5. William Veitch to Ted Johnson, Tulsa, OK, May 22, 1996.

6. Levy shared the interpreter's job with Sergeant Peter Furst, a German-speaking American soldier who was a correspondent for *Stars and Stripes*, the official U.S. Army newspaper.

7. Paul M. G. Levy to Sam Dann, Brussels, January 21, 1994.

8. Ibid., August 23, 1996.

THROUGH THE LENS OF THE PHOTOGRAPHERS AND THE ARTIST

1. Transcribed from videotape, Rainbow Division reunion, Louisville, 1994.
2. Ted McKechnie to Sam Dann, Falls Church, VA, October 5, 1996. Also, Ted McKechnie conversation with Sam Dann, New York City, August 15, 1997.
3. Excerpted from wartime diary of Fred Bornet, New York; Rainbow archives.

COMPLETING THE PICTURE

1. Defilade is natural defensive position protected by the terrain against direct enemy fire. Often it is the reverse slope of a hill.
2. The gunner who fired at the tank is believed to be Corporal Henry J. Andrzejewski, 1st Platoon, A Company, 692d TD Battalion.
3. Donald Downard to Dee Eberhart, Boerne, TX, May 17, 1988.
4. Robert Flora to Sam Dann, Chesapeake, VA, August 1, 1995. In World War II infantry regiments, the letters D, H, and M identified the heavy-weapons companies. Flora was a member of H Company, which consisted of two platoons, each equipped with four Browning water-cooled .30-caliber machine guns and one platoon armed with six .81-mm mortars.
5. Forrest Eckhoff, conversation with Charles Paine (transcribed), Cole Camp, Missouri, June 3, 1995.
6. Olin Hawkins to Sam Dann, Sand Springs, OK, November 8, 1996.
7. William "Hap" Hazard to Art Lee, Aurora, IL, February 6, 1994.
8. Anthony Cardinale to Sam Dann, Walnut Grove, CA, July 25, 1994.
9. Joe Balaban to Sam Dann, Aventura, FL, July 30, 1994.
10. Below general staff levels, very few if any officers knew the facts about or even the existence of Dachau. Certainly, this information was not yet available to the battalion commanders.
11. Alvin Weinstein to Sam Dann, Asbury Park, NJ, March 4, 1994. The physician who directed these experiments is identified as a Dr. Holzlohner. They were conducted for the Luftwaffe to study how flight crews shot down in the seas during winter and suffering from freezing could be restored to health. See Distel, *Dachau Concentration Camp*, p. 11. Experimentation at Dachau and other camps is well documented in the Holocaust literature.
12. George Jackson, Rainbow reunion, Louisville, KY, July 15, 1994; George Jackson to Sam Dann, Santa Rosa, CA, December 6, 1996.
13. The 88 was a notorious weapon in the German arsenal. A multipurpose artillery piece, it was effective against planes, tanks, and

personnel. For the targeted infantry, the 88 was dreaded for its terrifying shriek, its fast fire, its deadly explosions, and its awful accuracy.

14. Rainbow soldiers were warned repeatedly that feeding people could be dangerous, even fatal, yet how could one not be moved by the desperation in the eyes of those ravaged, skeletal human beings? It simply went against the normal instinct of giving food to those who so obviously needed it. At times, pity overwhelmed common sense.

15. Hobart Lewis to Sam Dann, Yuma, AZ, May 11, 1994.

16. Edwin Rusteberg's undated story was forwarded in a letter from Suzy and Bill Rusteberg to Sam Dann, Brownsville, TX, September 11, 1995.

17. Earl Schabloski to Sam Dann, Scottsdale, AZ, March 7, 1995.

18. Dixon Rogers to Dee Eberhart, Fayette, MO, May 19, 1988.

19. William Mayberry to Sam Dann, Crossville, TN, July 8, 1994.

20. Paul Rogers to Sam Dann, Los Gatos, CA, November 4, 1993.

21. Henry De Jarnette to Sam Dann, Cedar Rapids, IA, August 24, 1994. The "Kapos" he mentions were inmates who were well treated by the SS. In return, they "disciplined" their fellow prisoners. Recruited from some of the worst criminal elements of the camp, most were as brutal and sadistic as the guards.

22. Warren Dunn to Sam Dann, Monterey, CA, March 18, 1994.

23. Burton Sides to Sam Dann, Mebane, NC, July 19, 1994.

24. William Clayton to Sam Dann, Tucson, AZ, August 23, 1996.

25. Donald Hathaway to Sam Dann, Beach, ND, November 16, 1996.

26. Norm Thompson to Ted Johnson, Orange, CA, undated.

27. Robert Sherrard, Jr., to Sam Dann, Gainesville, FL, November 11, 1994.

28. Buster Hart to Charles Paine, Minneapolis, MN, September 3, 1996.

29. William Darmofal to Sam Dann, Somerdale, NJ, November 12, 1996.

30. Russell McFarland to Charles Paine, Portland, TX, April 11, 1994.

31. This was not an uncommon reaction. The sight was so overwhelming that it had a numbing effect on many who were suddenly exposed to it. A natural reaction was to tell oneself, No, it isn't real; it isn't happening.

32. Howard Margol's story was originally published in the Rainbow *Reveille* and is reprinted here with permission; Rainbow archives.

33. Neil Frey to Charles Paine, Red Cloud, NE, October 7, 1994.

34. Kenneth Ivey to Sam Dann, Fayetteville, AR, November 15, 1994. Ivey's comments highlight the theme of denial, which existed everywhere around Dachau. At least there was a consistency about it. If local residents claimed (as they did) that they couldn't see or hear or know what was going on "in there," naturally they couldn't admit that they could smell the place either. Yet the camp was about a mile away from the center of town, and many passed near it daily.

35. James Dorris, Jr., to Sam Dann, Chattanooga, TN, January 2, 1994.

36. Sam Platamone to Sam Dann, Thousand Palms, CA, November 29, 1996.

37. Morris Eisenstein, conversation with Sam Dann (transcribed), Delray Beach, FL, May 21, 1994.

38. Robert Perelman to Sam Dann, Omaha, NE, Aug. 17, 1997.

39. Carlyle Woelfer to Sam Dann, Fayetteville, NC, November 15, 1996.

40. Fred Peterson to Sam Dann, Sylvania, OH, March 10, 1994.

41. After four months of combat, and despite replacements, it was not unusual for many units to be understrength.

42. Herbert Butt to Sam Dann, Independence, MO, August 8, 1994.

43. Clifford Barrett to Sam Dann, West Orange, NJ, July 4, 1994.

44. Every military unit had a Table of Organization. This listed every rating, every specialty, every assignment. It accounted for the number of men and the task each was to perform.

45. When Rainbow soldiers talk about the numbers of dead bodies, it should be understood that a soldier who suddenly encounters a line of boxcars that seem to be filled with cadavers, plus those already lying dead on the ground, can only guess at the figure. It is remarkable how close most of these impressions were to the numbers that were accepted later.

46. Cliff Lohs to Charles Paine, Elgin, IL, September 27, 1994.

47. Quentin Naumann to Sam Dann, Houston, TX, August 8, 1994.

48. James McCahey, Jr., to Sam Dann et al., Bratenahl, OH, January 26, 1995.

49. Darrell Martin to Sam Dann, Wathsena, KS, November 6, 1994; telephone conversation with Charles Paine, December 12, 1996.

50. American soldiers may have considered the K-ration as mere subsistence, but to people almost dead from starvation it could be rich indeed. The food part of the average K-ration consisted of some crackers, a tin (the size of a can of shoe polish) of Spam, a candy bar, and a packet of powdered coffee.

51. Jack Westbrook to Sam Dann, Tulsa, OK, May 31, 1994.

52. Parts of Robert Calongne's account appeared in the Lake Charles (LA) *American Press*, June 12, 1992; additional comments are from a conversation with Sam Dann (transcribed), July 2, 1997.

53. Bill Keithan to Sam Dann, Seattle, WA, November 10, 1996.

54. Bill Kenny to Sam Dann, Morristown, NJ, December 2, 1994.

55. Robert Russ to Sol Feingold, Elkhart, IN, Sept. 25, 1988.

56. Daniel Cogar to Sol Feingold, St. Petersburg, FL, May 4, 1994.

57. Martin Arterburn to Sol Feingold, Owasso, OK, October 14, 1996; Martin Arterburn to Sam Dann, Owasso, OK, September 15, 1997.

THE CHAPLAINS

1. On June 21, 1996, Karl Leisner was beatified in Berlin by Pope John Paul II.
2. Father Charles G. Erb to Sam Dann, Bordentown, NJ, November 24, 1994.
3. Mueller is a common German name. The sadistic guard mentioned here should not be confused with Oskar Mueller, a member of the IPC mentioned earlier.
4. Rabbi Eli Bohnen to Eleanor Bohnen, May 1, 1945; used with permission.
5. Eli Heimberg to Sam Dann, South Dartmouth, MA, May 3, 1995.

DACHAU FROM WITHOUT

1. Roy W. Dodd, conversation with Donald Downard, August 3, 1987.
2. The Alpine redoubt, or the Alpenfest, was where Hitler and his last-ditch loyalists would make their dramatic last stand. Here, in his "eagle's nest," Hitler and his followers would die the heroic warrior's death. It didn't work out that way, because actually no one, including Hitler, himself, showed up.
3. Ted Johnson to Sam Dann, Ely, IA, November 13, 1996.
4. This tank, an American Sherman, mentioned in several of our accounts, is still a matter of controversy. It has been claimed, on the one hand, that the Germans captured it and on the other, that it was a 45th Division tank out of its zone that fired by mistake. Various official investigations have been unable to determine the facts, and since none of our people were hurt, the matter rests.
5. Howard J. Hughes to Sam Dann, Joplin, MO, November 21, 1994.
6. Harry D. Gruel to Sam Dann, Baltimore, MD, September 15, 1994.
7. Harold Collum, Rainbow Division reunion videotape, Louisville, KY, July 15, 1994; letter to Sam Dann, Kansas City, MO, November 4, 1996.
8. Bob Jecklin to Sam Dann, Belen, NM, October 6, 1995.
9. Elwin W. Davis to Sam Dann, undated letter.
10. Charles Rhealt to Ted Johnson, Dover, MA, November 5, 1996.
11. This was another "tank incident." Unfortunately, "friendly fire" is one of the everpresent hazards of warfare.
12. Charles Paine to Ted Johnson, Bridgewater, CT, August 3, 1995.
13. Dee Eberhart to Sam Dann, Ellenberg, WA, November 7, 1996.
14. Jack Summers to Sam Dann, Los Altos, CA, September 6, 1995.
15. There is another instance of a lifelong friendship that was forged between a liberator and an inmate: Klein and Glucksman, discussed in chapter 5.
16. Sid Shafner to Sam Dann, Denver, CO, June 5, 1995.

JUST OUTSIDE OF DACHAU

1. See Franz Hain, *The Furnace and the Fire: The Story of a Regiment of Infantry* (Vienna: Privately printed, 1946), Rainbow archives.
2. Walter Brophy to Sam Dann, Portland, OR, November 28, 1995.
3. Les Bruns to Sam Dann, Rushville, NE, February 23, 1995.

STORIES FROM BEHIND THE WIRE

1. Western Europeans were not treated as brutally, as a rule, as the others. Just below them were southern Europeans. Poles were treated badly, but Russians and other Slavs were treated even worse. At the very bottom of the non-Jewish totem pole were the Gypsies.

Of all the groups in the camps, the Jews suffered the worst abuses. See Falk Pingel, *Haftlinge Unter SS Herrschaft (Prisoners Under Nazi Control)* (Hamburg: Hoffman und Campe, 1978), pp. 91-96. Anti-Semitism had been Hitler's basic gut issue. Jews were given less to eat, when they were given anything at all. They were worked harder, even though much of their labor consisted of meaningless but murderous physical exercises. And they died faster.

2. Gleb Rahr to Sam Dann, Munich, October 24, 1994.
3. Potemkin Village was named after General Grigori Alexandrovitch Potemkin, a lover of the Empress Catherine the Great. She gave him funds to construct a model village with beautiful buildings. It is said that he pocketed the money, and when the Empress decided to visit this new village, he lined the shabby road with pretty facades of houses; rounded up some poor, hungry peasants, dressed them decently, stuffed them with a hearty meal, and assembled them to cheer the Empress. Afterward, the "sets" were struck and the village reverted to its "normal" sorry state. "Potemkin Village" has come to describe a "magnificent fake." When international investigative bodies, including the Red Cross, visited Theresienstadt, they were restricted to a part of it that was a carefully constructed Potemkin Village, where they could see inmates who were well-treated, usefully employed, and even enjoying leisure activities. Of course, when the inspectors left, the camp would revert to its brutal self. Thus, Theresienstadt was the showplace of the Nazi concentration camp system. For a full treatment of what it was like in Theresienstadt, see H.G. Adler, "Theresienstadt, 1941-1945," *Das Antlitz Einer Zwangsgemeinschaft Geschichte Soziologie 2, verbesserte ubd erganzte Auflage* (Tubingen: 1960).
4. Ibid.
5. An SS doctor who tried to save an inmate was surely exceptional. That doctor, the brave medical non-com, and those compassionate nursing sisters were shining examples of the fact that even the most virulent propaganda of hatred cannot burn out the humanity in everyone.

6. Seinfeld could make and conceal notes because he was usually assigned to some office job where he had ready access to paper and opportunities to hide his writings. But this was a most hazardous activity if these notes were ever discovered. In his book *Zeugen des Abenlandes* (*Western Witnesses*) (Saarlouis: Welten Verlag), Father Franz Gold-schmitt, a Catholic priest and prisoner in Dachau from 1942 until liberation, wrote, "I made notes secretly, very secretly, the rope already tightening around my neck, for whoever was caught collecting information about the National Socialists was hanged."

7. Ernest Seinfeld to Sam Dann, New Milford, CT, October 23, 1994.

8. The prospect of being transferred from one camp to another was frightening for most of the prisoners, as Barbara Distel describes: "The prisoners, who had with difficulty adapted themselves to the life of their present camp, having learned to appraise the people and the dangers of their surroundings, feared transport to an unknown camp where the new conditions for the newcomers were almost always worse. The SS also used these transports as a means of ridding themselves of prisoners who stood up for the rights of their fellow prisoners, and through their own upright behavior, strengthened prisoner solidarity"; *Dachau Concentration Camp*, p. 13.

While there was no such thing as a good camp, one might be marginally better than another. Compared to the camps where Seinfeld had been imprisoned previously, Dachau was better. For Glucksman, Dachau was worse. An inmate might consider one camp to be better because of his personal treatment there. He might have been assigned to a less back-breaking job: office, infirmary, servant to one of the officers. His particular group might be supervised by a guard who happened to be too lazy, or didn't care, or perhaps had some semblance of humanity. He may have been in a barrack or a block with inmates whose spirits had not yet been completely broken. They would work together, try to protect each other, share their meager rations. Seinfeld did have more luck than Glucksman (whose name, oddly enough, means "lucky man" in German). Dachau was in Germany. Seinfeld, an Austrian, knew the language and the customs. It helped him get easier jobs. Although both men were Jewish, Glucksman was Polish. Thus, he had the misfortune to be a member of the two peoples the Nazi's considered most undesirable.

9. Part of Sidney Glucksman's account appeared previously in the *Connecticut Jewish Register*, November 4, 1994; used with permission.

10. Jerome Klein to Sam Dann, New York City, NY, September 24, 1996.

11. For more on the Nazi doctors Schilling and Rascher, see chapter 5. For information on medical experiments at Dachau, see *Dachau*, National Archives, pp. 31, 32; Nuremberg Documents #1602 PS, and #428; Distel, *Dachau Concentration Camp*, pp. 10-12.

12. The soldier could also have been a member of the 692d Tank Destroyer Battalion, which supported the Rainbow.

13. Steve Ross to Sam Dann, Newton, MA, September 19, 1996.

14. Admiral Nicholas Horthy was regent of Hungary (1920-44), a country that had no navy. His rank was a holdover from the defunct Austro-Hungarian Empire.

15. Wannsee was a Berlin suburb where the Nazis planned the complete extermination of all the eleven million Jews of Europe. Quotas and timetables were set for each occupied country. Ironically, Wannsee was also where a group of German generals, realizing that the war was lost, set in motion their failed plot to assassinate Hitler.

16. Joseph Knoll to Sam Dann, Budapest, May 8, 1995.

17. Bill Lowenberg to Sam Dann, Los Angeles, CA, May 2, 1995.

18. Nico Rost, *Goethe in Dachau* (Berlin, 1948; new edition, Hamburg, 1981), p. 201.

THE RAINBOW AFTER DACHAU

1. Ted Johnson, conversation with Sam Dann (transcribed), September 9, 1995.

2. Thomas Kean, speech delivered at Drew University, Madison, NJ, November 1994. Text of speech on deposit at the archives of the Drew University Center for Holocaust Study.

3. Distel, director of the Dachau Memorial Museum in Dachau, is considered the preeminent authority on the history of the Dachau camp. Distel oversees archival materials dealing with the lives and deaths of more than two-hundred thousand persons in this first of the Nazi concentration camps.

4. Denson has written about his experiences as a war crimes prosecutor over the years. There have been feature articles written about him in various publications; see, for example, *Newsday*, April 23, 1990; and the *New York Times*, May 6, 1990. Some of the incidents that occurred at the trial are mentioned in his talk.

5. Despite Nazis' protests that they had to follow orders, an extensive literature exists proving that Nazis did not have to obey orders to commit murder. Himmler and many *Einsatzgruppen* (death squad commanders) apparently believed that only those who were dedicated and up to it would be asked to kill Jews. See Goldhagen, *Hitler's Willing Executioners*, p. 380. An SS colonel named Ohlendorf said at his Nuremberg trial, "I had sufficient occasion to see how many of my Gruppe did not agree [to the killing] in their inner opinion. Thus, I forbade their participation in these executions and sent them home"; official transcript, American Military Tribunal No. 2A v Otto Ohlendorf, et al., defendants at Nuremberg, Germany, 15 September 1947, p. 593, in *Dachau*, National Archives. For other accounts of SS who did not carry out orders to commit murder and were not punished, see Ernest Klee et al., *The Good Old Days: The Holocaust as Seen By Its Perpetrators and Bystanders* (New York: Free Press, 1988), pp. 80-87.

6. Victor Wegard, Drew University conference, November 1994.

7. Dick Tisch, Drew University conference, November 1994.

8. Bill Keithan to Sam Dann, Seattle, WA, November 10, 1996.

9. "And even after the gates of this notorious Camp were forced open on April 29, 1945, the truth about this hotbed of crime and slavery did not appear for a long time, for much that could have been shown to the world in names and numbers, the kind of inhumanities committed within its walls, *had been destroyed in the last moments by those responsible for the atrocities.*" Neuhausler, *What It Was Like,* pp. 12 ff. The bishop adds, "So it was that so much was concealed, denied or minimized, and declared mere Allied war propaganda. 'Let the grass grow over it,' was heard in public and private."

10. "Revisiting Bluebeard's Castle: The Imaginal Legacy of Nazi Genocide," master's thesis, Sonoma State University.

11. George Jackson to Sam Dann, Santa Rosa, CA, December 6, 1996.

12. The Holocaust is supposed to be taught in German schools. However, since there was such overwhelming support for Nazism, there are still many who participated and are living today. For this reason, perhaps, the depth of commitment to this kind of education varies.

13. Dee Eberhart to Sam Dann, Ellenberg, WA, March 1997.

14. Major General Harry J. Collins, *A Year in Progress.*

15. Ibid. Austria is the remnant of what was once the Austro-Hungarian Empire, which comprised Austria, Hungary, Czechoslovakia, Yugoslavia, parts of Poland, and northeastern Italy.

16. Nowinski's story of his experiences as displaced persons control officer was set down in an unpublished monograph titled *The Will To Live,* adapted here by permission of Mrs. Stanley Nowinski.

17. The number eighteen (Chai) means life in Hebrew. Twice Chai equals thirty-six, which is represented by the letters Lamed and Vov. To plant thirty-six trees is a wish that someone will live twice as long. Thirty-six is also a legendary number. It is believed that the Lord will permit the world to exist as long as He can find thirty-six people whose hearts are completely pure. Thus, these people—the Lamed Vovniks—are saving the world.

18. Aba Gefen and R. Reginald, *Defying the Holocaust—A Diplomat's Report* (San Bernardino: Borgo Press, 1993).

INDEX

257

Index